D1118914

Modern Japanese Drama: An Anthology

Modern Asian Literature Series

現代日本戯曲選集

Modern Japanese Drama

An Anthology

Edited and Translated by
TED T. TAKAYA

NEW YORK
COLUMBIA UNIVERSITY PRESS
1979

The Japan Foundation, through a special grant,
has assisted the Press
in publishing this volume.

All inquiries concerning rights, including
professional and amateur production rights,
to Kōbō Abe's *You, Too, Are Guilty*
should be directed to
Katharine Brown,
ICM (International Creative Management),
40 West 57th Street, New York, N.Y. 10019.
Cable Address: INCREATIVE

Inquiries regarding all rights to the other four plays
in this volume should be directed to
Columbia University Press,
562 West 113th Street,
New York, N.Y. 10025.
Cable Address: CUPRESS

Library of Congress Cataloging in Publication Data
Main entry under title:

Modern Japanese drama.

Bibliography: p.
CONTENTS: Abe, K. You, too, are guilty.—
Mishima, Y. Yoroboshi.—Yashiro, S. Hokusai
sketchbooks. [etc.]
1. Japanese drama—Translations into English.
2. English drama—Translations from Japanese.
I. Takaya, Ted T., 1927–
PL782.E5M6   895.6'2'5   79-4288
ISBN 0-231-04684-7

Columbia University Press
New York   Guildford, Surrey

Copyright © 1979 Columbia University Press
English translation of Kōbō Abe's *You, Too, Are Guilty*
copyright © 1979 Kōbō Abe

All rights reserved
Printed in the United States of America

For
Masako

MODERN ASIAN LITERATURE SERIES

Editorial Board

Kathleen R. F. Burrill
Pierre Cachia
C. T. Hsia
Donald Keene

Barbara Stoler Miller
Edward Seidensticker
Marsha Wagner

CONTENTS

PREFACE

The selections for this anthology were based on two main consid-
erations. First of all, the authors would be firmly established figures in the modern Japanese theater. Second, the plays, besides
those of Kōbō Abe and Yukio Mishima, would be written by
playwrights who, at present, would be relatively unknown to
Western readers. Since no anthology of recent modern Japanese
drama has so far been published in English and the plays now
available in translation are pitifully few, the number of can-
didates for possible inclusion in this volume was practically un-
limited. Out of this number, some of the finest examples of modern Japanese drama may remain untranslated because their
uniquely Japanese character may forever elude the best efforts of
potential translators. Even if a successful translation emerges
from this category, it may prove too exotic and mystifying except
for a select readership. Thus, in choosing the plays, heavy emphasis was placed on the immediate appeal to the Western
reader, in addition to the recognized merit as important dramatic works.

At a time when translations of modern Japanese drama are
quite scarce, it is easy to understand that there are those who
would like to see their own favorites substituted for the works
included here. However, when translations in this general area
are obviously meager, any play whatsoever probably can be con-
sidered a contribution.

Both Abe and Mishima are already familiar to the West
through a variety of translations, mostly in prose. These two authors also happen to be among the foremost playwrights of postwar Japan. Their clearly divergent approaches to the modern Jap-

anese theater which may be described in general as modern and neoclassical, respectively, offer a convenient framework for positioning the other playwrights in this anthology. These terms when applied to these dramatists probably best describe their most outstanding artistic outlook and is apparent throughout their works. Seiichi Yashiro, Masakazu Yamazaki, and Minoru Betsuyaku—the other three playwrights in this collection—are also counted among the major dramatists of the modern theater although they are being seen for only the first time in an American publication.

Since the theme and style of their plays reveal considerable variation, these dramatists cannot be easily fitted into a neat classification that is presently meaningful to a Western reader. Only the gradual increase in the number of translations of modern Japanese plays will allow for legitimate comparisons between plays and afford greater opportunities to view them in relation to each other. In this sense, it is hoped that the present anthology can be a preliminary step toward the full establishment of a vital program which can serve not only as a source for reading pleasure but also as a source for serious scholarly research by the West.

All of the translations found in *Modern Japanese Drama: An Anthology* are intended primarily to be read as dramatic literature and not to be used in their present form for immediate stage presentation. Therefore, a deliberate compromise has been made between a literal translation and a face translation more suitable for the stage. The bias, however, is clearly in favor of fidelity in translation under the rationale that a stage version can readily be adapted from it.

A word or two can perhaps be said in defense of the course chosen. A stage version has the added task of making certain that the performances do not "lose" the audiences. This requirement inevitably leads to the minimizing of the odd or the unfamiliar in the interest of "smoothing out" the plot. To be sure, much in these plays has to do with themes and issues that transcend national boundaries, but, clearly, the specifically Japanese perceptions of them run the risk of being lost in a stage version.

The "Japaneseness" of these plays can best be obtained, then, at some cost to stageworthiness. More items of specific cultural and historical interest can be retained and, it is hoped, can be of some profit to students and specialists of the Far East. Seiichi Yashiro's *Hokusai Sketchbooks* is a conspicuous example of the need for a somewhat more literal translation. The reader is even provided with a set of extensive footnotes to aid in his understanding of what is basically a biographical play of a highly individual and quite celebrated Japanese *ukiyo-e* artist.

The titles of all Japanese plays and novels available in English translation are given under their translated titles without an accompanying title in Japanese. The year given in parenthesis following the name of a play refers to the year of the initial stage performance. After the title of a novel, the year designation is its publication date. In the Introduction and elsewhere, the Japanese personal names are usually written with the given name followed by the surname, according to Western custom. The notable exceptions in this anthology are in the play translations and their footnotes where the presence of Westernized Japanese names may seem rather incongruous with their proper cultural and historical settings; hence, the Japanese practice of setting down the surname first has been adopted.

Because the term New Theater (*Shingeki*), commonly includes the prewar as well as the postwar theatrical movement, it tends to submerge a distinct break in tradition between the two periods. Hence, "modern Japanese theater" has been used throughout the Introduction to avoid this problem in our discussion.

ACKNOWLEDGMENTS

I would like to thank Professor Donald Keene of Columbia University for his warm support and valuable counsel during the preparation of this volume. As the leading translator of modern Japanese drama, he—more than anyone else in recent times—has been responsible for the growing interest in this long neglected field among the Western readers and theatergoers.

My special acknowledgment goes to Mr. Tad T. Takeuchi, a friend of many years, for his various suggestions and generous assistance on this project. Although a student of American history, his deep, abiding interest in Japanese history and culture offered me a rigorous but always discerning critic to whom I owe a deep debt. I have also benefited from the kindness of Mr. George Durham, who read over the manuscript and contributed helpful comments.

I wish to thank the various persons in this country and in Japan for their cooperation and assistance: Mr. Kōbō Abe, Mrs. Mutsuko Aiyama, Mr. Minoru Betsuyaku, Miss Katharine Brown, Mr. Yukio Fujino, Mr. Scott Harrison, Mr. Tom Kassa, Mrs. Yōko Mishima, Mr. Hiroshi Nitta, Mr. Toshio Takano, Mr. Masakazu Yamazaki, and Mr. Seiichi Yashiro.

The Chinese characters depicting *gendai nihon gikyoku senshū,* literally, "modern Japanese drama: an anthology," were written by Mr. Yūgō Satō, one of the most distinguished calligraphers in Japan today. I would like to express my appreciation for his gracious contribution.

For the fine photographs of the productions and the permission to use them, I am indebted to the following sources: Shinchōsha, THEATRO Magazine, and Mr. Seiichi Yashiro. The striking pictures of the five playwrights were made available through the courtesy of Shinchōsha.

I am grateful to Mr. William F. Bernhardt, Associate Executive Editor, of Columbia University Press, for his helpful guidance, which has made the otherwise arduous task of publishing, an enjoyable experience. My thanks are also due to Miss Joan Mc-Quary for the prompt and efficient work of her editorial staff.

Grateful acknowledgment is made to Miss Elizabeth T. Massey of the Japan Society (New York) for permission to refer the readers to the Society's *A Brief Bibliography of Modern Japanese Plays in English Translation* (1978) for a listing of the latest unpublished plays in translation.

Useful reading and research facilities were provided by the East Asian Collection, University of Wisconsin-Madison; Far Eastern Library, University of Washington-Seattle; International House of Japan Library; Japan Foundation Library; and Waseda University Library.

I wish to express my appreciation to the Japan Foundation for its Professional Research Fellowship (1975), which granted me a year of overseas study on the modern Japanese theater, and also for its Translation Grant (1977), which contributed to the final preparation of this book.

Middleton, Wisconsin   Ted T. Takaya
December 1978

INTRODUCTION

This anthology includes five plays by the leading postwar dramatists of Japan. All belong to a much larger group of plays, num-
bering in the hundreds, which make up the rapidly growing repertory of the modern Japanese theater. With the exception of
Kōbō Abe (1924—) and the late Yukio Mishima (1925–1970),
whose novels and short stories have early appeared in translation, the works of these dramatists are almost unknown to Westerners. This is true of Seiichi Yashiro (1927—), Masakazu Yamazaki (1934—), and Minoru Betsuyaku (1937—), whose plays
appear in this volume. Fortunately, the English translations of
some Abe and Mishima plays, especially during the past decade,
have prepared the way for the introduction of other important
playwrights whose works further reveal the wealth of creative talent and stylistic variety within modern Japanese drama. No single anthology of plays selected from among the many notable
works written since World War II can remedy the neglect shown
this vital area of artistic and cultural activity. The present collection, however, may provide a useful approach to the understanding and appreciation of the most recent examples of modern
Japanese drama. Worldwide recognition of this remarkable genre
is long overdue.

Why has the modern theater of Japan attracted so little attention overseas? Historically, Western interest and scholarship
have focused mainly on Japanese classical theaters such as Nō,
Kabuki, and Bunraku (puppet theater). This nostalgic-exoticist
tendency of the prewar period remains strong today as more and
more general and specialized studies of works devoted to the Japanese theater, together with plays in translation, continue to

maintain their popularity. These older forms of theater dating from before the Meiji Restoration (1868) are, of course, deserving of their international acclaim as being among the finest theatrical traditions of the world.

In fact, the very existence of such a rich and diversified theatrical tradition in Japan tended to discourage the development of a modern Japanese theater. This was especially an effect of interest in Kabuki, the most popular form of classical drama, which has a long history extending back to the early seventeenth century. It was mainly through this genre that the Japanese had acquired their accepted notions about what constituted good theater. Its familiar conventions, like the female impersonator (women were banned from the stage in 1629), highly stylized acting, colorful costumes, bold makeup, standard plots, and stage settings were essential elements of that theatrical experience. Kabuki made use of both realistic and stylized forms of acting, and the dialogue could follow either natural speech or an artificial declamatory style. It freely employed music and dancing to create spectacular extravaganzas.

There is little doubt that the flourishing stage of traditional costume drama inhibited the development of another form of contemporary theater during the nineteenth century. On the other hand, efforts to incorporate the new ideas, attitudes, and customs of the modern and Westernizing era into this traditional theater failed. In short, Kabuki with its well-known repertory of favorite plays from earlier times continued to be the dominant theater.

The only important innovation during this period was the emergence of New Faction Theater (Shimpa)—as opposed to Kabuki, the "old faction theater." It started out in the late 1880s as a stage vehicle for political propaganda by young activists who opposed certain governmental policies. To avoid arrest, they chose to express their ideas indirectly through the characters on the stage. These amateur performers frequently staged fight scenes so realistically that the audience found the productions far more exciting in comparison with those in Kabuki, which were mannered and predictable. The later New Faction Theater used women performers, up-to-date costumes, Western music, and other examples of modernity although it retained much of the essential acting style of Kabuki and prominently featured the female impersonator. This theater survives today, mainly staging sentimental period pieces that depict the early modern period. It commands only a small but devoted following among women and the older generation.

Though much spirited discussion concerning the need for a modern Japanese theater occurred during the early years of modernization, no significant step was taken until Hōgetsu Shimamura (1871–1918) proposed an ambitious plan to create the Literature and Arts Society (Bungei Kyōkai) to thoroughly reform literature, the arts, and drama. Shimamura had studied at Oxford and the University of Berlin and was familiar with the Western theater. With the strong support of Shōyō Tsubouchi (1859–1935), a leading intellectual and a specialist in both English and Japanese drama, who had been his former teacher and was now a colleague in the literature department at Waseda University (Tokyo), this organization was started in 1906. As part of their program for promoting the serious study of Western drama, they gave Tsubouchi's translations of *The Merchant of Venice* and *Hamlet* as well as experimental plays by Tsubouchi himself that combined both Japanese and Western theatrical elements.

By 1909 Tsubouchi founded an actors' school. Two years later its first graduates presented Tsubouchi's translation of *Hamlet*, followed by Ibsen's *A Doll's House* and other works of European dramatists. When the Literature and Arts Society was eventually forced to dissolve in 1913 because of differences between the two men, Shimamura immediately organized the Arts Theater (Geijutsuza). Under his leadership, this new group continued to perform translated plays by such playwrights as Maeterlinck, Ibsen, Wilde, and Tolstoi along with some plays by Japanese writers, until Shimamura's death in 1918 soon led to its breakup.

In the meantime, Kaoru Osanai (1881–1928), novelist, poet, dramatist, and director; and Sadanji Ichikawa II (1880–1940), a Kabuki actor with an enthusiasm for the Western theater, founded the Free Theater (Jiyū Gekijō), a group also specializing in Western plays. This troupe, largely consisting of Kabuki actors, also included some actresses trained in the Kabuki tradition. Its opening production of Ibsen's *John Gabriel Borkman* in 1909 featured Ichikawa in the leading role. This first Ibsen play on the Japanese stage made a strong impact, especially among intellectuals, and roused additional interest in the development of a modern Japanese theater. The Free Theater also offered plays by Chekhov, Gorki, Maeterlinck, and Hauptmann among its Western dramas. In December 1912, Osanai traveled abroad for several months to study the Western theater, beginning in Russia and then going on to Western Europe. By then, due largely to Ichikawa's outside theatrical activities, the troupe was well on its way toward dissolution. After sporadic activity, it finally disbanded in 1919.

Subsequent to the demise of the Free Theater, Osanai finally founded Tsukiji Little Theater (Tsukiji Shōgekijō) with Yoshi Hijikata (1898–1959), another key figure in the modern theater movement. Hijikata had studied drama in Berlin and had attended performances in the Moscow theaters before returning to Japan in 1923. Their Gothic-Romanesque style playhouse, seating nearly 500, was the first structure built expressly for staging Western plays. Prior to its opening in June 1924, Osanai delivered a lecture at Keiō University (Tokyo) declaring he would devote himself exclusively to translated plays because those written by his countrymen were inadequate. True to his word, he gave forty-four consecutive programs of Western drama that included Shakespeare's *Julius Caesar*, Chekhov's *The Cherry Orchard*, Ibsen's *Ghosts* and *Enemy of the People*, Kaiser's *From Morn to Midnight*, Strindberg's *Miss Julie*, O'Neill's *Beyond the Horizon*, Rolland's *Les Loups*, and Pirandello's *Six Characters in Search of an Author*.

Finally, in March 1926, Osanai presented *The Hermit* (En no Gyōja), a Tsubouchi play, noted for its unforgettable portrayal of the classic struggle of man against the forces of evil based on Japanese mythology; thereafter, he offered his own plays along with works by other Japanese writers and more Western dramas. The Tsukiji Little Theater left a valuable legacy of talented and experienced performers and directors. They contributed much to the later development of the modern theater movement. In December 1928, Osanai suddenly died. This important theater group disbanded in March of the following year.

During the early years of the modern theater movement, a few like Osanai, Shimamura, and Hijikata had studied abroad and were directly exposed to the Western theater. For this reason, and with great enthusiasm, they regarded the presentation of plays in translation as the cornerstone of a modern theater for Japan. But this approach also had its limitations. In fact, this partiality for translated plays bypassed and thereby delayed the development of young, serious dramatists who could hasten the realization of a new theater that would be less dependent on foreign dramaturgy. By the late twenties and early thirties, neglect of native playwrights became apparent, much time had been lost, and no significant progress in playwriting occurred until after the war.

In any event, a creative Japanese dramatist found himself in a difficult situation. The novelist or the poet can freely express himself in whatever style or form he wishes and can even publish his works privately if there is no market for them. For his part, the playwright requires the cooperation of both his performers and his audience in order to fully realize his own artistic goal. This meant that the playwright for the early modern theater needed to work tirelessly to create the agreeable overall conditions for presenting those modern Japanese plays that applied sound Western dramaturgy but were adapted to Japanese needs. The dramatist Kunio Kishida (1890–1954), who had studied in France before he joined the Tsukiji Little Theater, was a rare example of a playwright who tried to carry out a comprehensive program to this end. Since he had disagreed sharply with Osanai over the latter's preference for Western plays, Kishida could not implement his own ideas until the thirties, when he helped form other groups more compatible with his point of view.

Undoubtedly, many aspiring young writers recognized the untenable position of a modern Japanese playwright and preferred instead to be poets, novelists, teachers, critics, or journalists. Perhaps Kan Kikuchi (1888–1948), who started out as a serious playwright but later became a popular novelist and also the publisher of a leading omnibus magazine, *Bungei Shunjū*, may be cited as an outstanding example. The part-time dramatists from among their ranks wrote, for the most part, undistinguished though popular plays that often appeared in magazines, to be read. These writers generally followed the accepted theatrical conventions and offered little stimulus to the development of a truly modern Japanese drama. Their occasional experimental works, incorporating such Western notions as psychoanalysis, stream of consciousness, surrealism, dadaism, and expressionism, seem rather contrived and self-conscious for today's sophisticated Japanese play-readers or theater audiences.

Hijikata, after the death of his associate, Osanai, organized the New Tsukiji Drama Group (Shin-Tsukiji Gekidan) from among the members of the Tsukiji Little Theater. He had a long-standing disagreement with some of his colleagues over the basic question of the proper function of the theater. A leftist, Hijikata believed that the theater should serve as a medium of political action. This view, which was held by a large number of participants in the modern theater, gained much momentum after World War I. Through stage presentations, they addressed their political message to an audience that often consisted of members of labor unions and the intelligentsia. After Hijikata left, the remaining members of Tsukiji Little Theater, who had formed the Drama Group Tsukiji Theater (Gekidan Tsukiji Gekijō), could not long maintain a politically neutral policy. Suffering internal strife that was aggravated by further ideological differences, this group disbanded in 1930. Later on, after other reorganizations, the original members from Drama Group Tsukiji Theater became the nucleus for the Literary Theater (Bungakuza), established in 1937.

During this same period, the proletarian troupe led by Hijikata continued to exercise influence over the leftist theater movement by helping to organize new acting groups. In August 1940 the government disbanded his New Tsukiji Drama Group along with the New Cooperative Drama Group (Shinkyō Gekidan), another proletarian theater company founded in 1934. With the rise of militarism and increasing international tension, governmental suppression increased through censorship, harrassment, and even imprisonment of members of the left-wing theater groups. Despite these obstacles, this movement produced many major figures in the postwar modern theater, although plays written by the leftist dramatists are mostly forgotten.

The threat of government interference was not limited to the proletarian theater troupes. In fact, from its very inception the entire modern theater movement constantly faced this danger.

When Tsubouchi and Shimamura founded the Literature and Arts Society in 1906, it was the year following the end of the Russo-Japanese War (1904–1905). In subsequent years Japan built up its military preparedness, and its people lived under a highly authoritarian political system that restricted freedom of speech and action. This national policy included strict censorship of all public entertainment, including both the traditional and modern theaters. Each script was subject to a close examination before its performance, and the stage presentations were attended by government censors. Objectionable ideas, attitudes, or expressions were removed from the script or altered to suit the authorities. In some cases, the plays never opened; others were allowed to be performed in their watered down versions.

There is no practical way to assess the impact of such a restrictive governmental policy on the growth and development of the modern Japanese theater. The rapid advance of this movement soon after World War II suggests that only a free and open Japanese society would provide an environment conducive to creative artistic expression.

The years following the outbreak of World War II forced untold hardships on the modern theater movement. The ban on the proletarian theater groups had significantly reduced the strength of the movement as a whole. The government imposed a heavy amusement tax on the remaining groups. They were also obliged to perform plays with patriotic themes and to participate in government-sponsored programs aimed at raising the morale of the civilian and military population, both at home and abroad. By the end of the war, the Literary Theater was the only major company surviving from the prewar era. This was largely due to its nonpolitical position.

In August 1945, peace finally came. Two months later, Hijikata, a long-time advocate of the proletarian theater, was released after four years of imprisonment. Jailed for his leftist activities, Hijikata would have remained longer in prison had not the Pacific War ended. For him and other members of the proletarian theater, the Occupation meant liberation and a chance to resume their previous professional activities without fear of further harassment and possible imprisonment. The former militarist government had regarded the labor unions with suspicion as a disruptive force that conspired to undermine its authority. The Occupation, on the other hand, viewed the same organizations as a positive force in aiding Japan's democratization. Since the left-wing theater had always relied on the support of the working class, the increasing strength of the labor unions favored its box office.

December 26 through 28—less than four months after the Occupation began—saw the first major postwar production of the modern theater to survive the devastating air raids. On this special occasion, performers from three separate troupes—the Tokyo Arts Theater (Tokyo Geijutsu Gekijō, a new troupe formed by the Tōhō Theatrical Enterprises), the Literary Theater, and the Actors' Theater (Haiyūza), organized in 1944—presented Chekhov's *The Cherry Orchard*. This notable production featured a brilliant cast of seasoned players that included Koreya Senda (1904—), Osamu Takizawa (1906—), and Masayuki Mori (1911–1973) as well as Chieko Higashiyama (1890—), Akiko Tamura (1905—), and Haruko Sugimura (1909—), all actresses with distinguished careers.

The Cherry Orchard, bringing together important performers from the modern theater who were previously in opposing ideological camps, foreshadows the consolidation of the theater movement in the direction of a common goal. Indeed, the more orthodox, nonpolitical acting companies such as the Literary Theater and the major troupes with a proletarian background have drawn closer together artistically as the leftists accepted a wider repertory extending beyond the narrow confines of socialist realism. The revival of the left-wing theater greatly enlarged and strengthened the entire modern theater movement.

The successful recovery by the modern theater is illustrated by the careers of the Literary Theater, the Tokyo Arts Theater, and the Actors' Theater in the years immediately after the war. When it reopened in March 1946, the Literary Theater was already burdened with serious financial difficulties stemming from the war period. Its first production, *River* (Kawa), by Katsuichi Wada (1900—), turned out badly. The struggle for economic recovery continued. Eventually, Kaoru Morimoto's (1912–1946) *A Woman's Life* (Onna no Isshō), presented in August 1947 and starring Haruko Sugimura, was a smashing success that led to its financial solvency. The sense of futility and dispair found in this tragic story of a woman who sacrifices her whole life for the sake of the family may have mirrored the prevailing somber mood of the audience, whose lives had been drastically changed by the war. When it was first performed during April 1945, the frequent air raid alerts usually cut short a full performance.

Along with its repertory of contemporary Japanese plays, the Literary Theater also offered Western dramas. The choice of these was clearly influenced by the group's own playwrights, such as Kishida, who had studied contemporary French drama abroad before the Pacific War. They selected works by Marcel Pagnol, Jules Romains, Jean-Victor Pellerian, Simon Gantillon, and Roger Martin du Gard.

Michio Katō (1918–1953), a brilliant young playwright, joined the Literary Theater in 1949. Four years earlier he had written *Nayotake*, a play based on *The Tale of a Bamboo Cutter*, a Japanese classic of about the tenth century. Katō's drama about a beautiful young child found inside a bamboo tree who grows up and eventually returns to her heavenly home is still acclaimed as a highly imaginative work that preserves the lyricism and the mood of the ancient tale. In 1951 Kabuki actors successfully performed *Nayotake*, which has now become a popular modern piece in the Kabuki repertory.

In addition to Katō, Junji Kinoshita (1914—) deserves recognition as being one of the two major dramatists in the immediate postwar period who provided the impetus for the modern theater to once again seek a dramatic literature within the Japanese cultural tradition and to build a new theater that would no longer depend exclusively on the West for its guidance and inspiration. Kinoshita was a charter member of the Grape Society (Budō no Kai), a small group of young performers assembled under the leadership of Yasue Yamamoto (1906—), a seasoned actress once associated with the Tsukiji Little Theater. In 1948 the Grape Society presented *Tales of Hikoichi* (Hikoichibanashi), a humorous story drawn from the folk tale tradition that describes the extraordinary exploits of a wily young man who happened to be a skillful liar. Other similar Kinoshita works performed by the Grape Society and elsewhere finally led to the production of the well-known *Twilight Crane* in 1949. Konoshita's play as well as Yamamoto's performance as the tragic crane became a perennial favorite.

Yukio Mishima's *Kantan*, a modern Nō play, was given by the Literary Theater in 1950 and was followed by another work of his in a similar style, *Sotoba Komachi*, in 1952. His close ties with this troupe continued until November 1963, when he withdrew, along with Seiichi Yashiro and others, to establish the Neo Littérature Théâtre (NLT), the following year. In 1965 NLT performed *Yoroboshi*, one of his later modern Nō plays, included in this anthology. Subsequently, in 1969, Mishima and his faction broke off from NLT and established the Romance Theater (Roman Gekijō) where his final dramatic works were performed before he died in November 1970.

After receiving his degree in French literature from Waseda University, Yashiro joined the Literary Theater in 1949. The previous year his translation of Molière's *Les Femmes Savantes* had been accepted for one of its productions. Yashiro's career as a dramatist did not begin until *Castle* (Shiro). This play, presented in 1954, dealt with people of differing backgrounds soon after the war and explores the meaning of love. He remained with the Literary Theater until he joined NLT in 1963. His *Hokusai Sketchbooks*, a selection in this anthology, was an independent production produced in 1973.

The Actors' Theater—a small troupe made up of ten performers, including Koreya Senda, its present leader and director—was formed in August 1944. Some among them, like Senda, were important members of the prewar leftist theater movement, but for the duration of the war, the activities of the Actors' Theater remained ostensibly patriotic and non-controversial. The majority of its members who had left Tokyo because of the air raids organized a touring company that traveled throughout Japan. Its postwar performance back in Tokyo began in March 1946 with Gogol's *The Inspector General*, followed by plays by Rolland, Strindberg, Kliest, Molière, O'Neill, and Chekhov, along with plays by established Japanese playwrights. By 1949 it had also established a three-year actors' school and later assembled additional acting troupes from among the graduates.

In April 1954 this group opened the Actors' Theater playhouse, owned exclusively by the membership. One of the persistent problems in the modern theater movement was a lack of theater space, and for that reason tight program schedules in rented halls were generally necessary. There were few opportunities for long-running productions. After Osanai's death, the Tsukiji Little Theater was often rented out to various acting companies. An air raid in 1945, however, destroyed this structure. Now, at least, the Actors' Theater could set up a more independent schedule based solely on its own specific requirements, as the Tsukiji Little Theater had been able to do during its prime under Osanai's leadership.

The Actors' Theater gave Mishima's first successful drama, *House Fire* (Kataku), a one-act play, in February 1949, and his *The Damask Drum*, a modern Nō play, in 1952. One of Abe's initial efforts, *Slave Hunting* (Doreigari), was performed by this company in 1955. So were his other notable works, such as *The Ghost Is Here* (Yūrei wa Koko ni iru; 1958), *Tale of a Giant* (Kyojin Densetsu; 1960), and *You, Too, Are Guilty* (1965), translated in this anthology. In 1963 the Actors' Theater presented *Zeami*, a major play by Masakazu Yamazaki, describing the life of the great Nō actor, Zeami (1363–1443).

Organized by Osamu Takizawa and other members of the proletarian faction, the Tokyo Arts Theater began in March 1946 with a production of Ibsen's *A Doll's House*, directed by Hijikata, but it immediately disbanded in the following year. In July 1947 some of the charter members of the group, including Mori, Takizawa, and Jūkichi Uno (1914—), another active leader in the left-wing theater, formed the People's Arts Theater (Minshū Geijutsu Gekijō), usually called Mingei. For its opening performance in January 1948, the People's Arts Theater gave Tōson Shimazaki's (1872–1943) *The Broken Commandment*, adapted from one of his early novels in the realistic style. The original work, written in 1905, describes a schoolteacher who reveals to his students that he is a member of the pariah class, thus breaking his vow to his dying father. During the first period of the People's Arts Theater, which ended in July 1949, it presented Schiller's *Intrigue and Love*. Among Japanese plays, it offered Kinoshita's *Mountain Range* (Yamanami). This early work by Kinoshita depicts one woman's courageous struggle to escape the traditional restrictions of her farming community and to triumphantly realize her own personal happiness.

Reorganized in April 1950, the People's Arts Theater opened with Saneatsu Mushanokōji's (1885–1976) *The Sister* (Sono Imōto), a melodrama depicting the tragedy of a blind artist and his younger sister, who falls in love with their mutual benefactor. Mushanokōji had written the original story in 1915. In spite of the vast political changes and the Occupation, the theatrical groups of this period frequently chose plays based on prewar literary works and traditional themes. The basic modification in the mores and attitudes of a society occurs slowly, and the modern theater clearly indicated the truth of this general rule.

The People's Arts Theater performed works of many Japanese playwrights and also Miller, Tolstoi, Schiller, Gorki, Synge, O'Neill, Williams, and O'Casey. By including Western and Japanese plays portraying socialist realism on its season's program, this group still defends its proletarian principles.

Unlike the performers associated with the nonpolitical troupes, the members of the proletarian theater movement continued to be influenced by political changes at home and overseas. The cold war, the establishment of the People's Republic of China (1949), and the outbreak of the Korean war in June 1950 created sharp ideological disagreements among the membership of the left-wing theater. Because of the Korean situation, the Japanese government announced its plans to purge communists and sympathizers from national and municipal government in September 1950. This sweeping policy soon affected the modern Japanese theater. On October 3 the Actors' Theater reported to the Tokyo ward office that it had voluntarily disbanded its communist cell. In November and in December certain key members of the People's Arts Theater renounced their communist affiliations. While repercussions from these events also involved other organizations, the Literary Theater remained unaffected.

This "red purge" particularly affected the performers who worked for the motion picture industry. Since the newspapers listed communists and their alleged sympathizers, certain individuals were forced out of their jobs. The impact of the purge, fortunately, was short-lived, but the consequences clearly demonstrated that members of the proletarian theater were held accountable for their political ideology, even after the war.

The Korean armistice (1953), the relaxation of East-West tension in the late 1950s, and the amazing Japanese economic recovery leading to unprecedented prosperity in the 1960s has helped to stabilize the modern Japanese theater. With the rise of living standards among the Japanese, with more leisure time for workers and their families, the entertainment industry enjoyed a spectacular boom. The phenomenal growth of government and commercial television networks has provided new opportunities among the performers, whose income was previously limited to radio and motion pictures. Television appearances offer far higher wages and immediate public recognition than is found in the theater, often without the customary long apprenticeship and seniority demanded by the theater. The new medium has created greater mobility and freedom of action, especially for the younger actors, by shaking up the rigid structure and policies of the established acting companies.

The government-operated television network has brought stage performances to millions of additional viewers by televising entire theatrical productions. For example, in 1975, both *A Streetcar Named Desire,* staged by Literary Theater and starring Haruko Sugimura (who performed the role of Blanche for the seventh time since her first appearance in it in 1953), and *Death of a Salesman,* staged by People's Arts Theater with Osamu Takizawa as Willie Loman (a role he had first played in 1954) were televised in full-length versions soon after their commercial performances. Through these television programs, which are accompanied by carefully prepared commentaries, the public can appreciate the latest modern plays by Japanese dramatists as well as translated versions by popular Western playwrights.

The 1950s created a significant change in the modern theater movement. This occurred largely through the gradual rejection of two assumptions long held by the prewar modern Japanese theater: only translations of Western plays given on the contemporary stage would raise the quality of the theater, and only plays written according to Western dramaturgy would improve Japanese playwriting. The tendency in this direction was already evident in the case of Katō and Kinoshita, who dared to find their inspiration in Japanese culture and to create fresh modern plays that faithfully expressed their own true feelings and artistic ideas.

While these two dramatists were basically of a generation that had already turned professional before the war, others, like Mishima and Abe, represented playwrights from the 1950s who were also pursuing a similar goal. Mishima's modern Nō plays, like the plays by Katō and Kinoshita, attempt to interpret faithfully and to restage in a contemporary setting the essential mood of the traditional Nō drama. Abe, for his part, shifts his attention away from the past and focuses on the dynamic, changing reality of current Japanese society, where he perceives universal themes and perplexing issues shared by the rest of mankind.

In novels such as *The Woman in the Dunes* (1962), *The Face of Another* (1964), and *The Ruined Map* (1967), Abe addresses himself directly to the problems confronting modern man. The enigmatic, Kafkaesque quality of these works suggest the nagging perplexities of the existential situation. In his effort to find new approaches for presenting these issues, Abe constantly experiments. To force his audience into a deeper awareness of the basic intention behind his plays, he offers stage pyrotechnics deliberately calculated to expose the ironies and paradoxes of man's existence. *Friends* (1967) and *The Man Who Turned into a Stick* (1969) reveal his vigorous playwriting that demands an alert and perceptive audience. Although as a dramatist, Abe appears, at times, to be unconventional, incomprehensible, and even unJapanese, his basic aim is nothing less than a constant dissection of his society, which is forsaking many of its traditional assumptions and values and becoming part of "one world."

Abe's recent works include *Green Stocking* (Midori-iro no Sutokkingu; 1974), *Wē: New Slave Hunting* (Wē: Shin-Doreigari; 1975), *Guide* (Annainin; 1976), *Underwater City* (Suichū Toshi; 1977), and *Image Exhibition* (Imēji no Tenrankai) and *The Crime of Mr. S. Karuma* (S. Karuma-shi no Hanzai)—both given in 1978. All of these plays were performed by his own company, the Abe Studio.

You, Too, Are Guilty, presented in January 1965, takes place in a modern apartment and treats with sardonic humor the possible bond between the living and the dead. The strangeness of the "social contract" that Abe uses as an arresting theatrical device is reminiscent of his best-known novels.

In the modern Nō plays such as *Yoroboshi* (1965), Mishima may seem to espouse a radical, nonrealistic technique unfamiliar to the modern Japanese theater. Yet his approach is very much part of the existing Japanese theatrical tradition, which has always treasured its poetic, symbolic, and nonrepresentational elements—the Nō being its best example. His *Yoroboshi*, performed during May and June 1965, is an adaptation of a well-known Nō drama. The elegance and economy of this traditional theater is brilliantly evoked on the contemporary stage in a context of firestorms and universal guilt. Although his modern Nō play has no dancing, classical music, or chorus, and the performers appear without masks and are dressed in modern clothes, nevertheless, Mishima is able to effectively produce that mysterious mood unique to the Nō theater.

Among the classical theaters of Japan, whether Nō, Kabuki, or Bunraku, realism per se was never an issue, for the elements of drama, dance, and music were integral parts of the total theatrical experience. Thus the renewed appreciation and interest in the richness and diversity of the Japanese classical tradition heralded by playwrights like Mishima provided the necessary impetus for redirecting the modern Japanese theater to its own cultural past as a valuable source for creative inspiration.

Mishima's familiar neoclassicism is deeply rooted in his attachment and admiration for the past traditions of both Japanese and Western cultures. To readers in English, his early novel, *The Sound of Waves* (1954), may be reminiscent of first love as depicted in the classic story of Daphnis and Chloe. Besides the modern Nō plays and numerous works on both classical and modern themes, Mishima has also written several Kabuki plays. In order to create his own versions of Kabuki drama, he has employed old, familiar themes and also experimented with distinct writing styles from different periods in the development of the Kabuki theater. For one such work, Mishima adopts the theme from *Phèdre*, by Racine, who is regarded by literary historians as the most representative among all the French writers. Another Mishima play, *Madame de Sade*, presented in 1965, with a setting about the time of the French Revolution, once more illustrates his successful effort to re-create the highly sophisticated drawing room atmosphere reminiscent of an eighteenth century French aristocracy, although written as a modern Japanese play.

Though Abe and Mishima appear poles apart—one taking a modern position and the other a neoclassic one—they are, nevertheless, involved in creating new plays entirely independent of those in the realistic tradition, the mainstay of the prewar modern Japanese theater. Their plays are also unequivocal departures from rather ineffectual past efforts to create modern Japanese plays incorporating Western elements, then too culturally alien to the dramatist, the performers, and the audience.

As a professional dramatist, Seiichi Yashiro employs various styles ranging from the realistic to the theater of the absurd. He also incorporates elements from the traditional Japanese theater. Yashiro's urbane approach to playwriting represents the middle position that may provide the widest possible means of enriching the repertory of the modern Japanese theater. His unusual talent lies in his fresh, sparkling dialogue, skillful stagecraft, and warm humor. His plays reveal a consummate gift for capturing the subtle nuances and flavor of the Tokyo dialect, which has direct links to the common people of Edo (former Tokyo). *Hokusai Sketchbooks* is typical of this easy, balanced mood, which accounts for his wide popularity.

But Yashiro is not simply an entertaining playwright. He is a deeply moral writer who always reveals his own personal concern with the basic problems that have troubled Western man and particularly Christians. This aspect already appeared in his first successful work, *Castle* (Shiro), performed by the Literary Theater in 1954.

The drama focuses on a young wife bound in a loveless marriage to a much older man. The locale is a theater with a castle for a Western play as its stage setting. The woman, desperately infatuated with a young hoodlum clarinet player who is intimate with a thirtyish actress, intends to kill her rival as a means of seizing happiness for herself. When the principals confront each other on the rehearsal stage, however, they discover that their relationships to those they claim to love are actually quite ambiguous. The wife, realizing she is not loved by the young man, shoots herself.

On one level, Yashiro describes accurately the young people of the immediate postwar period who had lost all idealism and joy of life. For them, death was a perfectly reasonable alternative to the dreary, monotonous future without hope. The abrupt ending to this play poignantly underscores this philosophy. The perplexing problems of love, egoism, self-sacrifice, sin, and redemption—those issues that the young wife in *Castle* refused to face—become the recurring themes of his later works.

While dramas about religious conversions are familiar in the West, the subject is still rare in modern Japanese drama. Yashiro's *They Vanished at Dawn* (Yoake ni Kieta), presented in 1968, offers a candid testament on his final acceptance of the Catholic faith.

Among his most recent accomplishments, Yashiro has completed a series of three plays depicting the lives of outstanding *ukiyo-e* artists during the late Tokugawa period (1600–1867): *Sharaku* (Sharaku Kō; 1971), *Hokusai Sketchbooks* (1973), and *Eisen* (Inransai Eisen; 1975). In these works Yashiro fully demonstrates his mastery over the uninhibited ribaldry drawn straight from Edo culture expressed in his lively language and quick humor. Yet, it is his serious effort to explore the basic motivations behind the intriguing careers of Sharaku (fl. 1794–1795), Hokusai (1760–1849), and Eisen (1790–1848) that displays his full power as an outstanding playwright of this generation. A revival of these plays, including *Hokusai Sketchbooks*, was held as a three-part series in May and July 1977. Yashiro's most recent works include *The Fate of the Castaways* (Hyōryūmin no Hate; 1976) and *Bewitching* (Ayakashi; 1978).

In *Hokusai Sketchbooks*, performed in July and August 1973, Yashiro explores the individualistic philosophy of a famous creative artist who stubbornly defends his lifestyle and artistic freedom within the closed feudal society. The play presents an assortment of colorful characters whose diversity could not be dimmed by a regimented social system. The triumphant free expression by an individual whose zest for life overcomes seemingly insurmountable human adversities has universal meaning.

If Yashiro's versatility and range of dramatic expression ranks him among the important postwar dramatists, Masakazu Yamazaki also belongs in this category. Yamazaki is in addition a distinguished biographer, literary critic, and teacher, and a perceptive observer of the American cultural scene. While Yashiro represents a rare exception among modern Japanese dramatists who can successfully devote his whole career to playwriting alone, Yamazaki's various achievements outside the theater mark him as an individual with singular intellectual breadth. This extensive knowledge and background, especially in the history of ideas, literature, and the arts—both Japanese and Western— allow Yamazaki to present a lucid commentary on modern Japanese society through his plays and by extension on the universal human condition.

Similar to Yashiro, Yamazaki's approach to playwriting is open-minded and inventive, defying ready classification. In his first important play, *Zeami* (1963), based on the life of the celebrated master of the Nō stage, Yamazaki portrays him as the total embodiment of consecration.

Though Zeami has been favored by Shōgun Ashikaga Yoshimitsu (1358–1408), he is deeply disturbed because he must always remain within the shadows of his patron's benevolent protection and cannot assert his own selfhood. The time finally arrives, however, when he is no longer accorded such cordial treatment and is openly persecuted by one of the succeeding rulers. Zeami is even exiled to an offshore island. Later, his second son, also a Nō actor, enters the priesthood, and the eldest son in whom Zeami had placed so much hope suddenly dies while away from home. Now he must give up his title as the Nō master to a successor favored by the ruler. Zeami courageously registers his disapproval by refusing to give up the celebrated teachings of his Nō school.

An English version of this play was performed in a short run in New York during December 1965 while Yamazaki studied at Yale Drama School in the United States under a Fulbright grant.

The Boat Is a Sailboat, included in this anthology, was given in January 1973 by the Hands Group (Te no Kai), a small theater troupe founded jointly by Yamazaki and Minoru Betsuyaku. In this drama Yamazaki skillfully develops themes of alienation and confused identity in likeable, ordinary protagonists in the setting of modern Tokyo. The erosion of old, universally accepted values and the emergence of ambiguous new values is expressed by in-direction, and personal happiness seems less accessible than ever. For example, Tatsuno, the principal character, has no genu-ine passion or zeal for life. He compulsively moves from job to job and constantly forms new human ties, desperately trying to acquire a temporary respite from gnawing anxiety and a sense of isolation. Some readers may be reminded of Pirandello or the theater of the absurd, but Yamazaki is not bound by any narrow dramaturgy, as was often the case among the prewar modern playwrights.

In *Sanetomo Sets Sail* (Sanetomo Shuppan), presented in 1973, Yamazaki tells of a courtier-poet, Minamoto Sanetomo (1192–1219), who was mysteriously assassinated. The dramatist attempts to offer a modern psychological interpretation of the enigma surrounding the main character's short but colorful and compact career. For Yamazaki, Sanetomo's effort to accomplish so much in his brief life revealed within himself a profound spiri-tual vacuum, and he was desperately trying to fill up this void by immersing himself in feverish activity. In the end, Sanetomo builds a huge ship sturdy enough for a voyage to China. The boat, however, is too heavy to set sail. Despite the disaster, Sa-netomo is undaunted, for this ambitious project had kept him oc-cupied and had served the essential function of filling the ever-present emptiness within. Both Tatsuno in *The Boat Is a Sailboat* and Sanetomo lack the capacity to become totally committed to anything they undertake. Yamazaki seems to regard this phe-nomenon as a basic predicament plaguing modern man. This play was also performed in English at Washington University (St. Louis, Missouri) in 1976.

Yamazaki has also written *Oh, Héloïse!* ($\overline{O}$, Eroizu!), performed in 1972, with a medieval setting that explores the nature of pure love through the well-known romance of Abélard and Héloïse. He even has a musical comedy to his credit. Yamazaki's latest play is *Hideyoshi and Rikyū* (Mokuzō Kakukei; 1978).

By the early fifties Abe was already experimenting with exis-tentialism and surrealism in his writings, and his own use of these modes in dramatic works clearly placed him at the forefront of an important trend departing from the prewar tendency toward realism. He was at least a decade ahead of his countrymen, whose popular interest in the writings of Sartre, Brecht, Beckett, and others started in the sixties.

Minoru Betsuyaku, who began writing plays in the early sixties, represents a younger group of dramatists who were strongly affected by the theater of the absurd. His first important work, *The Elephants* (Zō), was performed at the Actors' Theater in April 1962 by the Free Stage (Jiyū Butai), a troupe consisting mainly of drama students associated with Waseda University.

The Elephants is a strange play, set in a hospital and centering on a young man and his uncle, a victim of the atomic bomb. Before being hospitalized, the uncle had long relished making a public display of his horrible scars. As the one-act play ends, the uncle dies and is carted away. Now the young man, who had also survived the bomb, is beginning to show symptoms of the dreaded radiation sickness. He must remain in the hospital.

Like many plays in the theater of the absurd, the characters in *The Elephants* have no specific names, there is scarcely any plot, and little dramatic action takes place on the stage. The burden, therefore, is placed on the dialogue for sustaining dramatic tension and driving the play forward toward its ironic conclusion. Betsuyaku successfully achieves this effect in the dialogue by the constant repetition of key words and phrases found within the play. These are often delivered like a chant—that is intended to create a hypnotic influence over the audience. Much of this technique, so effective in Japanese, is lost in an English translation, where a faithful rendition of the original passages would sound monotonous and even distracting. The playwright builds up the play to a high emotional pitch through the skillful alteration of the ordinary language pattern, subtly modifying and rearranging its rhythm and tempo. He boldly challenges his performers to invent new ways to effectively deliver the lines and to convey precisely the emotion and meaning behind the spoken words.

To those already familiar with Ionesco's *Rhinoceros* (1959), where his characters turn into rhinoceroses because of a strange disease, *The Elephants*, given two years later, may ominously suggest that everyone in the hospital will eventually die, and so may the rest of mankind, still very much under the threat of a nuclear war. Betsuyaku's other works, such as *A Little Girl Who*

Sells Matches (Matchiuri no Shōjo; 1966) and *Alice in Wonderland* (Fushigi no Kuni no Alisu; 1970) retain the style of his earlier plays where he developed a unique stage language for expressing his distinctive, forbidding view of the world. He often presents a modern allegory whose simple language and seemingly ordinary actions veil the bittersweet ironies and inescapable absurdities of the human predicament. His more recent works include *The Buried Scenery* (Uzumareta Fūkei) and *Abuku tatta! Niitatta!*, both performed in 1976, and *Ni-shi-mu-ku Samurai* (1977).

The Move, which appears in this anthology, was presented in September 1973 by the Hands Group. In this strangely haunting play, Betsuyaku offers an abstract treatment of human existence and destiny, focusing on a single family as it embarks on a journey to nowhere in a futile and pathetic quest for a better life. The agonizing trip reduces the original party of grandparents, a couple, and their baby to only the husband and wife. Yet, despite the mounting terror and anxiety, they desperately press onward as though eagerly anticipating their ultimate doom.

In addition to his playwriting, Betsuyaku is recognized as one of the founders of the "little theater movement" (shōgekijō undō) of the sixties. This new movement had its beginnings in such groups as the Free Stage, which performed on the second floor of a coffee shop in back of Waseda University. It was the forerunner of the Waseda Little Theater, also organized by Betsuyaku and others in 1966. This second theater finally closed in 1975 after a remarkably long existence. Now the reorganized membership has moved out to the foothills of Mount Fuji where they perform in a village farmhouse.

During the late fifties, many members of the postwar generation of college students and intellectuals voiced their political and more general discontent by rallying around the opposition to the U.S.–Japan Mutual Defense Treaty (1960). Among those youths, many also belonged to existing leftist theater groups where they expected open public support, denouncing the terms of the Treaty through political activism and appropriate theatrical presentations. The great outcry against the Treaty never materialized. To the disappointed youths, the modern theater movement as a whole had rejected its political and artistic responsibilities by remaining aloof at a critical moment in Japan's history. Their frustration and a deep sense of alienation from the mainstream of the modern theater movement were translated into practical terms by the formation of drama groups made up entirely of the younger generation who would now challenge the authority of the "established" theatrical companies—both proletarian and apolitical. While this new movement—also identified as "underground" or *"angura"* in Japanese—was at least a decade behind its Western counterpart, it helped, nevertheless, to reshape and redirect the course of the modern Japanese theater.

Betsuyaku and his associates who led this fresh movement believed that the major modern theater companies had become too self-satisfied and inflexible to seriously commit themselves to vigorous experimentation and greater artistic growth. On the other hand, they would put forth their own ideals by forming a small, dedicated group—free of the shortcomings often associated with large, commercially oriented groups. Even though the Waseda Little Theater had a capacity of about 80, it belonged entirely to the young troupe, which could set policies suited to its particular artistic needs. After the mid-sixties, these little theater groups arose all over Japan, performing in coffee shops, rented apartments and basements, tents, public squares, open fields, and on backs of trucks. Many soon failed because of their youthful inexperience and poor financial resources, and only a handful have successfully survived into the seventies.

Their long-range effect, however, has been significant. These little theater groups opened up unprecedented opportunities for the younger generation in the modern Japanese theater to gain first-hand experience as directors, playwrights, and performers. This movement also helped to dissipate, once and for all, the inveterate, deferential attitude toward the Western theater that had persisted throughout the prewar period. From its inception, it has encouraged a healthy, eclectic approach among the young people which has, in turn, fostered greater freedom and creativity in the entire modern theater.

By greatly reducing the former emphasis on the realistic theatrical tradition borrowed from the West, this new movement put to rest the limitations imposed on playwriting early in the twentieth century. It has readily abandoned the conventional method of presenting plays within the framework of the familiar Western theater architecture and the proscenium stage, which were imported. The young dramatists like Takayuki Kan (1939—), Jūrō Kara (1941—), and Makoto Satō (1943—) boldly pursue their own distinctive careers with the modern theater but share in common a fresh and imaginative approach to playwriting. They freely combine techniques and themes from the Japanese theatrical tradition with more recent ideas from both at home and abroad.

Nearly fifty years have passed since Osanai and Hijikata helped to build the Tsukiji Little Theater, where so many future leaders of the modern Japanese theater were trained. Today the established groups that are the legacies of the earlier Tsukiji Little Theater are finally being challenged by the younger members, who demand greater artistic freedom, earlier professional recognition, and better financial rewards. The growing exodus of these younger people from the leading theatrical troupes and the increasing number from among their ranks who prefer to work independently reveal a crucial problem still unresolved within the modern Japanese theater. The departing dissidents often express their strong dissatisfaction with the autocratic nature of the leadership within these older organizations. In a wider cultural context, this allegation is only symptomatic of the changing Japanese society whose traditional authoritarian relationships are gradually breaking down, and the younger generation is taking advantage of its newly gained freedom and self-determination.

BIOGRAPHICAL NOTES

KŌBŌ ABE (1924–) was born in Tokyo but spent his early years in northern China (Manchuria). Although a graduate of the University of Tokyo Medical School, he has devoted himself entirely to writing plays and novels. (See *YOU, TOO, ARE GUILTY*)

YUKIO MISHIMA (1925–70), who was born in Tokyo, received a bachelor of law degree from the University of Tokyo. During his brief but brilliant literary career, he distinguished himself as both a playwright and a novelist. (See *YOROBOSHI: THE BLIND YOUNG MAN*)

SEIICHI YASHIRO (1927–), who is a native of Tokyo, graduated from the Department of French Literature at Waseda University (Tokyo). After spending some time as a translator of French drama and as a stage director, he gained recognition as a playwright in the mid-fifties. (See *HOKUSAI SKETCHBOOKS*)

MASAKAZU YAMAZAKI (1934–) was born in Kyoto but lived in northern China (Manchuria) during his childhood. He graduated from the Department of English at Kyoto University and also attended Yale Drama School under the Fulbright Program in 1964–65. Yamazaki first attracted public notice as a dramatist in the early 1960s. (See *BOAT IS A SAILBOAT*)

MINORU BETSUYAKU (1937–), who was born and raised in northern China (Manchuria), was later repatriated to Japan after the war. In 1960, he withdrew from the Department of Political Science and Economics at Waseda University (Tokyo) and joined the staff of a labor union. His writing career began in the early Sixties. (See *THE MOVE*)

Modern Japanese Drama: An Anthology

You, Too, Are Guilty

KŌBŌ ABE

Originally published in Japanese as
Omae nimo Tsumi ga aru
(Tokyo: Shinchōsha)

Copyright © 1978 Kōbō Abe
(Authorized revised version)
All rights reserved

This play was first performed at the Actor's Theater (Tokyo) on January 1, 1965. The performance was directed by Koreya Senda. In July 1978, Kōbō Abe completed a major revised version of the original Japanese play. The present authorized English translation is included in *Modern Japanese Drama: An Anthology* with the playwright's special permission.

CHARACTERS
(in order of their appearance)
MAN NEXT DOOR
WOMAN SHOPPER (walk-on)
WOMAN NEXT DOOR
NEWSPAPER BOY (walk-on)
MAN
DEAD BODY
WOMAN
POLICEMAN A
POLICEMAN B (walk-on)
POLICEMAN C (walk-on)
PLAINCLOTHESMAN D (walk-on)

Scene One

A single door at stage center.

(Mysterious MAN NEXT DOOR *enters from stage right. While carefully glancing around, he assumes an outwardly nonchalant air. Upon reaching the door, he knocks lightly.)*

MAN NEXT DOOR: No answer.

(As he takes out a piece of wire with a bent tip from his pocket and moistens it with his tongue, suddenly there is the sound of wooden clogs at stage left. It is WOMAN SHOPPER, *who carries a towel, washbasin, etc., as if she will go to the public bath and plans later to shop for her supper on the way back. Flustered,* MAN NEXT DOOR *retreats from the door and pretends to exercise. He makes a friendly bow to the passing woman. He gazes after the woman, who had eyed him rather nervously.)*

Act as though nothing's the matter, and no one will suspect the worst. Just look at the gasman, the postman, the insurance salesman, and the cosmetics salesman. These fellows can walk around freely from street to street and from door to door without arousing any suspicion. In other words, you might say that society is built on mutual trust. So, if you want others to trust you, you have to start out by trusting them.

(Again he moistens the tip of the wire, nestles against the door, and glancing around once more, quickly inserts the wire into the keyhole. With his free hand, he pinches his ear, trying to steady his nerves. At the sound of the yielding lock, he jumps back and looks about.)

Meow! *(Imitating a cat.)*

(At that moment, from stage right WOMAN NEXT DOOR *runs in, pushing a baby carriage loaded with a dead body. As if expecting her,* MAN NEXT DOOR *quickly opens the door while* WOMAN NEXT DOOR *rushes inside, pushing the carriage.)*

WOMAN NEXT DOOR: I forgot the shoes! Will you hurry and get them!

(Nodding, MAN NEXT DOOR *closes the door behind him and walks quickly toward stage right. Inside the door, the thud of a body falling to the floor. Startled,* MAN NEXT DOOR *stops short.)*

MAN NEXT DOOR: If you trust society, there's nothing to be afraid of.

(He exits to stage right. NEWSPAPER BOY enters from stage left and slides the evening paper under the door. He goes to stage right as MAN NEXT DOOR returns with a pair of shoes. MAN NEXT DOOR looks about as he opens the door.)

Hurry!

WOMAN NEXT DOOR (rushes out, pushing the empty baby carriage):

May he rest in peace. May he rest in peace . . .

(She runs off to stage right. MAN NEXT DOOR neatly arranges the shoes and shoves them inside the door. After looking over the apartment, he closes the door. With his coat sleeve, he wipes off the fingerprints around the doorknob and walks casually toward stage right with perfect composure.)

The stage darkens.

Scene Two

A studio apartment. To stage right, a door. At stage center, a bed set apart by a curtain. At stage left, a desk and a chair. A high window. Farther stage left, presumably a kitchenette and the toilet. A room without walls is preferable.

The spotlight is on the dead body lying at the center of the room.

As the spotlight fades, the entire room becomes dimly lit. The evening sky is seen through the window. Street noises. The sound of approaching footsteps outside the apartment. The snapping bark of a dog.

(Whistling accompanies the approaching footsteps. Both stop and the door opens. MAN enters. He holds a briefcase in his left hand and carries a load of groceries under his right arm.)

MAN: That's funny. The door's unlocked . . . (Mystified, MAN inclines his head to one side but immediately recovers and starts humming. Shifting the briefcase to his right hand, he closes the door. Still facing the door, he switches on the light and hastily slips off his shoes without untying them. Suddenly, he notices a strange pair of shoes by the door and stops humming. Turning around, he discovers the dead body.) I wonder who it is? (Frowning, he approaches the dead body.) Did a drunk get in by mistake? Hey! Wake up! (Clicks his tongue.) Damn it! (Laying down his burden on the desk, MAN puts his hand on the shoulder of the dead man

and tries to peer into his face. MAN *finally realizes he is dead.)*
. . . He's dead! . . . *(Slowly backing up to the front door.)* Wait
a minute! Better look him over before I call the police . . .
(Fearfully, MAN *goes back and gets on all fours next to the dead
body and looks into his face.)* I don't remember this face. Never
saw him before . . . *(Rising suddenly.)* It's blood! Might be
murder! . . . What a mess! *(Pressing both hands against his
temples, he glances about anxiously.)* But he's a total stranger
. . . There's no way they can suspect me . . . *(Walking toward
the door.)* Still, what a nuisance . . . *(Taking a look at his
watch.)* . . . And she'll be here in another thirty minutes . . .
Our date is completely ruined . . . The police detectives and
the rest will barge in one after another . . . A house search!
. . . *(Glancing around.)* With her here, that'll be a bit awkward
. . . Really awkward! Before I call them, I'd better, at least, get
rid of those two things . . . *(Disconcerted, walks toward the
desk but stops short in front of the dead body.)* Why in my apartment of all places? *(Turns about abruptly and gazes anxiously in
the direction of the kitchenette at stage left. Appears relieved that
no one else is present.)* I just don't understand it . . . And the
police may find it hard, too . . . That's bad! If they're
stumped, that spells bad news for me, too. Of course, there's
no proof that I'm the murderer. On the other hand, there's no
further proof that I'm in the clear, either . . . What a disaster!
(Pause.) All I need is an alibi! . . . *(Pondering.)* An alibi . . .
But for that I'd have to know the time of his death . . .
*(Glances over the dead body. Then fearfully picks up a coat sleeve
and lifts an arm. Horrified,* MAN *drops it.)* Hmm, no rigor
mortis yet . . . How many hours before that sets in? . . .
Anyway, he must have just died . . . Damn it! It's getting
worse for me!
*(The following dialogue should be presented as an imaginary exchange
between* MAN *and a hypothetical police detective, with the actor
playing* MAN *speaking both parts.)*
Police Detective: Tell me. Where were you and what were you
doing for an hour before you came back to this apartment?
MAN: Oh, mostly walking around town.
Police Detective: Walking around? What for?
MAN: Just walking. No particular reason.

Police Detective: That's strange. Didn't you invite your girlfriend to the apartment today? Why did you walk around when there was such a pleasant time to look forward to?

MAN: I didn't want to get back until the very instant that she promised to come.

Police Detective: I see . . . In other words, you wanted her to find the body first . . .

MAN: That's ridiculous! Can't you understand? A lonely apartment can be such a dull and empty place for a bachelor in love.

Police Detective: Don't you have any self-control? You only had to wait an hour!

MAN: Let me ask you. Suppose I'm guilty? What's the motive?

Police Detective: You know that better than I do. As far as I'm concerned, you're guilty as long as there's no proof of your innocence . . .

(*The imaginary dialogue is interrupted by approaching footsteps. Startled,* MAN *holds his breath. He dashes to the door and locks it. The footsteps pass by.*)

. . . That's absurd. If I'm innocent, I'm innocent . . . What was I going to do? . . . Yes, go to the police . . . That's right! Before I do, I should tend to my own affairs . . . (*Runs to the desk and ransacks the drawers.*) Where's the diary and the picture album? . . . (*Heading back toward the door.*) Such things that might stir up misunderstanding should be . . . (*Suddenly halts.*) Hold on! The outside garbage bin may not be the place for them . . . It's a case of homicide . . . Likely places for disposing of the murder weapon will be thoroughly searched . . . I'll burn them!

(*After ripping a few pages from the diary,* MAN *lights a match and sets fire to them; then he heads for the kitchenette. The frantic sound of running water to extinguish the fire.* MAN *returns.*)This is stupid! I've got more important things to do. (*Approaching the dead body,* MAN *is about to reach out with his hands to turn it over on its back but wavers. Although he kneels down beside the dead body,* MAN *cannot bring himself to touch it and finally rises.*) Damn it! When my Old Man died, I left it all to the mortician and didn't have to lift a finger . . . (*Glancing around, he brings a chair and uses it as a lever to turn over the body. Peers fearfully into the face of the dead body.*) What a miserable way to end up . . . What did he do to deserve this? (*Looks carefully at the body's forehead.*) The weapon used wasn't a knife. Must have been a hammer or a club . . . (*Uncovers the inside pocket of the topcoat.*) The name tag is torn off . . . Definitely a professional job . . . (*Going around the dead body, he checks through each pocket.*) Suppose he has my name card or something which can be traced back to me. Then it wouldn't matter how hard I claimed that he was a total stranger . . . They're empty . . . That's a relief . . . (*Relieved, stands up. Suddenly, glancing back toward the kitchenette.*) I shouldn't have done that! What would the police think if they saw the ashes? . . .

(*A light knock on the door.* MAN *stands frozen. Again, knocking. He quietly shoves the body under the bed. Third knocking. Disconcerted, he looks for a place to hide the rest of the diary and the picture album. He throws them into the toilet and flushes. Smoothing down his hair,* MAN *takes a deep breath, forces a smile, and heads for the door.*)

    Yes, coming . . .

(*As* MAN *opens the door, it is* WOMAN NEXT DOOR, *who barges in.*)

WOMAN NEXT DOOR (*smiling*): You're certainly back early today.

MAN: What's wrong?

WOMAN NEXT DOOR: Well, if nothing's wrong, that's fine . . . That's simply fine . . . (*As she observes* MAN's *expression, her smile fades.*)

MAN: . . .

WOMAN NEXT DOOR: Don't you always get back after ten?

MAN: I had special business today.

WOMAN NEXT DOOR: Well, since you're back now, a strange noise is nothing to fuss over, is it?

MAN: Did you hear something?

WOMAN NEXT DOOR: Well, if you didn't hear anything . . . (*Suddenly her eyes are fixed on the dead man's shoes.*) But there are so many frightening stories lately . . .

MAN (*becoming aware of her gaze, he replies in confusion*): Oh, I don't think so.

WOMAN NEXT DOOR: What time did you get back?

MAN: What are you suspicious about?

WOMAN NEXT DOOR: Suspicious? That sounds terrible.

MAN: Then don't look in and stare so hard.

WOMAN NEXT DOOR: I'm not trying to look in . . . Just smelling.

MAN: What smell? . . .

WOMAN NEXT DOOR: As if something is smoldering . . . You think it's a short circuit?

MAN: Oh, that? . . . I burned some paper . . . The air in this room is so muggy.

WOMAN NEXT DOOR: The air, you say . . .

MAN: Yes, two, three sheets of paper . . .

WOMAN NEXT DOOR: Two, three sheets? . . . Well, I'm sorry to have bothered you . . .

(She quickly exits. Pressing against the door, MAN heaves a sigh of relief. Locking the door, he picks up the dead body's shoes from the doorway.)

MAN: Whew! I nearly forgot to take care of those shoes . . .

(A light shines over the bed and through the gauze curtain, revealing DEAD BODY sitting on top of the bed.)

DEAD BODY: What are you doing with my shoes?

MAN (startled): Who's that?

DEAD BODY: It's me . . . The body you shoved under the bed.

MAN (relieved): So you were alive.

DEAD BODY: Of course not! (Crawls off the bed.)

MAN (backing away): Never mind. Don't bother coming out.

DEAD BODY: Don't be so irresponsible.

MAN: What's irresponsible about it? Besides, I'm the one whose being imposed upon!

DEAD BODY: I'm asking about those shoes . . .

MAN: Shoes?

DEAD BODY: What are you trying to do with them?

MAN (looking at the shoes): . . .

DEAD BODY: If you're not guilty, why change the scene of the crime?

MAN (distracted): Well, I'm expecting a visitor soon . . .

DEAD BODY: Then why not call the police immediately? Stop this strange cover-up . . .

MAN: You bet, I'll call them! I wouldn't live with a dead body, for the world! But before I do . . . (Glances about.)

DEAD BODY: These shoes are different from your diary and the nude photographs. You can't flush them.

MAN: I know that! (Lured into checking the toilet.) The damned thing is stuck!

DEAD BODY: What a shortsighted fellow you are! . . . No, you're probably afraid.

MAN (*throws the shoes down in their original place*): Once you're dead, you've got nothing to be afraid of! (*Gets a plunger from the kitchenette and attempts to unplug the toilet.*)

DEAD BODY: You'll make it worse!

MAN: . . .

DEAD BODY: Are you sure you're doing the right thing by making all these changes? . . .

MAN: I'll soon put everything back the way it was . . .

DEAD BODY: Isn't it too late already?

MAN (*continues to struggle with the plunger*): . . .

DEAD BODY: You seem to act entirely on the assumption that it was murder. But maybe I just collapsed from a heart attack or something. However, thanks to your hasty meddling . . .

MAN (*startled, stops working*): Were you a burglar or a sneak thief?

DEAD BODY: I won't deny that possibility. Maybe I was and maybe not.

MAN (*shaken*): Then how about the wound on your forehead?

DEAD BODY: I staggered and bumped against the corner of that desk. And although I tried to stay on my feet, I couldn't make it, and finally fell down here. (*Pointing to the floor.*)

MAN: Who'd believe such a story? It sounds a bit fishy . . .

DEAD BODY: I suppose so . . .

MAN (*subdued*): Please . . . What really happened to you?

DEAD BODY: I can only leave that up to your own imagination. You know, dead men tell no tales . . .

MAN: Tell no tales? . . . Aren't you chatting freely now?

DEAD BODY: Well, there's a difference between chatting and expressing an opinion. Unfortunately, the dead are only permitted to speak within the limits of the listener's own powers of imagination.

MAN: Can't you make this an exception?

DEAD BODY: If an exception is made to raise me from the dead . . .

MAN (*desperately*): What can I do?

DEAD BODY: Do exactly as I told you.

(*A woman's footsteps are heard approaching down the corridor.*)

MAN (*holding his breath*): Could it be her?

DEAD BODY: Don't say I didn't warn you.

(*The footsteps pass by.*)

MAN (*sighs with relief*): It wasn't her!

DEAD BODY: Muster up your courage!

MAN (*suddenly snapping back*): Courage? Don't sound so smug! How can the dead ever understand my situation!

DEAD BODY: Don't talk like a coward. You know, women are, as a rule . . .

MAN: Shut up!

DEAD BODY: Now, don't get so excited!

MAN: I admit there are sudden disasters in this world. Auto accidents, beams falling at a construction site, getting stabbed in the street by a mad killer . . . But this was in my apartment . . . And there's no insurance against such a disaster.

DEAD BODY: You're exaggerating . . . It's too early to give up . . .

MAN: No, I give up.

DEAD BODY: As I told you before, I was only chatting within the limit of your own power of imagination. If you'd like, I can give you a totally different deduction. For example—ready? That housewife next door . . . What was her reason to come snooping around?

MAN: . . .

DEAD BODY: Suppose you chose this line of argument . . . Follow me?

MAN: No, I don't . . .

DEAD BODY (*sharply*): Maybe she's the real culprit!

MAN (*mumbling*): Don't try to kid me.

DEAD BODY (*speaking pursuasively*): Now listen. You seem to have already made up your mind that this room was the scene of the crime. But where's the evidence?

MAN: . . .

DEAD BODY: The murder might have been committed somewhere else entirely different . . . And I might have been carried in here after I was killed.

MAN: There's no end to making that kind of assumption.

DEAD BODY: It doesn't have to be an assumption. For example, take a look at the doorway . . . When you observe closely from this angle, you can see two faint lines.

MAN: Two lines?

DEAD BODY: Like tire tracks.

MAN (*looking closely at the entrance from various angles*): Now that you mention it . . .

DEAD BODY: By that width, I'd say it was a baby carriage . . .

MAN: A baby carriage?

DEAD BODY: Too bad the precious evidence is terribly faint because you've been walking around so carelessly . . .

MAN: You mean the body was carried in here by a baby carriage?

DEAD BODY: That's why the housewife next door was so anxious . . .

MAN: But why does it have to be her?

DEAD BODY: Why? Would she come snooping around without any reason?

MAN: Could have been the manager. He has a pass key to all the apartments . . .

DEAD BODY: Oh, the locks in this building can be picked open with a single nail.

MAN: . . . You're right, there's something strange about that couple next door . . .

DEAD BODY: You see?

MAN (*looking preoccupied*): Are you serious about all this?

DEAD BODY: Well, as I've said repeatedly, I can only speak within the limits of your own imagination . . .

(MAN *leaves for stage left.*)

DEAD BODY: Where are you going?

MAN'S VOICE: How about a drink?

DEAD BODY: Don't be foolish! If you smell of alcohol, the police will get a less favorable impression of you.

MAN (*returns with a glass of whiskey in his hand*): None of your business! (*Takes a drink.*)

DEAD BODY: You're the one who's going to be sorry. Since you seem to like detective stories, you must have read somewhere about "dead spots." These purple spots under the skin of a corpse are caused by the precipitation of blood. So if you move the body, the position of these spots naturally changes. You can't fool the experts. Don't you realize that your situation is getting steadily worse?

MAN (*after a final drink from his glass*): It's too late anyhow.

DEAD BODY (*flustered*): Too late? Don't be so callous! What are you planning to do with me?

MAN: How should I know? If you're already dead, why can't you act more resigned to your present fate?

DEAD BODY: The dead can only stay alive within the memories of those who are still living. To a dead man, the place where he died is the final door linking him to life. Isn't it only natural that the dead man would have a special attachment for the place where he died—for all eternity!

MAN (*taking out the canned goods, etc., from the paper bag on the desk*): I'll have to get ready for her visit . . .

DEAD BODY (*anxiously*): It's in such bad taste to leave me here like this and to carry on with your girlfriend. You're young, and you've still got a long life ahead of you. For your own good, listen to me . . .

MAN: I'll just repeat what happened to me with someone else. Don't worry about it.

DEAD BODY: And what will you do?

MAN: Pass the buck.

DEAD BODY: Pass the buck?

MAN: Just as someone tossed you into my apartment, this time I'm going to toss you into someone else's. Plus and minus equals zero . . . Hurry up and disappear! . . . Listen, it might be her . . .

(*Approaching footsteps.*)

DEAD BODY: You're a fool!

MAN: I may be a fool, but I'm not a coward.

DEAD BODY: But plus and minus may not equal zero. For example, look! What do you plan to do with that bloodstain!

MAN (*startled*): Bloodstain?

DEAD BODY (*pointing*): That bloodstain . . . A test will instantly give you away!

MAN: Damn it!

(*Frantically, MAN puts a cup over the bloodstain. Then removing the cup, replaces it with an ashtray. Again, sound of knocking. MAN acts as if he is driving away DEAD BODY. The latter disappears. MAN starts to head toward the door but changing his mind, removes the ashtray, takes a book from his desk, and covers the spot instead. Again, goes to the door.*)

Scene Three

MAN: Who is it?

WOMAN'S VOICE: It's me . . .

MAN (*becoming aware of* DEAD BODY's *shoes, he grabs and hides them behind his back as he opens the door*): Come in.

WOMAN: Have you a visitor?

MAN (*surprised*): Why?

WOMAN: I thought I heard voices . . .

MAN: Must be some other apartment. You know how cheaply this building is made.

WOMAN (*gazing suspiciously at the rather absent-minded* MAN): Is it all right?

MAN (*recovering himself*): Of course. Please come in . . . (*Glances around the room over his shoulder as he remains constantly in her line of vision with reference to the bed.*) Where can you sit? . . . I know, that chair is the best . . .

WOMAN (*concerned that there is only one chair*): How about you?

MAN: Who—me? Oh, I can sit anywhere. (*He walks backward and sits on the bed.*)

WOMAN: But I don't feel very comfortable . . . Why don't we sit together on the floor?

MAN (*flustered*): No, not down there! It's unhealthy.

WOMAN (*starts sniffing around*): . . .

MAN (*startled*): What is it?

WOMAN: Don't you smell it?

MAN: That's odd. (*Pretending to smell under the bed.*) I didn't think it would start smelling yet . . .

WOMAN (*sniffing*): Like something got scorched . . .

MAN (*relieved*): Oh, that . . . (*Pointing to the kitchenette.*) I just burned some wastepaper over there. Let's open the window.

WOMAN: Never mind. It'll get cold in here.

MAN (*rises, without heeding her*): I'll turn on the electric heater right away.

WOMAN (*speaking bluntly*): What's that? (*Gazes apprehensively at the pair of shoes* MAN *forgot he held behind his back.*)

MAN (*confused*): They're shoes.

WOMAN: I know that . . .

MAN: It's nothing . . . (*Quickly throws the shoes on the bed.*)

WOMAN: Is the bed over there? (*Rises and is about to go toward the bed.*)

MAN (*frantically*): Stay where you are! (*Inadvertently kicks the book that conceals the bloodstain.*)

WOMAN (*notices* MAN *returning the book to the same spot*): What's that book?

MAN (*stepping on the book*): It's nothing at all!

WOMAN (*stunned*): . . .

MAN (*apologetically*): Now, don't worry about it. It's really not important.

WOMAN: . . .

MAN: I'll make some tea . . . (*Realizing that* WOMAN *refuses to take her eyes off the book hiding the bloodstain.*) Did you know that a person dies every thirty seconds in Japan? So at this very instant, somewhere, someone is dying. But if you concern yourself with every such instance, you'll go crazy. The living have their hands full, simply trying to keep alive.

WOMAN: Does the book say that?

MAN (*impulsively*): Who cares! (*Regretting his outburst.*) It's just a detective story called "You, Too, Are Guilty . . ."

WOMAN: Oh?

MAN: . . . But if you concern yourself with each person who dies every thirty seconds . . .

WOMAN: I suppose you're right . . .

MAN: Don't you believe me?

WOMAN: Regarding what?

MAN: Say, how about a soft drink? I'm so thirsty.

WOMAN: Maybe it's better if I go home.

(DEAD BODY *appears with a faint smile on its face.*)

MAN (*startled*): Keep out of it! This is no time for you to butt in!

WOMAN: What!

MAN: I wasn't talking to you.

WOMAN: Then who were you talking to?

MAN (*taking a side-glance at* DEAD BODY): Of course, you may not understand, but . . .

WOMAN: How could I?

MAN: If you did, it'd be dreadful. (*Desperately.*) Damn it! Naturally, I know that death may be a crucial issue for the individual concerned. But isn't he a total stranger? Why should I give a damn?

WOMAN (*somewhat uneasily*): What do you mean?

DEAD BODY: You should have listened to my advice . . .

MAN (*about to reply harshly to* DEAD BODY *but quickly changes his mind and pleads with* WOMAN, *instead*): All right! I'll tell you everything! I'm having a hell of a time! You may not believe me even if I tell you. But will you at least try?

WOMAN: Yes, go on.

MAN: Yeah, I will.

DEAD BODY: Don't strain yourself. It's so shameful to put up such a fruitless struggle.

MAN (*inadvertently, to* DEAD BODY): Can't you shut up! (*To* WOMAN.) Sorry. I wasn't talking to you! Heard someone's voice in my head.

WOMAN: Have you a fever?

MAN: Let me see . . . (*Placing a hand on his forehead.*) Now that you mention it, there may be a touch of it.

DEAD BODY: Why don't you stop this. It's so ludicrous!

WOMAN: Isn't there a flu epidemic going on?

MAN: Maybe that's it.

WOMAN: Then you'd better not exert yourself. I'll make you something hot.

(*Suddenly,* DEAD BODY *marches out and in an exaggerated manner attempts to kick the book.*)

MAN (*frantically leaps on the book and tries to hold it down under his arms*): Cut it out!

WOMAN (*dumbfounded*): . . .

MAN (*irritated*): Sorry. Made a mistake . . .

WOMAN: You may be sicker than you think.

MAN: I wonder?

(*Again,* DEAD BODY *gets ready to kick the book.* MAN *instinctively prepares to stop* DEAD BODY *and can barely restrain himself.*)

WOMAN (*consoling* MAN): All right. I won't let that book bother me anymore . . .

MAN: Yeah. At any rate, in Japan alone a person dies every thirty seconds . . .

WOMAN: You're not going to die so easily from the flu . . .

MAN: Of course, it's a crucial issue for the individual concerned. But, after all, I'm not a mortician, so there should be no grounds for complaints.

WOMAN (*suddenly, turning serious*): I see . . .

MAN: Eh?

WOMAN: I'm shocked . . .

DEAD BODY: Isn't she under a misapprehension of some kind?

MAN: I bought some fine black tea. (*Starts rising.*)

DEAD BODY: But the bloodstain won't disappear.

WOMAN: I'll put away this book.

MAN (*desperately, tries to stop her*): No, you can't!

WOMAN (*stunned*): . . .

DEAD BODY: Serves you right!

MAN (*pleading with* WOMAN): Don't worry about that anymore.

WOMAN: So, wouldn't it be better to put it away?

MAN (*pretending not to hear*): I'll put the kettle on the gas burner. (*Goes to stage left.*)

WOMAN (*glancing around*): Even I'm beginning to get the chills . . . (*Calling toward stage left.*) Listen, can I turn on the heater?

MAN'S VOICE: Absolutely not! When the temperature goes up, rotting . . . I mean, it promotes the growth of harmful bacteria.

DEAD BODY (*jeeringly*): He's afraid I might start rotting . . .

WOMAN (*while watching stage left,* WOMAN *quietly approaches the book on the floor. Peeking at the title*): "You, Too, Are Guilty . . ."

DEAD BODY (*as if goading her on*): Pick it up! Pick it up!

(WOMAN *slowly stoops over and is about to reach out for the book. She suddenly withdraws at the sight of* MAN, *who returns from stage left with a tea set for the black tea on the tray.*)

WOMAN: What would *he* think if he knew you were treating him like he was dead?

MAN: Who?

WOMAN: . . . Well, aren't you?

MAN: Who are you talking about?

WOMAN (*as if trying to cover up her inadvertent slip, she takes the tray from* MAN *and carries it to the desk*): Isn't it obvious? . . . The one who gave you that book.

MAN (*thrusting back at her*): What for?

DEAD BODY: What a strange state of affairs. (*Laughs ironically.*)

WOMAN (*groping for words*): You're the one who brought it up!

MAN: I did? Brought what up?

WOMAN: Don't be so evasive!

MAN: What a way to pick a fight!

WOMAN: Maybe I should go home, after all.

MAN (*pleading*): Please, I'm begging you . . .

DEAD BODY: Good grief!

WOMAN: Then why don't you get rid of that book!

DEAD BODY: There you go! Now you're talking!

MAN: So, what I'm trying to say is . . .

WOMAN: Well, tell me!

MAN: You might call that book a metaphor . . . A metaphor for my desperate condition . . .

WOMAN: You can't expect me to understand a metaphor!

MAN: All right . . . I'll tell you everything . . . When I came back here, I found that a mysterious corpse had been tossed into my apartment. I mean, a body of a stranger who had nothing to do with me. Obviously, that's a crucial issue . . . Especially for the person who was killed . . . But am I responsible for taking care of that dead body, even at the risk of getting all involved?

WOMAN (*angrily*): I've had enough of your metaphors.

MAN: But it's not a metaphor!

WOMAN: Then, is it true?

DEAD BODY: Come on, you're almost there!

MAN (*flustered*): Well, assuming it's generally true . . .

DEAD BODY: Why don't you give up . . . Either show her what's under the book or let her peek under the bed.

MAN: Shut up! . . . No, I don't mean you! (*The sound of a kettle boiling over on stage left. Happily.*) Oh, it's boiling! (*Runs off stage left.*)

(DEAD BODY *walks around the dumbfounded* WOMAN *with a sardonic smile on his face.* MAN *returns with a steaming kettle.*)

WOMAN (*as if obsessed by the kettle*): Give it to me . . . Black tea won't steep properly unless the water is at a boil . . . (*Grabs the kettle. She begins to prepare the black tea.*)

DEAD BODY: Just look at the way she's behaving!

MAN (*unable to discern the truth behind* DEAD BODY'*s remark*): . . .

DEAD BODY: I'll bet she was all nerves, worrying you might dash the hot water over her head.

MAN: I can't believe it!

WOMAN: What?

DEAD BODY: If you don't believe me, holler and act as if you're going to attack her.

WOMAN: The tea's ready.

(As MAN approaches the desk, there is a noise under the bed. He inadvertently drops the teacup.)

WOMAN: Wasn't that under the bed?

DEAD BODY (laughs scornfully): Rigor mortis is setting in.

MAN: Must be a mouse.

WOMAN: A mouse?

MAN: You don't expect a tiger to jump out, do you?

WOMAN: You're right, I suppose . . .

DEAD BODY: I was shoved under the bed in a rather cramped position. And my arm which turned stiff sprang back and pushed up from under the bed. Well, suit yourself! . . . But don't forget that a debt has a set rate of interest.

WOMAN: Why not take a look?

MAN: There's nothing breakable down there.

WOMAN (suddenly, hysterically): Please, tell me! What's that book all about? Can't you put it away somewhere!

(Pause. Sound of knocking on the door. It offers partial relief from the existing tension.)

Scene Four

MAN (stiffly): Who is it please?

MAN NEXT DOOR (obsequiously): It's me, your next-door neighbor . . .

DEAD BODY: You see! They've come back to spy again! This time it's the husband.

MAN (momentarily wavers but with WOMAN present, he is compelled to act casually and advances to the door): Can I help you?

MAN NEXT DOOR: I'd like a serious word with you . . . But it's a little awkward standing in the doorway . . .

DEAD BODY (mischievously): Finally, we've got three witnesses!

MAN (*rather grudgingly opens the door, slightly*): I'm sorry, I have a visitor . . .

MAN NEXT DOOR: A visitor? (*Appears openly interested.*) I won't take up much of your time . . . (*Quickly forces himself in, glances about, and sees* WOMAN. *He displays obvious disappointment.*) I'm sorry to have disturbed you at a time like this . . . (*Bows knowingly to* WOMAN.)

MAN: I can drop in to see you later . . .

MAN NEXT DOOR: No, no! I couldn't let you do that . . . (*He looks over the area occupied by* DEAD BODY.) It'll only take a moment—five, six minutes . . . Or even two or three . . .

MAN (*angered*): Earlier, your wife came around using the same excuse. What's going on?

MAN NEXT DOOR (*appearing surprised in an exaggerated manner*): You say my wife did? Imagine that! . . . I hope she wasn't trying to borrow money . . .

MAN: Don't be absurd! In fact, she never got around to the point . . . But it looked too obvious for an excuse.

MAN NEXT DOOR: An excuse?

DEAD BODY: Hey! Why give yourself away! You'd better watch what you're saying!

MAN (*becoming obstinate*): But isn't it merely an excuse to peek into my apartment? . . . And don't you think I'm aware of that? After all, we hardly exchange greetings when we see each other . . .

MAN NEXT DOOR: Hmm. An excuse, you say? . . . Then, you mean there was some big happening at your place . . . And people are even willing to invent excuses to come around for a peek? (*Glancing around boldly.*) Lately, I haven't had much time to read the newspaper carefully . . .

MAN: Why don't you quickly tell me your business . . . You said two minutes?

MAN NEXT DOOR: Yes, two or three . . .

MAN: Well?

MAN NEXT DOOR: Now, don't keep me in suspense. What's the story?

(*While this exchange is taking place, the following action also occurs on the stage.* WOMAN *stealthily picks up the book on the floor as*

MAN's *attention is distracted by* MAN NEXT DOOR. *However, she does not see the bloodstain under the book. She examines the book from various angles. Then she carefully opens it and rapidly leafs through the pages. Finding nothing, she now grabs hold of its spine and shakes it to see if anything has been concealed inside. If time permits, she can glance at* MAN *once more, return to her chair, and start reading. Meanwhile,* MAN NEXT DOOR *carefully observes the apartment, especially places where a body can be hidden, but gradually focuses his attention on the area around the bed. Moreover,* MAN *unconsciously tries to obstruct* MAN NEXT DOOR's *view.*)

DEAD BODY (*mockingly*): You're really in a spot now . . .

MAN (*trying to eject* MAN NEXT DOOR): If you've got business, come right out with it! You're certainly exasperating!

MAN NEXT DOOR: Hmm, I see you're quite excited . . .

MAN: And why not! . . . With the two of you taking turns to come spying on me without any reason!

MAN NEXT DOOR (*in an exaggerated fashion*): Spying?

MAN: Why don't you state your business!

MAN NEXT DOOR (*undaunted*): Oh, I thought you might let me peek under the bed . . . (*Takes off his sandals and tries to step farther into the apartment.*)

MAN (*immediately grabs* MAN NEXT DOOR *and thrusts him back*): No! You're making an unlawful entry!

MAN NEXT DOOR: Please, no violence! . . .

(WOMAN *rises after laying the book on the desk.*)

    . . . Listen, young lady. (*Gives her a friendly smile.*)

MAN (*almost speechless with excitement*): Of all the nerve! . . . Imagine looking under a bed in someone else's apartment! . . . How would you feel if I'd asked you, all of a sudden?

MAN NEXT DOOR: Who—me? I wouldn't mind in the least. You're welcome to do that this instant . . . Go ahead . . .

MAN (*restraining himself*): And what's the point of looking under a bed?

MAN NEXT DOOR: . . . Then if you'll excuse me . . .

MAN: You can't!

MAN NEXT DOOR (*looking puzzled*): Why not?

MAN: None of your business! You're impossible!

MAN NEXT DOOR (*rather presumptuously to* WOMAN): Listen, young lady, can't you put in a word for me . . .

MAN: Well, why not state your purpose clearly!

WOMAN: Yes, why can't you be more specific . . .

DEAD BODY: "The mouth is the fount of misfortune."

MAN NEXT DOOR (*after a momentary reflection*): And if I tell you my purpose, will you promise to let me see under your bed?

DEAD BODY: I thought he'd use that approach. Now you're really cornered.

MAN: Never!

MAN NEXT DOOR (*showing no particular surprise*): You still refuse?

WOMAN: Why not listen to his reason, anyway?

MAN: I refuse! Please go now!

MAN NEXT DOOR (*with amazing good grace*): I see . . . Goodby. (*Exits.*)

(*After* MAN NEXT DOOR *leaves,* MAN *closes the door, locks it, and stands in a daze for a while. Looking rather anxious,* WOMAN *suspiciously peers, in turn, under the bed and around the shoulders of* MAN.)

Scene Five

DEAD BODY: . . . He's quite an imposter. He's worked it out so that he'd have a perfect alibi in case you charge him with suspicious activity by simply saying, "He didn't even listen to my reason." Besides, how ironic that his main witness happens to be your girlfriend!

(MAN *abruptly turns his head toward* WOMAN.)

WOMAN: What a strange man . . . What sort of interest would he have in looking under someone else's bed?

MAN: He had no honest reason!

WOMAN: But I'm a little curious.

DEAD BODY: Let me see. He might have asked: "Is there a rat hole going straight through the wall?" Or, "Has the stain on the ceiling from the leaking rain spread over to your side?" . . .

MAN: It's an excuse!

WOMAN: What excuse? Wasn't he accusing you of the same thing? . . .

MAN (*getting angry*): Are you suspicious of me, too?

WOMAN (*tries to humor him*): I'm just curious. Who knows? A rat might be there clutching the neighbor's diamond ring it its mouth. Let's pretend as if we were duped and take a peek . . .

MAN: Stop it! (*Cuts her off.*) As it is, we've wasted a lot of valuable time. Let's not go on with this nonsense . . . (*Suddenly realizes that the book on the floor is missing and catches his breath.*)

WOMAN (*fearfully, picking up the book from the desk*): I'm sorry . . . (*Grabs the book by its spine and shakes it.*) Still, it doesn't explode or give off smoke . . . It's only a book . . . I'm so relieved . . . Nevertheless, the important thing is to find out . . .

MAN (*distracted by the bloodstain*): I suppose so.

WOMAN (*returning the book to the desk*): I think the water for the tea has turned cold. I'll reheat it. (*Picks up the fallen teacup and exits with the tea kettle toward stage left.*)

MAN: Thank goodness.

DEAD BODY (*sardonically*): It's just a sweet smile before she starts clamoring for something.

(MAN *quickly pulls out a handkerchief from his pocket. As he cautiously watches for* WOMAN's *return, he soaks the handkerchief in the black tea on the desk and begins wiping away the bloodstain on the floor.*)

DEAD BODY (*in confusion*): What are you doing! Stop it!

MAN: I might as well go all the way!

WOMAN's VOICE: I'll wash these dirty dishes, too.

MAN: Oh, thank you . . .

DEAD BODY: That bloodstain might have been the only pathway to the truth left open to me . . .

MAN (*rubbing intently*): I hope all the truth disappears.

DEAD BODY: Why should it? Truth may change, but it never disappears. And a bloodstain is more persistent than any artist's colors. You may block the truth, but that, in turn, will only open up a pathway to misunderstanding.

(*As* DEAD BODY *has asserted, the bloodstain is rather difficult to wipe away, and* MAN *begins to slightly lose his self-assurance.*)

WOMAN's VOICE: . . . Is the white bottle with the label missing, the detergent?

MAN: . . . Probably . . . (*As if intrigued by* WOMAN's *question, begins to rise.*)

DEAD BODY: Why put up such a useless struggle?

MAN: Can't you just resign yourself to your fate! (*Stands up and goes to stage left.*)

DEAD BODY (*annoyed at* MAN's *actions*): Damn it! Thanks to you, I'm about to get killed for the second time . . . First, it was my physical death, and now—within the hearts of living men . . . How can the law be so lopsided? It only punishes killers who are charged with physical death and winks at the second kind of murder . . . Since judges have never died before, I guess it can't be helped . . . But, in fact, the second kind is far more terrifying. . . . For the victim his having been alive becomes a total waste. It's as though he had never lived at all! It's like turning into a mate for a worn-out wooden clog or into a half-eaten piece of bread—floating down a pitch-black sewer forever—without being recognized by anyone. What a frightening thought!

(*The rather vulgar laughter of* MAN *and* WOMAN. *Finally,* MAN *returns, with his head facing stage left. In his hand, he carries a bottle of detergent.*)

DEAD BODY: Are you still going through with it?

MAN (*begins wiping away the bloodstain with the handkerchief soaked in detergent*): I said I wouldn't listen to your orders!

DEAD BODY: Later, you're going to be really sorry.

WOMAN'S VOICE: This tomato catsup is all moldy!

MAN: Get rid of it.

DEAD BODY: Wouldn't it be kinder to tell her the truth before she gets too wrapped up with her maternal love in the kitchen?

MAN (*applies saliva to the bloodstain and begins wiping again*): Who invented the *tatami*,[1] anyway? It's so hard to clean off!

DEAD BODY: If I were you, I'd either put her in full charge or let her face the truth that's under the bed . . .

MAN: Plots and situations are only interesting in novels. In real life, you're better off without them. Since people hate to be bothered with such things, they pay a high tuition to get through college and to settle down in white collar jobs. Isn't that right? (*Carefully examining the bloodstain.*) Is it all gone now? Well, this should take care of it . . .

DEAD BODY (*full of irony*): I wonder?

[1] Mats covering the floor of a Japanese-style room.

MAN: No problem! It's perfectly white, like a brand-new *tatami*.

DEAD BODY: Yes, perfectly white—only where you wiped it . . .

MAN (*rather disconcerted*): Does it show?

DEAD BODY: Why not ask her?

MAN: But it's not the color of blood!

DEAD BODY: For an expert, there's more than enough evidence if
he has a spot that's been deliberately wiped away. You might
fool the naked eye, but there's always the luminol test . . .

MAN: . . .

DEAD BODY: That whiteness has a certain meaningful ring . . .
Like sending a signal by flashlight in total darkness . . .

WOMAN'S VOICE: The water's boiling!

MAN (*frightened*): What should I do?

DEAD BODY: So, perform your duty!

MAN: Why does this have to happen to me?

DEAD BODY: Because you happened to be you . . .

WOMEN: Get the hot water, will you?

MAN (*to* WOMAN): Coming! (*To* DEAD BODY.) Will she believe me?

DEAD BODY: Why not test her?

MAN: . . . At this point, I don't intend to become your sacrificial
victim . . . I've always kept out of all union activities no matter how they urged me . . . I've always refused to sign all pe-
titions though I may have been in favor of some . . . And I've
always made it a point to tag behind, when I've had to join in
demonstrations . . . so I wouldn't be noticed at all. Besides,
even if I put up a big fuss, how could that influence world affairs? . . . But despite all that effort . . . Now, I have to sacri-
fice myself for a corpse who's a total stranger . . .

WOMAN'S VOICE: What's keeping you? I'm busy now. I've started
to wash the rice . . .

MAN (*to* WOMAN): Coming right away! . . . (*Starts leaving but
glances back once again.*) I feel anxious about doing anything,
but it's far worse not doing anything . . . Still, I've been able
to put up with this anxiety, so far . . .

DEAD BODY: Probably she was impressed by that perseverance.

MAN: And how did you bear up when you were still alive?

DEAD BODY: Dead men tell no tales. I can't say anything more
than what you can imagine for yourself.

MAN (*suddenly, has an idea*): I've got it! Why not make a lot of

identical spots all over? . . . A single spot may look conspicuous, but if you have a hundred . . . That makes it normal . . . (*Walking toward stage left and looking back at* DEAD BODY.) How about that? There's a difference between being inactive and being helpless . . . I'm not as stupid as you think. (*Leaves.*)
(*Shaking his head,* DEAD BODY *gazes after* MAN. DEAD BODY's *shoulders suddenly droop. He stares at the spot where the bloodstain has disappeared.*)

WOMAN: Be careful now. It's hot. I'll keep the burner on and start cooking the rice . . .

MAN'S VOICE: Wow ! I can hardly believe my eyes! It's so tidy!
(*Sniffing,* DEAD BODY *gets down on his knees and peeks under the bed.*)

DEAD BODY: What's so tidy about it? I'm all twisted up like a pretzel! (*Rises, sits on the edge of the bed, and holds his temples with both hands.*)

WOMAN'S VOICE: Listen! Don't you wish there was a shelf here?

MAN'S VOICE: For a bachelor, a convenience can be a nuisance.

WOMAN'S VOICE: Well, if you don't know inconvenience, I suppose, you'll never know what convenience is about, either. That's how ideas are born.

DEAD BODY: That's how ideas are born, she says . . . As a matter of fact, I was only hoping for the birth of an idea, too . . . Of Memory Insurance on which I paid premiums while I was still alive . . . (*Rises, and his delivery gradually assumes an oratorical flavor.*) Indeed, social living itself is the premium for this kind of insurance to assure the proper distribution of your memory after you are dead . . . Does not this tacit understanding account for the utmost mutual respect shown to nationality, status, date of birth, name, etc.—all signs meant for others to recognize? Therefore, the preservation of Memory Insurance should be the collective responsibility of every individual as long as he is alive. And the task of redeeming the payments on behalf of the dead is a sacred duty that no living person can evade. (*Points brusquely toward stage left.*) So, naturally, you, too, are no exception . . . (*Suddenly, resuming his former composure.*) Hmm. The idea of Memory Insurance is quite clever . . . It really hits the mark . . . Perhaps I was quite intellectual before my death.

WOMAN'S VOICE (*suddenly, with a scream*): It tickles!

MAN'S VOICE: I'm sorry! It's so narrow in here . . .

WOMAN'S VOICE: Everyone says I'm too sensitive. They're all women, of course . . .

(*They return, with* WOMAN *holding the teacups and* MAN, *the kettle.*)

DEAD BODY: Why must they act so cozy? It's disgraceful!

MAN (*his eyes shift rapidly between* DEAD BODY *and the white spot on the floor*): Now that you mention it, I'm beginning to get that kind of feeling, too.

WOMAN: Feeling? (*Takes the kettle from* MAN *and starts pouring the hot water into the teapot containing the black tea.*)

MAN: Well, like that growth of the idea of convenience . . .

WOMAN (*as if she had finally managed to get her own way*): I told you so.

MAN: I may not look it, but deep down I'm quite a stickler for cleanliness. (*Looks around for other stains and soiled spots to wipe off.*)

DEAD BODY: How could he say that after stuffing a dead body under the bed!

WOMAN (*having poured the tea*): The important thing is that feeling. Rather than feeling, it's more like . . . How can I put it . . . You could call it a plan, but it's actually a much earlier stage . . . I guess feeling will do . . .

MAN (*absent-mindedly*): I guess so . . .

WOMAN (*inviting* MAN *to drink the black tea*): One or two lumps of sugar?

MAN: One, please . . .

WOMAN: Don't thank me each time . . .

MAN: I'm not.

WOMAN: Oh? (*Taking a sip.*) Let me see. What did I start to say?

MAN: Yes, what was it? . . . I'll have another lump.

WOMAN: I'm sure it was rather important.

MAN: Yeah, right . . . (*Unable to recall, he busily sips the tea.*)

DEAD BODY: What's more important than me?

WOMAN: I remember now! You can call it a first step . . . Or, a precondition . . .

MAN: . . . Yeah, that reminds me. A while ago, I started to have this strange feeling . . .

WOMAN: What kind?

MAN: It's an odd desire I've never had before . . . You know, I began to tell you earlier . . . Call it a kind of awakening to cleanliness. (*Turns around completely as he surveys the room.*) A desire to wipe away all the soil and stain around me . . .

DEAD BODY: Don't overdo it!

WOMAN (*swallowing the tea in her mouth*): It's exactly the same feeling as mine . . .

MAN (*hopefully*): You, too?

WOMAN (*passionately*): In my case, it's more like maternal love . . . For example, how to fill up all the wasted space in this apartment with necessary things . . .

MAN: But I'd rather wipe away first before I fill up . . .

WOMAN: Means the same thing. (*As if trying to convince herself.*) I've made a bet . . . Yes, a bet! . . . (*In a daze.*) That's strange . . .

MAN (*fervently*): What's strange about it? We're not starting a business deal now. Isn't the very fact that you came to visit a bachelor apartment like this . . .

WOMAN: I realize that, but . . .

MAN: I've written you six letters already. So my feelings should be perfectly clear to you. And you responded by your actions. What could be clearer than that?

WOMAN: That's true . .

MAN (*encouraged*): We must be entirely frank with each other . . .

(WOMAN *smiles bashfully.* MAN *turns toward* DEAD BODY *and proudly sticks out his chest.*)

DEAD BODY (*pointing to the bed*): Next, you're finally ready for the bed-in ceremony? Oh, don't worry. After all, I'm dead. I won't get excited and jump up. Good timing is crucial at a time like this. What are you stalling for?

WOMAN (*suddenly*): How wide is that bed?

MAN (*surprised*): Eh!

WOMAN: Well, I'll have to know . . . If I want to balance the bed with the rest of the space in here . . .

MAN: I haven't measured it . . .

DEAD BODY: You're so dense! She's inviting you to measure it with her!

WOMAN: How about an estimate? . . .

MAN: I don't even have a tape measure . . .

WOMAN: I'm just asking whether there's enough space for the two of us.

DEAD BODY: Here comes the charge!

MAN (*immediately*): I think it should serve our needs . . . (*Extends both arms in a vague fashion.*)

WOMAN (*suddenly becoming her usual self*): That's wonderful! After all, ordering a brand-new bed is a big investment . . . (*Taking out a notebook from her handbag, she leafs through the pages.*) I've tried to set up various plans, ranging from the cheapest to the most expensive . . . This is Plan A . . . This is Plan B . . . This is Plan C . . . And this is Plan D . . . Since we can leave out the bed, we might even try Plan B on the budget of Plan C.

(WOMAN *takes out a pocket calculator and starts operating it with remarkable skill.* MAN *and* DEAD BODY *appear dumbfounded for a moment.*)

WOMAN: Surprised?

MAN: . . . Not especially.

WOMAN: But half of all your letters were like budget reports . . . The fixed rates of your salary increase is so many percent, your average bonus is such and such, and the compounded interest on your time deposit comes to . . . That's right, I have your latest letter here . . . Let me show you what I mean by reading it.

MAN (*flustered*): Never mind!

WOMAN: As a matter of fact, my aunt was terribly impressed with your letter.

MAN (*surprised*): How could you let others see it?

WOMAN: Why should you mind if she was impressed? Guess what she said? It was sheer poetry!

MAN: Poetry?

WOMAN (*nodding*): Yes, poetry . . .

MAN: What made her say that?

WOMAN: I'll read it anyway.

MAN: I understand now.

WOMAN: If you really understand, that's fine, but . . . Then do you also understand what I've just done? (*Thrusts the notebook and the pocket calculator in front of him.*)

MAN: It's a declaration of your love, but in your aunt's style.

WOMAN (*happily and innocently*): I knew you'd understand! My aunt says marriage based on such notions as love, mutual understanding, and union of two hearts never lasts.

MAN: Sounds a bit arbitrary . . . Even I wouldn't go that far . . .

WOMAN (*sniffing*): Wait! I have to see about the rice . . . (*Thrusts the notebook at him.*) Can you glance through this page? (*Trots out toward stage left.*)

DEAD BODY (*tries to take a peak at the notebook over* MAN's *shoulders*): She must be either extremely stupid or extremely smart . . .

MAN (*abruptly turning around*): Don't be so loose with your tongue!

DEAD BODY (*taken aback by* MAN's *retort*): I understand . . .

MAN (*snapping at him*): I'm in love with her! I'll marry her no matter what others say!

DEAD BODY (*balking*): I know . . . But how about her mental condition? . . . It looks quite precarious to me . . . At first glance, she's like a clear blue sky. Yet, when I strain my eyes and gaze near the western horizon . . .

MAN (*laying down the notebook and the calculator*): You're enough of a nuisance by being a dead body lying under that bed. I'm begging you not to hang around here anymore.

DEAD BODY: I'm not down there for the fun of it!

MAN: By midnight, I promise to move you somewhere else.

DEAD BODY (*soberly*): Shouldn't you carefully reconsider that . . . After all . . .

(WOMAN *returns with energetic steps.*)

WOMAN: What do you think of it?

MAN: Very systematic. . .

WOMAN: I'm so glad!

MAN (*pointing toward the kitchenette*): How about the rice?

WOMAN: Another ten minutes . . . Where shall we start on our plan?

MAN: For instance. . .

WOMAN: In Plan B. . .

MAN: TV's a must. . .

WOMAN: That goes without saying. What I'm talking about in Plan B is. . .

DEAD BODY: What an arrogant attitude! I'd give her a whack on the mouth. . .

MAN: Don't butt in!

WOMAN: Who—me?

MAN (*confused*): I don't mean you . . . I hear ringing in my ears, again. Like it was a strange voice . . . (*Feels his pulse.*) That's odd. Didn't you hear it? . . .

WOMAN (*quickly recovers her presence*): It's all in your mind. Now, will you listen to my plan? . . . First, I'd like to start with a carpet.

MAN: A carpet? (*Anxiously.*) Why?

WOMAN (*looking around the floor*): Well, isn't it about time to change the *tatami*? We can add a little more to that expense and . . .

(MAN *follows* WOMAN's *gaze and realizes it is fixed on the spot where the bloodstain has been wiped away. Suddenly, he takes the bottle of detergent at the foot of the table, sprinkles a stain in a different place, and starts rubbing vigorously.*)

WOMAN: What are you doing?

MAN (*pretending to be casual*): Remember? I told you. It's that impulse toward cleanliness . . . (*Pointing to the spot where the bloodstain had been previously.*) See! I tried wiping there a while ago . . . It's white here, too! (*Finds another stain, moves over, and continues to wipe.*)

WOMAN (*anxiously*): Listen, I'll do that later with a damp cloth . . .

MAN (*continues working*): This is entirely different from cleaning up . . .

WOMAN (*becoming gradually discouraged*): Then what is it?

MAN (*changing his position, continues to work*): If you don't mind, could you lend me a hand?

WOMAN: Explain it to me.

MAN (*suddenly weakens and wears a pleading expression*): There are, at most, thirty or forty more . . . And if I can, I'll work on twenty or so, on each of the four walls . . . Then, I'll stop altogether . . .

WOMAN: Are you being sarcastic?

MAN: Why?

WOMAN: What's wrong with a carpet? If you spread a carpet, those stains will disappear instantly.

MAN: But that won't help. Unless we wipe away all those stains, the whole carpet will become a giant stain. (*Shifting, he continues to work.*)

WOMAN: Please stop!

MAN (*continues working*): Maybe you think I'm crazy . . .

DEAD BODY: No, you look more like a turtle!

MAN: I can't help it! . . . Though I'm completely sane!

WOMAN: If you are, please stop it.

MAN (*suddenly stops*): Oh, the rice is burning. You see, I'm sane enough to recognize that . . . But I realize also that, at this moment, that's of minor concern to you . . . And if you ran into the kitchenette now, it would look too absurd . . . You have to admit I'm must be quite sane if I can size up your situation to this extent . . . Still, I mustn't stop . . .

WOMAN: I never imagined you'd be like this . . .

MAN (*rising, he surveys the area already wiped away and again chooses a spot to continue his work.*) What do you mean by that? . . . I wonder how you regard my misfortune?

WOMAN (*drawing the folds of her dress together*): It's getting chilly . . .

MAN (*rising*): The smoky smell is getting much worse . . . I'll turn off the burner.

(MAN *goes to stage left.* WOMAN *remains standing. Suddenly, remembering, she glances toward stage left and quickly stoops down to take a peek under the bed.*)

DEAD BODY (*excitedly*): Now's your chance! Stick your head in!

(*At the same time,* MAN *rushes out and stands in front of* WOMAN.)

MAN: Don't do that!

WOMAN: You mean that the neighbors had a good reason to come spying, even by inventing excuses?

MAN: Of course not!

WOMAN: Then, why not let me look?

DEAD BODY: We're finally coming to a showdown! (*Gleefully, rubbing his hands together.*)

MAN (*slowly shaking his head*): I don't want you to . . . And I can't stand being suspected by you like this.

WOMAN: . . .

DEAD BODY: He's cleverly talked his way out of that!

MAN: You must find it difficult to understand why I keep acting the way I do, especially if I've got nothing to hide . . . But there are lots of others things which can't be explained, either . . . In the first place, how can I possibly explain why I'm so intent on wiping away the stains this way? . . .

DEAD BODY: You've said a mouthful!

MAN (*facing* DEAD BODY, *directly*): I'm not lying . . . At this moment, everything I say is true . . . I don't have to invent an ounce of excuse . . . Right now, you're simply an excuse.

WOMAN: I'm an excuse . . .

MAN (*to* WOMAN): I was complaining to my ringing ears . . .

WOMAN (*like an incantation*): The shoes you hid and carried behind your back . . . The book on the floor I can't touch . . . The bed I can't get near . . . And the bed I can't look under . . . The electric heater I can't turn on without opening the window . . . Your fever without running a temperature . . . Your ringing ears always skulking nearby . . . Your stains on the floor and walls which must be wiped away . . . (*Covering her face and sniffling.*) Though I never believed a word of what my aunt said before. . .

MAN (*attempting to console her*): Are you upset about the furniture and the electric appliances? Quit worrying then. We'll get the carpet and anything else, just as you planned it . . .

WOMAN: But won't the entire carpet become a giant stain unless you wipe away the rest of those stains?

MAN: So, if you'd be patient for a bit longer . . .

WOMAN: I must have misread it . . .

MAN: You mean, your balance for measuring him and me?

WOMAN: Yes.

MAN: I wonder how well I did on the scale of your broken balance?

WOMAN: I can't tell you. . . I'm so cold . . .

MAN (*as if resigning himself to his own despair*): I guess you'll be leaving me for sure.

WOMAN: But I don't think I can . . .

MAN (*with mixed feelings of anticipation and anxiety*): Why not?

WOMAN: Because you're more like him than he was himself. And I thought I had finally escaped from him . . . (*Shakes her head sadly.*)

MAN (*in desperation*): I'm like him? In what way?

WOMAN: The shoes you hid and carried behind your back. . . The book on the floor I can't touch . . . The bed I can't get near . . . And the bed I can't look under . . . (*Runs out of breath.*)

MAN (*following suit*): The bed I can't get near . . . And the bed I can't look under . . . The electric heater I can't turn on without opening the window . . . Your fever without running a temperature . . . Your ringing ears always skulking nearby . . . Your stains on the floor and walls which must be wiped away . . .

DEAD BODY: You seem to be strangely overrated.

WOMAN: . . . I couldn't believe that this was happening to me. And remembering my aunt's advice, I desperately tried to fill up the empty space in your apartment with imaginary furniture . . . But even before I had a chance to choose the color of the carpet . . . I realized I couldn't get away anymore.

MAN: And what did you talk about with your ex-boyfriend every day?

WOMAN: Compared to you, he was so ordinary.

MAN: Well, for example?

WOMAN: He didn't talk very much . . . And when he did, it was mostly about how he didn't believe in his own words. So, as soon as he spoke them, they melted away like cotton candy . . . But sometimes his stories lingered without melting away . . . For instance, the one about some far-off country . . . In it, there's a plain as far as the eye can see . . . It has only short grass and swamps overgrown with water grass . . . Not a single tree is growing . . . And on this desolate plain, a child on the verge of starving to death cries on incessantly.

MAN: Why?

WOMAN: I haven't the slightest idea . . .

MAN: No nearby houses?

WOMAN (*shaking her head*): Not one . . . And it takes three, four days by car to reach the first house.

MAN: The child will become an easy prey for the wild dogs!

WOMAN: But there are no wild dogs or wolves. Since it's such a peaceful place, I suppose there may be some rabbits.

MAN: Go on.

WOMAN: So the child cries on and on.

MAN: Then what?

WOMAN: He gradually gets weaker and weaker. The hands that wildly clawed the air, drop limply to his chest, and he can only make convulsive movements. His cries become hoarse and disjointed. But he'll keep crying like a broken flute until he finally dies of starvation . . .

MAN: It's bound to turn out that way . . .

DEAD BODY: The issue here is not the effect but the cause. What an unpleasant story! (*In the meantime,* DEAD BODY *appears to be deeply absorbed in thought.*)

WOMAN (*inquisitively*): Did you ever meet my ex-boyfriend?

MAN: No, I've only heard about him through you.

WOMAN (*hesitantly*): It's hard for me to say this . . . And I'm sure it's just a coincidence . . . But that child's face . . . I mean the one who starved to death . . . Looks very much like you . . .

MAN: That's silly! . . .

DEAD BODY (*bursts out laughing*): . . .

WOMAN: Naturally, at first, I thought I had actually come back to a world where everything has a proper price tag and where every kind of question has a clear answer . . .

MAN: . . . You mean, back in a world without an examination where all the answers are already printed along with the questions on the same sheet . . . Where your station in life is guaranteed as soon as your write in your name . . .

WOMAN: Well, I was wrong.

MAN (*painfully*): I may have been under a misapprehension, but so were you.

WOMAN (*soberly*): That's true.

MAN: You don't understand. I don't mean it the way you think . . .

WOMAN: A stain on the floor that you can never entirely cover, even with the thickest of carpets . . . An empty space in the wall that you can never entirely fill, even with all the furniture in this world . . .

MAN: It's so hard to explain.

WOMAN: You're exactly like that child in the plain who is crying his eyes out . . .

MAN: Still, you should go back to your old boyfriend.

DEAD BODY: There you go! That's the spirit!

WOMAN (*shaking her head*): But he has only stories to tell.

MAN: You won't find anything here, either.

DEAD BODY: Unfortunately, I'm here.

MAN (*startled*): And that's no help at all! (*Puts detergent on his handkerchief and again starts wiping off the stains.*)

WOMAN: I'll help, too . . .

MAN (*stops working*): Don't do that! As long as you're sane, you'll never be convinced!

WOMAN: Then, are you convinced?

MAN: . . .

WOMAN (*puts detergent on her handkerchief and after finding a stain starts wiping*): . . .

MAN: Stop it! I'll stop, too!

WOMAN: It's like making a parachute jump for the first time in your life!

MAN: That's why you should stop.

WOMAN: But it's too late now. I've already jumped. What can I do if you don't catch me?

MAN (*desperately*): You don't understand! . . . You've got the wrong person . . . Besides, you misunderstand the situation . . .

WOMAN: Have you so little faith in me . . .

MAN: To you, this whole thing may seem to be in bits and pieces without any connection. But that's because you don't have the key to this situation! (*Unconsciously points under the bed.*) If you only knew . . .

(*Realizing where his finger is pointing,* MAN *hastily withdraws it. But* WOMAN *had not missed his behavior. She drops her handkerchief and quietly rises.* DEAD BODY *appears tense.*)

WOMAN (*whispering*): Tell me more.

MAN: . . .

DEAD BODY (*sympathetically*): Now, here's you're chance to make up your mind. I feel sorry for you, but having reached this point, what else can you do? . . .

WOMAN (*with deep sincerity*): I'd really like to take a look . . .

MAN: That's out of the question!

WOMAN: But I've already jumped!

MAN: It's all a misunderstanding!

WOMAN: I know! I know perfectly . . . About what's under the bed!

MAN (*startled*): What's down there!

WOMAN: Nothing . . . Isn't that right?

MAN (*flustered*): Yeah, I suppose . . .

DEAD BODY: Well, well . . .

WOMAN (*as if relieved*): Did I see straight through your trick? The key is "nothing." And your excuse to make me worry is "nothing." At least, this time you lose.

MAN: No, it's not entirely "nothing."

WOMAN: I say it's nothing.

MAN (*pointing to the bed*): There is a key! But I can't show it to you.

WOMAN (*ignoring him*): Obviously, you can't show me a "nothing."

MAN: It's not!

WOMAN: Then I'm going to take a look. If there's nothing there, I win . . . And if there is, I lose . . . (*Walks toward the bed.*)

MAN: I told you not to! (*Blocks her way.*)

(*When* WOMAN *tried to shake him off and advance forward,* MAN *inadvertently knocks her down.*)

WOMAN (*rises slowly*): . . . I'm all confused . . .

MAN: Excuse me . . .

(WOMAN *waits for him to continue.*)

WOMAN: "Excuse me." Is that all you can say?

MAN: . . .

WOMAN (*nods lightly*): Then I give up. (*She folds the handkerchief, picks up the notebook and the pocket calculator from the table and puts them away in the handbag. She walks slowly toward the door.*) It's getting late.

MAN: Goodbye . . .

WOMAN (*turns around*): I'm not as composed as I might appear to be. (*Leaves.*)

(MAN *stands frozen.*)

Scene Six

MAN (*groaning*): This is just too much . . .

DEAD BODY (*solemnly*): I'm really sorry . . . But wouldn't it have looked strange if I stepped out now as an intermediary?

MAN: I'd like to kill you again!

DEAD BODY: This may sound to you like an excuse, but your girlfriend was too demanding. If that's her way, I'd worry about your future. In the long run, breaking up with her might have been the best thing. I deduce from the fact that I met this kind of death that, well, I probably had quite a rich experience in life. And on the very day that I'm lucky enough to discover my true identity and can speak out as a personality with a proper name, I may even turn into an ideal witness for you. Unfortunately, in my present state, I'm just a common dead body. And what I say must, naturally, remain very common and ordinary.

MAN (*suddenly*): What did she say before she left?

DEAD BODY: Let me see . . . I'm sure it was: "I'm not as composed as I might appear to be."

MAN (*as if savoring* WOMAN's *words, he narrows his eyes*): Well, you can't tell from simply that . . .

DEAD BODY: Tell what?

MAN: What she actually thought was under the bed.

DEAD BODY: Naturally, she thought it was nothing.

MAN: She wasn't suspicious at all?

DEAD BODY (*looking puzzled, inclines his head to one side*): Only she would know that . . . A useless speculation is just a useless speculation. As a common dead body without a proper identity, I can only offer a common opinion . . .

MAN: I know! I haven't forgotten about you . . .

DEAD BODY: I can understand perfectly why you might hate me. But leave out your personal feelings for now . . .

MAN (*nods docilely*): I haven't given way to my feelings . . .

DEAD BODY: There's no assurance that you won't face sudden death at any time under some circumstance . . .

MAN: What's more, there's no assurance that you won't get mixed up in an unexpected murder at any time under some circumstance . . . And with a body of a stranger you've never laid eyes on . . .

DEAD BODY: You have no right to say such nasty things.

MAN (*as if refuting* DEAD BODY's *words*): No, it's resignation. Plain resignation . . . (*Looking about the floor.*) That mottled surface looks terrible . . .

DEAD BODY: . . . I hope it will serve some purpose and won't turn out to be just wasted effort . . . You've spent so much time on it . . .

MAN: "Serve some purpose"?

DEAD BODY: If it fools the police according to plan, and they don't see the blood stain . . .

MAN (*laughing*): Don't try to console me.

DEAD BODY: All right. It's already too late to bring this up, but you went too far in your cover-up . . .

MAN: Don't they call my kind of cover-up something like "confessionless confession"—in a legal jargon?

DEAD BODY: You're imagining things. First of all, you don't even know my name, and you have no motive whatsoever to kill me . . .

MAN: Don't count on it! If the police check on your identity, you may not be a total stranger . . . I'd better get ready to leave.

DEAD BODY: I'm much obliged to you . . .

MAN: If I'm proved innocent, I suppose she'll be disappointed . . . (*From next to the bed,* MAN *takes out a raincoat and puts in on.*)

DEAD BODY: Maybe it's because we've had this heart-to-heart talk, but somehow you don't seem like a stranger anymore.

MAN: The feeling's mutual . . . (*Nods lightly, turns off the light, and goes out the door.*)

DEAD BODY (*walking leisurely around the room*): He's a fine fellow . . . Exceptionally fine . . . If he's unlucky enough to land in jail, I wouldn't mind going over and visiting him occasionally . . . By then I'll be able to talk about the old days and . . . (*Abruptly closes his mouth and disappears.*)

Scene Seven

(*The door opens quietly. With a flashlight in hand,* MAN NEXT DOOR *sneaks in, followed by* WOMAN NEXT DOOR, *who enters pushing a baby carriage.*)

WOMAN NEXT DOOR (*whispering*): Where is he?

MAN NEXT DOOR (*shining the flashlight under the bed*): See! Didn't I tell you? . . . Hold the flashlight!

WOMAN NEXT DOOR (*taking the flashlight*): He's such a nuisance!

(MAN NEXT DOOR *crawls under the bed and drags out* DEAD BODY *by his feet.* WOMAN NEXT DOOR *lends a hand, and they attempt to put him in the baby carriage.*)

Isn't he much stiffer than before?

MAN NEXT DOOR: I guess it's about that time. I'll move him, so you go outside and see!

(WOMAN NEXT DOOR *opens the door slightly, takes a look, rushes out quickly, opens the door wide, and waves the flashlight.*)

WOMAN NEXT DOOR: Now's our chance!

(MAN NEXT DOOR *pushes the baby carriage with* DEAD BODY *and goes outside. At the same time,* WOMAN NEXT DOOR *comes back in a flurry, and as she shines the light on the floor she says:*)

His shoes! They're gone!

MAN NEXT DOOR: Look under the bed!

(WOMAN NEXT DOOR *frantically grabs the shoes, and after turning off the flashlight, rushes outside and runs. The door is closed, and only the dim light from the window is seen.*)

Scene Eight

(*A gentle knock. Long pause. Again, a knock. The door opens slowly and* WOMAN *peers in.*)

WOMAN: It's me . . . No one here? (*Comes in and gropes for the switch—use a lighter if necessary—and turns on the light.*) I wonder what happened to him? (*First, peeks into the kitchenette on stage left and then stands in front of the bed. After a long hesitation, looks boldly under the bed.*) There's nothing, after all. (*Quickly turns off the light and begins undressing. Down to her slip, she crawls into bed and draws the curtain.*)

Scene Nine

(*Sound of footsteps . . . The door opens revealing* POLICEMEN A, B, *and* C *in uniform;* PLAINCLOTHESMAN; *and* MAN. MAN *enters first and turns on the light.*)

POLICEMAN A (*glancing around*): Where's the murder victim?

(MAN *points toward the bed as he continues to face the audience.* PO-LICEMEN B *and* C *brusquely head toward the bed. One looks suspi-*

ciously at the spot on the floor where the stains have been wiped away. Suddenly, the whole scene becomes a tableau vivant—)

DEAD BODY (*abruptly appears, passes through the* tableau vivant, *stands at center stage, and addresses the audience*): Testing one-two-three . . . Testing one-two-three . . . (*Dropping his voice.*) Can you hear me? No, how can you? That's impossible. Testing one-two-three, testing one-two-three . . . (*Looking over the audience,* DEAD BODY *shakes his head vigorously.*) I know you can't hear me . . .

Quick curtain

Yoroboshi:
The Blind Young Man
Modern Nō Play

YUKIO MISHIMA

Originally published in Japanese as
Yoroboshi
(Tokyo: Shinchōsha)
Copyright © 1968 Yōko Hiraoka (Yōko Mishima)
All rights reserved

This play was first performed at the Art Theater–Shinjuku Bunka Hall (Tokyo) on May 19, 1965. The performance was directed by Yoshihiro Terasaki. In July 1976 a revival of *Yoroboshi* was offered at the small hall of the National Theater (Tokyo).

CHARACTERS
(in order of their appearance)
SAKURAMA SHINAKO, a member of the Board of Arbitration
KAWASHIMA, TOSHINORI's stepfather
MRS. KAWASHIMA, TOSHINORI's stepmother
MRS. TAKAYASU, TOSHINORI's real mother
TAKAYASU, TOSHINORI's real father
TOSHINORI, a blind young man

Time: Late summer—from afternoon to sunset.
Place: A room in a domestic relations court.

(*As the curtain rises,* SHINAKO *sits at stage center while the* KAWA-SHIMAS *and the* TAKAYASUS *are seated, respectively, at stage left and stage right. After a short pause.*)

SHINAKO (*an attractive woman past forty dressed in a kimono*): It's terribly humid, isn't it? As you can see, we don't even have a fan . . .

(*Everyone remains silent. With no other recourse, she laughs.*)

The domestic relations court has such a tiny budget. And though we are members of the Board of Arbitration, which sounds rather impressive . . .

(*Everyone remains silent. After a short pause.*)

Please. Speak up. This isn't a place for a quarrel.

KAWASHIMA: It was such a surprise . . . We never dreamed that we'd ever meet Toshinori's real parents . . . It's been fifteen years since we first found him . . . Fifteen long years . . .

MRS. KAWASHIMA (*wiping away her tears with a handkerchief*): And after fifteen years, he's just like our own child . . .

SHINAKO (*looking at papers*): Toshinori is twenty now?

(*The* TAKAYASUS *remain silent as their attention is constantly drawn toward the door.*)

KAWASHIMA: Yes . . . That's right.

MRS. KAWASHIMA: I can recall it so clearly. We had no children, but my husband and I discussed the possibility of adopting a child. And if we did, we wanted to personally save a child who was at the utmost depth of misfortune and to give him all earthly pleasures.

KAWASHIMA: Soon after the war in autumn when we began to feel the chill in the evening breeze . . .

SHINAKO (*leafing through papers*): You found Toshinori in an underground passageway in Ueno.

MRS. KAWASHIMA: Even today I can remember it clearly. We saw a helpless, blind child in rags, begging. He was sitting on a dirty straw mat, next to his grimy boss . . . After one glance, I knew this child had to be ours . . . Although he was blind, he had serene eyebrows and a fair, noble face. In that dark and sour-smelling underground passageway, there was a special glow around this child. He looked like a prince.

KAWASHIMA: I offered his boss a satisfactory sum, and we promptly took charge of him. His natural refinement became apparent when we brought him back to our house and bathed him. First, we provided him with a warm bed and hot meals. He accepted them so naturally. Next, we tried to restore his sight. This is one thing we have been unable to accomplish, so far. His eyes were burned by the flames as he ran about in confusion during an air raid.

MRS. TAKAYASU (*as if obsessed, she begs* SHINAKO): Please let us see that child, immediately.

TAKAYASU: Now, shouldn't we do that after we hear their story, dear?

MRS. KAWASHIMA (*to* SHINAKO): He was just an innocent child, then. So we couldn't find out exactly what happened. He said that after his home was destroyed in an air raid—and probably after he lost his parents—he had lived by depending on others. We felt such compassion for him. Though things were scarce those days, we tried our best to raise him with utmost care and affection.

SHINAKO: It's fifteen years now . . . Toshinori is quite attached to both of you?

MRS. KAWASHIMA: Absolutely.

SHINAKO: And he was never fearful or aloof?

MRS. KAWASHIMA: No. As a matter of fact, he was totally spoiled.

KAWASHIMA: You'd better tell her the truth, dear. Frankly, Toshinori's personality has a strange aspect. It's like a hard shell that we simply can't penetrate.

MRS. TAKAYASU (*getting angry*): He's not like that!

KAWASHIMA: How would you know! You only had him for five years when he could still see. Unfortunately, that child's strange personality developed after he became blind.

MRS. TAKAYASU (*crying*): Poor darling! Poor darling!

TAKAYASU: And what do you mean exactly by saying you can't understand him?

KAWASHIMA: There's no simple explanation. Well, for example . . . That child shows no emotion. When he heard that his real parents were found, he didn't react at all. And on our way here, he looked extremely bored. But, at other times, he would suddenly get excited over something trivial and become unruly . . .

MRS. TAKAYASU: Toshinori isn't like that! Once he sees our faces . . .

KAWASHIMA: May I remind you that he's blind.

MRS. TAKAYASU: That doesn't matter . . . Once he hears our voices, the shell around his heart will melt away instantly, and he'll be his old, gentle self. Ahh, within the past fifteen years, there hasn't been a day that I didn't think of him. You've been living with his body for the past fifteen years, but I've been living with his spirit . . . We resigned ourselves to his death. We held his funeral and put up a tombstone. But even then, we still couldn't give up completely. And when my husband and I started to search among the waifs in Ueno . . . Ahh . . . By then Toshinori was already with you. We spent fifteen years living with two dreams about that child—about his being alive and his being dead. When we visited his grave covered with the red blossoms of crape myrtle, we felt as if he was alive somewhere. But when we saw the soiled faces of the homeless children, we felt as if he was already dead. We were haunted by feelings of both hope and despair. It was like not knowing exactly whether we belonged—out in the sun or in the shade. In other words, in the shade, we were distracted by the sunlight, and once in the sun, we could not forget the dreaded shade. When we saw a cloud at the seashore, we thought it looked just like our child. And when we heard the voice of the neighbor's child coming from across the fence, we were startled, thinking it was our own Toshinori's. When we saw the flowers blooming in the garden, we could not decide whether we should take them to his grave or arrange them in his empty study . . . and . . . Can you imagine our surprise when we found out quite by chance that he was being cared for by the Kawashimas!

KAWASHIMA: "Being cared for" is hardly appropriate, Mrs. Takayasu. Even legally, he's already our child.

MRS. TAKAYASU: But actually, you must be anxious to get rid of such a blind and twisted eccentric?

MRS. KAWASHIMA: How can you say that!

KAWASHIMA (*to his wife*): Let her have her say, dear. In any case, they can't do anything about it. That child has no desire to go back to his real parents.

TAKAYASU: You have such confidence!

KAWASHIMA: And why not! To be honest, that child is a kind of maniac. Since we've patiently endured his madness, we have the right to scoff at your naive sentimentality. We've stubbornly endured his madness and have even become as one with him in body and spirit. You'll never understand the horror of this bond. We've brooded over killing that child a number of times . . .

MRS. TAKAYASU: So they were treating him cruelly, after all!

KAWASHIMA: Toshinori's blindness saved his life and also saved us from committing a crime. You simply have no idea.

MRS. TAKAYASU: You call that adorable Toshinori a maniac!

TAKAYASU: They're trying their best to find fault with him.

MRS. KAWASHIMA: Well, just wait and see whether both of you can manage him.

MRS. TAKAYASU: What great educators you are!

TAKAYASU: You're the ones who drove him to madness.

MRS. KAWASHIMA: No. You who abandoned him to the flames are to blame. You were only thinking of yourselves . . .

MRS. TAKAYASU: We abandoned him? You say we abandoned him?

SHINAKO: Please restrain yourselves. You mustn't get emotional. In any case, this is a place of peace where all disputes should end with smiles. I hold an invisible balance in my hand and mete impartially to both parties their appropriate satisfactions and also dissatisfactions. In my eyes, the flames of anger are like a sculpture of agate . . . And the churning water of the rapids is like a crystal relief. For some reason, the tangled-up knitting yarn and the tightly clinging ivy are, to me, mere illusions—just deliberate tricks played by a strange, evil spirit. And all complicated situations are also illusions. The world is actually simple and eternally silent. At least, I believe that. So, I have the courage of a white dove that descends on the sand of a bull ring during a savage fight and waddles about awkwardly. Why should I mind if my white wings are spattered with blood? Blood and fighting are both illusions. And I can walk calmly among you . . . Just like a dove strolling on a beautiful temple roof next to the sea . . . Are you ready? It's now time for all of you to meet the individual in question. I'll bring Toshinori here. (*She exits.*)

(*A moment of anticipation. Off stage.*)

Toshinori, please come here.

(*Leading* TOSHINORI *by the hand,* SHINAKO *enters. He wears a well-tailored suit. He has on a pair of dark glasses and uses a stick.*)

TAKAYASUS: Toshinori! (*They try to embrace him.*)

SHINAKO: Please sit here. (*Leading* TOSHINORI *to a chair next to hers.*) The people sitting to your right are your real parents.

(TOSHINORI *is aloof.*)

MRS. TAKAYASU (*crying*): My, how he's grown! You can't see Mother? Poor darling. Dear, that child is so overwhelmed he's speechless. Touch my hands. Touch my face. Then you'll know I'm your real mother.

(MRS. TAKAYASU *draws near* TOSHINORI *and tries to take his hands. He abruptly brushes aside her hands. With reluctance she returns to her seat, crying.*)

TAKAYASU: Stop crying, dear. His behavior shows they've filled him full of bad opinions about us. We must be very patient and wait until his heart softens.

MRS. KAWASHIMA: You can imagine whatever you please. Hasn't it turned out exactly the way we imagined, dear?

KAWASHIMA: Well . . . It looks that way.

SHINAKO: What happened, Toshinori? Your mother's crying.

TOSHINORI: So what? I can't see anyway.

SHINAKO: But surely you can hear her voice.

TOSHINORI: It's a dear voice.

TAKAYASU: Toshinori! You're beginning to recognize us!

TOSHINORI: Recognize what? I only meant that I missed the sound of someone crying. I hadn't heard that for a long time. It's a typically human sound. When this world comes to an end, man will lose his power of speech and only cry out. I'm sure I've heard that crying once before.

MRS. TAKAYASU: You're gradually beginning to remember, Toshinori. Isn't it a voice you've definitely heard before?

TOSHINORI: There you go chattering again. You ruin everything through words. The humanness of the sound has faded away again . . . It's terribly hot. Like being in a furnace. The flames are blazing furiously on all sides. The flames are dancing around me in a circle. Isn't that so, Miss Sakurama?

SHINAKO (*smiling faintly*): No, it's summer now. Besides, you're wearing a suit like a proper gentleman.

TOSHINORI (*feeling himself*): This is what they call a necktie . . . A white shirt . . . A jacket. They're the clothes I wear just as I'm told. I don't exactly know how they look on me. This is what they call a pocket. It holds matches spilled out from matchboxes, loose change, transfers, safety pins, losing lottery tickets, dead flies, and pieces of an eraser . . . It's a worthless bag where you always find such things mixed in with lint. And this entire outfit is a perfectly safe uniform called a suit. It's proof that the wearer is faithful to the routine, daily existence.

MRS. TAKAYASU: He's grown up all twisted! Just listen to the way he talks.

TOSHINORI: You know, Miss Sakurama, I don't give a damn about appearances. What I understand is this feeling of being strangled and this feeling of the sweat-soaked underwear sticking to my skin. I've been forced to wear a silk collar and a cotton straitjacket. Isn't that so? I'm a naked prisoner.

MRS. KAWASHIMA: Of course, you are. You're a naked prisoner. You're forced to wear a collar and a cotton prison uniform.

TOSHINORI: Exactly. Mother is always so understanding.

MRS. TAKAYASU: How can I bear this, dear? He still hasn't called me "Mother."

TOSHINORI: You want me to call you "Mother"? Then you'll have to agree with what I say. Am I a naked prisoner with a collar?

MRS. TAKAYASU: That's absurd! You have on a fine suit.

TOSHINORI: You see? She's totally unfit to be my mother. Father, am I a naked prisoner?

KAWASHIMA: Of course, you are. You're a naked prisoner.

TOSHINORI: Uncle Takayasu?

TAKAYASU (*after a slight hesitation*): Of course. You're a naked prisoner.

MRS. TAKAYASU (*excitedly, following suit*): You're a naked prisoner! A naked prisoner! There's no doubt about it.

TOSHINORI (*laughing until tears roll out of his eyes*): Ha, ha, ha.

Now I've got two sets of parents.

(*Strange silence.*)

SHINAKO: Then let's get down to the main issue. First, we'll hear from the Kawashimas.

TOSHINORI: Miss Sakurama. Why do you speak? Why do you speak words? You should either be quiet or cry. You have such a beautiful voice. It's wasted when you speak.

SHINAKO: However . . .

TOSHINORI: "However," you say? I won't listen to excuses . . . Do you think mere words will sway me? They're like fog or mist. Do you think something visible will do that? I'm blind, you know. Something I can touch with my hands? I only feel unevenness. A human face? That's just unevenness, too.

MRS. KAWASHIMA (*with customary obsequiousness*): That's very true. The human face is just unevenness.

TOSHINORI: A light shines in all directions from the center of my body. Can you see this?

MRS. KAWASHIMA: Of course, I can.

MRS. TAKAYASU (*eagerly*): Of course, I can.

TOSHINORI: Good. You've got eyes solely for this purpose. To see this light. Otherwise, it's better you should lose your eyes somewhere.

MRS. TAKAYASU (*to* TAKAYASU, *in a whisper*): Poor darling. He's always worried about his eyes. What a pity.

TOSHINORI (*rising, highly excited*): What are you chattering about? Shut up!

(*As if dealt a blow, all become silent.* TOSHINORI *again sits down.*)

 . . . Now listen to me. You all have eyes just to see what I tell you to see. In other words, your eyes are a form of responsibility. Your eyes are responsible for looking at whatever I want you to see. And only then, your eyes become a noble organ taking the place of my own eyes. Suppose I want to see a large, golden elephant wending its way through the blue sky? You must see it instantly. A large yellow rose casts itself out of a window on the twelfth story of a building. When I open the refrigerator door late at night, there's a white, winged horse crouching inside. A cuneiform typewriter . . . A dark green, deserted island inside an incense burner . . . You must all instantly see that kind of miracle—any kind of miracle. You're better off blind if you can't . . . By the way, can you see the light shining in all directions from the center of my body?

KAWASHIMA: Of course, I can.

TAKAYASU: Ahh . . . Ahh . . . I can see.

TOSHINORI (*covering his face, sadly*): Ah, I have no form. When I touch my face and body like this, it's simply unevenness, everywhere. This can't be my form. It's only the extension of unevenness found everywhere on the face of the earth.

MRS. TAKAYASU: Toshinori!

TOSHINORI: I don't have a form, but I'm light. I'm a light inside a transparent body.

KAWASHIMA: Of course, you're a light.

TOSHINORI (*spreading open his jacket*): Look carefully. This light is my spirit.

MRS. TAKAYASU: Your spirit?

TOSHINORI: Unlike the rest of you, my spirit wanders naked around this world. Can you see my light shining in all directions? This light can burn another body, but it also relentlessly produces burns on my spirit. Ahh, it's such a struggle to live naked—like this. It's such a struggle . . . Since I'm a hundred million times more naked than the rest of you . . . You know, Miss Sakurama, maybe I'm already a star.

KAWASHIMAS, TAKAYASUS: Of course, you're a star!

TOSHINORI: That's right. A distant star, many light years away. Otherwise, unless the source of my light was so far away, how could I be living here, so serenely? Because this world is already gone.

MRS. TAKAYASU: What are you saying?

TOSHINORI: This world is already gone. Can you understand? If you're not a ghost, then this world must be. And if this world isn't a ghost . . . (*He points directly at* MRS. TAKAYASU.) You are!

MRS. TAKAYASU: Ahh! (*As she starts falling,* TAKAYASU *grabs her.*) That child has finally gone mad!

TAKAYASU: Get hold of yourself. If you lose your mind, too, it's the end of everything!

KAWASHIMA: Didn't I say he was a maniac? Nevertheless, he does say highly clever things. And rather than be his parents, we've become his good friends.

MRS. KAWASHIMA: Anyway, we knew you couldn't manage him.

TOSHINORI: Give me a cigarette. My tongue is coated since I've spoken so eloquently.

KAWASHIMA (*approaching him, opens a cigarette case*): Well, choose whichever you like.

TOSHINORI: You've kept an assortment of cigarettes in stock for me as usual. Watch me, Miss Sakurama. I can tell them apart by simply feeling them. (*Holds one between his fingers.*) This one? It's a Camel?

KAWASHIMA: Yes.

TOSHINORI: And this is a . . . Navy Cut. I'll take one.

(KAWASHIMA *offers him a light.*)

TAKAYASU (*to his wife*): You see. When he's like that, he's a completely normal individual. He acts exactly like a proper gentleman. (*To* TOSHINORI.) You like English cigarettes?

TOSHINORI: Yes.

TAKAYASU: I'll bring you some next time.

TOSHINORI: Oh, thank you. While I'm puffing on a cigarette, that time is for smoking.

KAWASHIMA: You can accept it with composure.

TOSHINORI: Exactly. I don't mind riding the subway or shopping at a department store. And there's no need to criticize the daily lives of others. Unfortunately, to those who can see, the picture of their daily lives is clearly visible. Fortunately for me, I can't. That's the only difference. And it's better not to see, for things are bound to have a frightening appearance . . . I don't mind watering the plants and flowers in the garden or using the lawn mower. And I can do frightening things without seeing! After all, isn't it frightening that flowers bloom in a world already ended? And to water the ground of a world already ended!

MRS. KAWASHIMA: Of course. It's frightening.

KAWASHIMA: We're all living in terror.

TOSHINORI: Even so, the rest of you don't recognize that terror. You're living like corpses.

KAWASHIMA: That's right. We're corpses.

MRS. KAWASHIMA: I'm a corpse, too.

MRS. TAKAYASU: It's bad luck to talk about corpses.

TAKAYASU: Now, now. You don't understand, dear.

TOSHINORI: What's more, you're all cowards. You're insects.

MRS. KAWASHIMA: Cowards!

KAWASHIMA: Insects!

MRS. TAKAYASU: That's how they spoil the child. Parents aren't insects.

TAKAYASU: But if you want Toshinori back, there's no other way except to agree with him.

MRS. TAKAYASU (*with extraordinary determination*): Then I'm an insect, too. But call me "Mother."

TOSHINORI (*without emotion*): Mother . . . insect . . .

MRS. TAKAYASU: He's finally called me "Mother"!

TAKAYASU: And I heard "insect", too.

TOSHINORI: You're all stupid morons.

(*Momentary hestitation.*)

KAWASHIMAS, TAKAYASUS: We're all stupid morons.

(*Short silence. The big window at upstage center gradually catches the colors of the sunset.* TOSHINORI *puffs on a cigarette as if thoroughly enjoying its taste.*)

SHINAKO: It may be partly my fault, but we're getting nowhere. I can clearly see that the Kawashimas and the Takayasus have the same splendid qualifications to be parents. Since both parties have such deeply sincere parental feelings, even I can't help being moved to tears. Unfortunately, at this point, the contest is a draw. The balance with Toshinori at the fulcrum doesn't seem to swing in either direction. As a member of the Board of Arbitration, I believe I should ask both parties to retire to another room. Then I'll have a long, heart-to-heart talk with Toshinori. How does that sound to all of you?

(*Both parties nod approval.*)

Then let's proceed accordingly . . .

(*As the* KAWASHIMAS *and the* TAKAYASUS *retire offstage,* SHINAKO *sees them to the door.* MRS. KAWASHIMA *reenters and then leads* SHINAKO *to a wing of the stage.*)

MRS. KAWASHIMA: Though I think you already know, that child is dangerous. Very dangerous. And you must be careful of the venom he carries.

SHINAKO: What do you mean by that?

MRS. KAWASHIMA (*smiling sweetly*): What do I mean? . . . I can't tell you that. I'm only speaking from my own experience.

(MRS. KAWASHIMA *leaves.* SHINAKO *walks to the window upstage center.*)

TOSHINORI: Have they all gone?

SHINAKO: Yes.

TOSHINORI (*with a cold smile*): . . . Hee, hee. I've cleverly driven them away!

SHINAKO: You mustn't talk that way about your parents who are so kind to you. They both love you from the bottom of their hearts.

TOSHINORI: The parents who adopted me are already my slaves. And my real parents are unredeemable fools.

SHINAKO: I don't want you to talk that way.

TOSHINORI: What does everyone want with me? I have no form at all.

SHINAKO: Form is important. After all, your form isn't your own. It belongs to society.

TOSHINORI: Then you're concerned about my form, too?

SHINAKO: Of course, I am. As long as I have eyes, there's no other way for me to make a judgment.

TOSHINORI: But I can't see your form. It's unfair. Stepmother says you're beautiful.

SHINAKO: That's silly. Besides, I'm already an old woman.

TOSHINORI (*rising, very angrily*): What is age? Age! Age is a single path in total darkness. And you can't see where you've been or where you're going. So distance doesn't exist. It's all the same whether you're walking or standing still. Or whether you're going forward or backward. On this dark path, the seeing become the blind, and the living, the dead. And like me, everybody uses a cane and wanders about, groping his way with his feet. In other words, the infant, the youth, and the aged are all huddled together quietly in the same spot— like insects swarming noiselessly on top of a withered branch in the evening.

SHINAKO: When you say that, it gives me courage. Society only judges people by age, especially women.

TOSHINORI: The seeing eye sees only form.

SHINAKO (*gazing through the window*): What a fantastic sunset!

TOSHINORI: The sun is setting, isn't it?

SHINAKO: The rays of the setting sun seem to be dancing all over the window.

TOSHINORI: The window you're looking through faces east, doesn't it? Isn't the sun about to set in the east?

SHINAKO: What are you saying? The sun sets in the west. The back gate below the window faces directly west. And beyond it across the wide road I can see the sun sinking into the tops of the trees in the park. Thanks to the park, the sky is open, and I can look across at a full sunset.

TOSHINORI: That's why the sun is setting in the east. You just said the western gate, but that rundown western gate directly faces the eastern gate of Hell.[1] And that invisible eastern gate of Hell faces this direction from beyond the sunset—with its dark mouth wide open. And before this gate, the black sand, always swept and purified, lies waiting for the footprints of the newly arriving guests.

SHINAKO: Your manner of teasing frightens people. Oh, now all the lights in the park have been turned on. The sky is like a blazing furnace, and the green of the forest is especially bright. So the row of park lights shines faintly like unpolished, blue gems . . . The windows of the moving cars are flaming red, reflecting the sunset.

TOSHINORI (*facing the window for the first time*): I can see it, too.

SHINAKO: What? . . . You can see?

TOSHINORI: Of course, I can see that flaming red sky.

SHINAKO: Toshinori! Can you really? Then why didn't you tell us that . . .

TOSHINORI: I can only see this flaming red sky. So clearly and in such detail . . .

SHINAKO: My!

TOSHINORI: You think that's the setting sun. And you think it's a sunset. You're wrong! That's the scene of the end of this

---

[1] It was believed in olden times that the sea east of present-day Osaka was connected with the Buddhist Western Paradise, and the western gate of Shitennōji Temple (Osaka) directly faced the eastern gate of Paradise. Mishima has incorporated this traditional notion into his modern version of the original Nō play.

world. (*Rising, he walks over to* SHINAKO *and places his hands on her shoulders.*) Now listen! That's not the setting sun!
(*Fearfully,* SHINAKO *withdraws herself beyond his reach and looks up at* TOSHINORI's *face. Standing by the window and facing the audience,* TOSHINORI *speaks. Eventually,* SHINAKO *turns her back to the audience and motionless gazes at the window. The deep red outside the window mysteriously intensifies.*)

I'm certain I've seen the end of this world. I've even seen that final flame which burned out my eyes during the last year of the war when I was five. Ever since then, the flames at the end of this world have been burning furiously in front of my eyes. Like you, I tried a number of times to convince myself that it was just a quiet scene at sunset. But that was no use. What I saw was definitely this world enveloped in flames. See! The countless flames rain down from the sky. Every house starts to burn. Every window of every building spews out flames. I can see it clearly. The sky is full of sparks. The low-hanging clouds are dyed in poisonous purple, and these same clouds are mirrored on a river which is already flaming red. The sharp silhouette of a large steel trestle . . . The pitiful sight of a big tree enshrouded in flames with its top completely sprinkled with sparks, swaying in the wind . . . The small trees and the thickets of bamboo grass all wear emblems of fire. In every corner, the emblems and border decorations of fire vigorously move on. The world is strangely quiet. And in this stillness, a single sound resounds and echoes from all directions like inside a temple bell. It's a curious sound like a groan, as if everybody is reciting the Buddhist scripture. What do you think it is? Can you tell me, Miss Sakurama? It's neither speech nor singing. It's the agonized cry of humanity. I've never heard such dear voices. And I've never heard such sincere voices. Humanity will never raise such sincere voices except at the end of this world. Can you see? Surely you can . . . the people burning here and there? Under the fallen beams, under building blocks, within imprisoned rooms—men burning everywhere. And naked, rose-colored corpses, lying here and there. The rose-colored ones—as if they had died of shame. And poppy-colored ones . . . And pure black ones—as if they had died of remorse . . . Naked corpses of every color . . . Oh, yes, the river is full of the dead, too. I can see it now. Its surface no longer reflects anything. And the closely packed, floating corpses slowly move toward the sea. Toward the sea where the purple-colored clouds overhang. The flames press forward everywhere, one after another. Aren't the flames pressing forward? Can't you see? You can't see that, Miss Sakurama? (*Running to the center of the room.*) The flames are everywhere. To the east, to the west, and to the south and north. A wall of flame looms quietly in the distance. A small flame rises from there. It flies directly for me waving its soft hair. It circles around me as if teasing. Then it stops in front of my eyes and seems as if it were peering into them. It's hopeless! The flame! It leaped into my eyes!

(*Covering both of his eyes,* TOSHINORI *collapses.* SHINAKO *looks back, but remains in a daze for a moment. Then she quickly runs over to him, kneels down, and grabs hold of him. At that moment, the sunset outside the window begins to fade rapidly.*)

SHINAKO: Get hold of yourself, Toshinori! Get hold of yourself!

TOSHINORI (*finally regaining consciousness*): Did you see the end of this world? You did, didn't you, Miss Sakurama?

(*Long pause.*)

SHINAKO (*after some hesitation comes to a decision*): No, I didn't.

TOSHINORI: You're lying. You're hiding it from me.

SHINAKO (*gently*): No. I didn't see it. I only saw the sunset.

TOSHINORI: You're lying!

SHINAKO: I don't lie!

TOSHINORI (*violently brushing her aside*): Go away! I hate women like you. They're always lying. Go away instantly!

SHINAKO (*rising quietly*): I'm staying here.

TOSHINORI: Didn't I tell you to go? You're disgusting!

SHINAKO: No, I won't.

TOSHINORI: Didn't you hear me say you were disgusting?

SHINAKO: Yes, but I'm still staying.

TOSHINORI: Why?

SHINAKO: . . . Because I'm starting to like you a little.

(*Pause.*)

TOSHINORI: You're trying to take the scene of the end of this world away from me.

SHINAKO: That's right. And that's my job.

TOSHINORI: I can't live without it. And you're going to take it away from me though you realize it?

SHINAKO: Yes.

TOSHINORI: You don't care if I die!

SHINAKO (*smiling*): You're already dead.

TOSHINORI: You're a disgusting woman! You really are!

SHINAKO: But I'm staying here. You want to make me leave? . . . Yes, I'll tell you how. Just ask me to do you a small favor. Something trivial having nothing to do with the end of this world or a sea of flames.

TOSHINORI: Do you want to go?

SHINAKO: No, I always want to stay with you.

TOSHINORI: I just have to ask you a small favor, Miss Sakurama?

SHINAKO: Yes.

TOSHINORI: Give me your hands.

SHINAKO (*extending her hands*): Like this?

TOSHINORI: You've got soft hands. I thought you'd suffered much more.

SHINAKO: No, compared to you, I don't know suffering.

TOSHINORI (*proud smile*): I only have to ask as if I were speaking to a servant?

SHINAKO: You should rather say, "Speaking to an older sister."

TOSHINORI: Hee, hee. I'm hungry.

SHINAKO: Yes, it's already supper time.

TOSHINORI: Can you give me something to eat?

SHINAKO: Shall I go out and get you something?

TOSHINORI: Just anything. As long as you can do it right away.

SHINAKO: Fine, leave it to me. (*Taking* TOSHINORI *by the hand, she makes him sit in his chair. The room is already dark.*) You wait here quietly for me.

TOSHINORI: Uh-huh.

(*As* SHINAKO *begins to leave through another door than the one used by the others, she presses the light switch. The room suddenly brightens up.*)

SHINAKO: I'll be right back.

TOSHINORI: Uh-huh.

(*Smiling,* SHINAKO *starts to leave.*)

Miss Sakurama . . .

SHINAKO: What is it?

TOSHINORI: You know . . . I don't know why, but everyone loves me.

(SHINAKO *leaves, smiling. In the brightly lit room,* TOSHINORI *remains, all alone.*)

Curtain

Hokusai Sketchbooks
A Play in Three Acts

SEIICHI YASHIRO

Originally published in Japanese as
Hokusai Manga
(Tokyo: Kawadeshobō-shinsha)
Copyright © 1973 Seiichi Yashiro
All rights reserved

This play was first performed at Kinokuniya Hall, Tokyo, on July 3, 1973. The performance was directed by Masayoshi Kuriyama. From May to July 1977, *Hokusai Sketchbooks* was again presented as part of a three-play series featuring Yashiro's dramatic works about well-known *ukiyo-e* artists.

CHARACTERS
(in order of their appearance)

TETSUZŌ (KATSUSHIKA HOKUSAI), thirty-five to ninety
O'NAO, unknown background, youth to after death
NAKAJIMA ISE, TETSUZŌ's father through adoption, fifty-five to eighty-two
SASHICHI (KYOKUTEI BAKIN), twenty-eight to eighty-two
O'EI, TETSUZŌ's daughter, fifteen to seventy
O'HYAKU, SASHICHI's wife, thirty-one to after death
GOSUKE, errand boy, youth
The other O'NAO, young girl
VOICE OF PRINTER A
VOICE OF PRINTER B
VOICE OF PRINTER C
VOICE OF PRINTER D
The action spans a period of fifty-six years—from 1794 to 1849.

Act One
Scene One

Place: The luxurious mansion of NAKAJIMA ISE, *the official mirror polisher, located in the Yokoami district* [1] *of the Honjo area* [2] *in Edo (later, Tokyo).*

Time: Early afternoon in the spring of 1794.

(TETSUZŌ *and* O'NAO *are sitting on tree stumps in the garden.* TETSUZŌ *is the later* HOKUSAI *when he was still known professionally as Katsukawa Shunrō. In the prime of life at thirty-five—both tall and robust—*TETSUZŌ *presents a strikingly dashing figure. There is an arrogant air about him.* O'NAO, *at twenty-four or -five, still retains traces of girlish innocence. However, she appears strangely sensuous for a respectable girl.*)

TETSUZŌ (*rather harshly*): Sometimes, I get fed up with everything for no reason at all. It's as though the sky suddenly turned dark, and there's a heavy thunder shower. And each time this happens, I hear some guys urging me to take cover under the eaves because it'll be over soon. But I'm not a sissie! I refuse to listen and start walking, knowing I'll get soaking wet. As I pick up more and more speed, I break into a run. And I keep running. No one knows where I'm headed. That's obvious. I'm not even sure myself. But there's one thing I'm sure of. I have to drop everything and start over again! I'm nearly bursting with that kind of feeling. You see, I'm not acting this way out of sheer desperation. And as I run, I keep telling myself, "Don't give up!" I slip and fall. I'm covered with mud. Still, it doesn't bother me at all. The guys waiting under the eaves laugh at my awkward appearance. Hmm, I'll never tell them how I actually feel at times like this. It's so refreshing! And how I can run! . . . That's right, once again I'm betting on myself. Being a woman, O'Nao, you probably wouldn't understand.

[1] A section of the Honjo area on the Sumida River.
[2] That part of Edo extending eastward from the Sumida River, east of Edo Castle (now the Imperial Palace); in present Sumida Ward.

O'NAO (*inclining her head to one side and with laughing eyes*): . . .

TETSUZŌ: It's those eyes again. (*He squeezes* O'NAO's *hand tightly and roughly embraces her. She stiffens.*) I won't do anything. I guess I could take you by force, but I wouldn't be winning. That'll only happen when you willingly submit to me.

O'NAO (*relaxing, buries her head in* TETSUZŌ's *chest*): Tetsuzō, is O'ei really your daughter?

TETSUZŌ: I'm not bragging, but she was born when I was just nineteen. That same year I left my wife on New Year's Eve because there was a thunder shower in my heart. (*Laughs.*)

O'NAO: And how many showers happened after that?

TETSUZŌ (*busily counts on his fingers*): . . .

O'NAO: Liar! I can't believe that!

TETSUZŌ: I'm telling the truth! I'm having trouble, O'Nao, because I'm so attractive to women.

O'NAO (*laughs innocently*): That reminds me. You seemed quite sure of yourself on the night we first met.

TETSUZŌ: I was convinced you were just a common streetwalker. That's why I made a far better pitch. Still, you were lucky it was me, though you needn't feel grateful. Any man would get hot and bothered if he saw a woman standing alone so late at night at the foot of Ryōgoku Bridge[3] and in the shadow of a willow tree—of all places.

O'NAO: I was lost and didn't know what to do.

TETSUZŌ: Even so, you were too naive.

O'NAO: And how about you? (*Again, her eyes are laughing.*)

TETSUZŌ: What do you mean?

O'NAO: I think it's far more naive for a person to swallow the story of a woman being lost and then letting her stay at his house . . .

TETSUZŌ: So, you think I'm naive. (*Laughs.*)

O'NAO: As an artist, you're naturally that way.

TETSUZŌ: You talk as though you knew everything about the cares of the world. And I adore you for that.

O'NAO (*looks somewhat embarrassed*): . . .

TETSUZŌ: Why don't you tell me about yourself? You haven't said anything about where you were born or how you were

[3] A bridge spanning the Sumida River in the busy entertainment area known as Ryōgoku.

brought up. Can't you be more friendly? After all, we've lived under the same roof for ten whole days.

O'NAO: Don't men find women wrapped in mystery more fascinating? No, I'm only joking. Actually, I'm a prostitute. (*Her eyes are laughing.*)

TETSUZŌ: I'm an artist of sorts and trust my own eyes. And they tell me you're not a whore. You please me. At the moment, you're a most handy subject for my pictures.

O'NAO: Oh, am I just a "subject"?

TETSUZŌ: What else? But who knows? Starting today, maybe it'll be "goodby!" for us.

O'NAO: Are you taking a trip?

TETSUZŌ (*for a moment, he has a treacherous expression*): No, probably you.

O'NAO: Why?

TETSUZŌ: Two, three nights ago when we were having noodles at the open-air stand, you said you liked older men.

O'NAO: Yes. They pamper you and also act as though they're being fooled.

TETSUZŌ: I've fed you three square meals a day for the past ten days. When a person forgets his gratitude, he's worse than a dog. (*His eyes gently caress* O'NAO's *entire body.*) Still, I'd have liked to draw you for a little longer.

(NAKAJIMA ISE *enters. He is dressed rather conservatively but in good taste. Despite his outward appearance of being a stubborn old man, he is still in the prime of manhood.* TETSUZŌ *suddenly changes his tune and becomes obsequious.*)

It's been a long time, Father.

ISE: What's on your mind?

TETSUZŌ: I want some money . . . Yes sir.

ISE: And who's this young lady? (*Stares sharply at* O'NAO.)

TETSUZŌ: I brought her along to see if you might like her, Father.

O'NAO: I'm happy to meet you. (*Perhaps bashful,* O'NAO *twists her body and bows lightly as she gazes at* ISE. *Her eyes are laughing.* O'NAO's *behavior is coquettish and unconsciously sensuous.*)

ISE: Do your eyes bother you, young lady?

O'NAO: No.

ISE: A near-sighted girl squints from force of habit whenever she looks at anyone. This gradually turns into a sensuous mannerism which tantalizes men . . . If your eyes aren't bad, you've got something special you were born with. You're not meant to be a respectable married woman.

O'NAO: What a terrible thing to say . . . (*Yet, she does not appear particularly offended.*)

TETSUZŌ: Don't take him seriously. My Old Man says frankly what's on his mind. He's not the silent type who whispers nasty things behind your back. So don't worry about it.

O'NAO: You mean he's being honest? I'm crushed. (*Smiles.*)

ISE: As for the money, Tetsuzō . . . After this time, I'm cutting you off from all further help.

TETSUZŌ: That's cruel, Father. When I've taken the trouble of bringing you such a fine girl.

ISE: Think back carefully, Tetsuzō. You once ran away from this house because you were going to become a professional artist. I could have disowned you then. But I couldn't do it. Listen to me. I had no son. I adopted you, so you could take over my business as the official mirror polisher.

TETSUZŌ: Then I'll take over. And I'll study art when I have free time.

ISE: You simply can't make a success of yourself because you have that sort of attitude. And how can you justify your past behavior? At seventeen, you became a pupil of Mr. Katsukawa Shunshō.[4]

TETSUZŌ: I know what you want to say, Father. I neglected my art study and lost my head over that girl who became my wife. But everyone makes mistakes when they're young. You were once pretty fast with the ladies, too.

ISE: Later on, you were a pupil of an engraver I've never heard of.

TETSUZŌ: That was . . . ah, when I realized, a picture can't be just flat. It has to show depth as well.

ISE: And why did you start a rental library? You claimed for studying the illustrations of chapbooks[5] and humorous novels.[6] And the rental library was the best way to read all the books for free. Rubbish!

TETSUZŌ: That was a bit naive.

---

[4] 1726–1792.

[5] *Kibyōshi*, illustrated stories in booklet form for adults, often satirical and humorous, popular in the latter half of the Tokugawa period (1600–1867).

[6] *Kokkeibon*, popular works of the late Tokugawa period.

ISE: And that so-called descendant of Sesshū,[7] the artist—Tsu-tsumi Tōrin[8] . . . You were completely taken in by him and took over a disreputable whorehouse in Shinagawa.[9] For how many days?

TETSUZŌ: About a month. I'm sorry about all that expense you had to bear.

ISE: I never knew Sesshū played around with women.

TETSUZŌ: Well, there was a thunder shower . . . Yes sir.

ISE: I've heard these days you go over to Mr. Kanō Yūsen's and you're involved with literati art,[10] and Chinese-[11] and Japanese-[12] style paintings. Just about anything you can get your hands on. What's it all about? You still belong to the Katsukawa School, but you're completely absorbed in Kanō style paintings. Don't you feel you're being disloyal to Mr. Katsukawa Shunshō? He was your teacher for such a long time. Remember, he even gave you the professional name of Shunrō.

TETSUZŌ: Well, ah, there are these sudden thunder showers . . .

ISE: So it's a thunder shower again. And what exactly is that?

TETSUZŌ: Once when there was a thunder shower, I wanted to im-itate the landscapes I saw in some Dutch copper engravings. Then, two years ago, the Russian warship, *Ekatrina*,[13] came to the port of Nemuro[14] in Ezo.[15] I thought I might see some in-teresting pictures . . .

ISE: And did you go all the way over there?

[7] A Buddhist priest and artist (1420–1506), one of the best among the Chinese-style painters in Japan.

[8] A self-proclaimed descendant of Sesshū who regarded himself as the thir-teenth in the line of succession. Active during the latter half of the eighteenth century through the first half of the nineteenth century—exact dates unknown.

[9] A station on the southern approaches to Edo on the Tōkaidō, the major high-way linking the Tokugawa capital with Kyoto. Its pleasure quarters ranked low in comparison with similar establishments in Ryōgoku or Fukagawa (see footnotes 3, 109).

[10] *Bunjinga*, paintings done by nonprofessionals, such as the literati, especially after the late Tokugawa period.

[11] *Kanga*, paintings following the Chinese tradition in technique and/or subject matter.

[12] *Yamato-e*, paintings following the Japanese tradition vis-à-vis Chinese-style paintings.

[13] The name of the vessel bringing Lieutenant Adam Laxman (1766–?) to Japan in late 1762 on the first official Russian mission.

[14] A seaport in eastern Hokkaidō.

[15] The present Hokkaidō, the most northern of the major islands of Japan.

TETSUZŌ: No, damn it! A fellow named Sashichi asked me to illustrate his chapbook stories, and I was just too busy . . . And I'm still sorry about that.

ISE: Your attitude toward life and your manner of studying art is a shambles.

TETSUZŌ: Oh, well, I can easily settle on a single goal when another thunder shower comes along soon. You think I'm too carefree?

ISE: You always think it'll work out somehow. And, in fact, up to now, it's worked out that way. But you know who made that possible?

TETSUZŌ: It might be my born, optimistic nature. Which reminds me, Sashichi said it was my upbringing. Doesn't that make you happy, Father?

ISE: You're hopeless. (*To* O'NAO.) This young man was raised in the poorest section of Edo in the Honjo area. His Old Man cleaned the sewers. His uncle was a clam peddler who came to my house. Tetsuzō used to follow behind him timidly through the servants' entrance. At least in those days, he seemed bright. So, I adopted him after his parents died of starvation.

TETSUZŌ (*gradually losing his patience*): What's the sense of telling all that to O'Nao?

ISE: Well, this time you should settle down at your teacher's place and seriously study. This advice and this money are my final acts of parental love. (*Taking the money from the fold of his kimono,* ISE *throws it down on the ground, in front of* TETSUZŌ.)

TETSUZŌ: This is outrageous!

ISE: Why don't you pick it up?

TETSUZŌ (*becoming angry*): I'm not a beggar or a dog! Are you telling me to hold it in my mouth and turn three times on my hind legs? (*He restrains himself.*) . . . No sir. It's still too early for a thunder shower. (*Self-mockingly, he gets on all fours and then picks up the money, like a dog.*) Thank you, sir. (*Putting it away in the fold of his kimono.*) Once I've got this, I can do as I please. Father, I've already cut ties with my teacher!

ISE: What did you say?

TETSUZŌ: If I stay there, that means I can only draw pictures which suit the teacher. And I'll still be imitating him no matter how good I become. And even if I get better than he is, at best, the public will only recognize me as Shunrō of the Katsukawa School. I hate that. I want to draw pictures only I can do. Or I'll no longer be me.

ISE: I feel refreshed. Now, I can disown you publicly without fearing criticism.

TETSUZŌ: That's fine with me, Father. But can I ask you for one more favor? (*To* O'NAO.) You listen carefully, too. Now that I've cut ties with the Katsukawa School, I also feel refreshed, Father. But something terrible has happened. All the print makers who used to buy my pictures of beautiful women, Kabuki actors,[16] *sumō* wrestlers,[17] and so on, won't have anything more to do with me. In other words, they're being loyal to my former teacher. So, for the time being, I won't make a copper until I switch over to the Kanō School.

ISE: So what!

TETSUZŌ: That's why I asked you before. How do you like this girl?

ISE (*looks at* O'NAO): . . .

O'NAO (*stares vacantly*): . . .

TETSUZŌ: How about making her your mistress?

ISE: Tetsuzō, what an utterly contemptible creature you are!

TETSUZŌ: I know this comes as a complete surprise to you, O'Nao, but try to understand. I'm sure, I'll be an accomplished artist some day. So, you must bear this, for my sake.

ISE: He's totally unscrupulous!

O'NAO: He's thick-skinned. (*Her eyes are laughing.*)

TETSUZŌ: I'm convinced she's the kind of woman you like, Father.

O'NAO: Now I understand. You let me stay at your place to carry out this scheme.

TETSUZŌ (*brazenly*): That's right. I was sure the two of you were suited for each other. You can decide what to do at your leisure from here on. And if everything works out, you can give me a generous reward for my services . . . (*Spreading his arms in front of them in an exaggerated fashion.*)

O'NAO: I don't like it. I think there's a thunder shower starting in my heart, too. Still, Tetsuzō's proposal sounds fresh and rather pleasant. (*To* ISE.) Don't you agree? (*Her eyes are laughing.*)

ISE (*scrutinizing both* TETSUZŌ *and* O'NAO): I don't think you two

---

[16] A popular theater from the Tokugawa period in which only male actors appeared.

[17] Japanese wrestling.

are conspiring. But you can't tell what young people will do these days.

TETSUZŌ: Well, then . . .

ISE: Then, what?

TETSUZŌ: I'll come again.

ISE: What!

TETSUZŌ: One of these days I'll come back again. (*He leaves.*)

(ISE *walks toward the arbor but notices that* O'NAO *is still there.*)

ISE: Have you some other business?

O'NAO (*again, her eyes are laughing*): . . . Oh? Do you mind if I leave?

ISE (*becoming gentle*): How old are you?

O'NAO: Don't you think I'm young enough for you?

ISE: Come with me. (*Leads* O'NAO *to the dimly lit arbor surrounded by trees.*) Do you know now what a shiftless fellow that Tetsuzō is?

O'NAO (*nods*): . . .

ISE: What a sensible girl you are. When a boyfriend is given such a cruel dressing down, a girl usually does a turnabout and defends him by raising his good points.

O'NAO: In this world, is there such a thing as a promising man? Though there are some who cleverly make their way through life . . .

ISE (*casually*): Have you made love with Tetsuzō?

O'NAO: That man loves to tease.

ISE: I can't believe that! He's probably restraining himself because he wants to sell you to me at a good price. Are you angry with me now? I'm a businessman, and naturally think in these terms. You can go if you're upset.

O'NAO: I thought a man who places drawing above women or luxury would be somebody different and interesting. So I lived with him. But I'm beginning to get tired of it. I can't help thinking I'm being lazy when I go through the same routine every day. Unless I'm constantly stimulated, I don't feel alive.

ISE: Then, shall I stimulate you?

O'NAO (*shaking her head in an ambiguous way*): . . .

ISE: After all, there are different kinds of men. You simply can't say that they're attractive because they happen to be young.

O'NAO: I guess you're right. You say you sold hand mirrors and mirror stands to the government?

ISE: That's right. I cleverly bribed my way in when Lord Tanuma Okitsugu[18] was chief councilor. And I made more money than I knew what to do with. Well, how about it? Don't you want to live in luxury? When that tight and inflexible Lord Matsudaira Sadanobu[19] was chief councilor, business was bad. But I turned the inner palace people against him and forced him to resign. And you could count on bribery again.

O'NAO: Please do.

ISE: Eh? What did you say just now?

O'NAO: I said, "Please do." (O'NAO *leans on* ISE.)

ISE: Are you serious?

O'NAO: I'm always serious.

ISE: With someone you only met for the first time?

O'NAO: Well, it was the same with Tetsuzō. And how can you know someone else's heart, even after spending ten years together?

ISE: I guess you've heard from Tetsuzō that my wife died two years ago.

O'NAO: Maybe I did, and maybe I didn't. I don't remember.

ISE: Are you planning to bear my child and eventually inherit this house and property?

O'NAO: I hate that sort of thing. I don't want to be tied down. If I suddenly feel like changing my way of life, I want to respect that feeling. I want to live freely, following whatever natural course it may bring.

ISE: I'm sorry for being suspicious. That's all the better. Now, will that, finally, make you angry?

O'NAO: Why should I get angry?

(ISE *embraces* O'NAO. *She puts up a token resistance.*)

ISE: You feel so soft.

O'NAO: Let's talk some more.

ISE: Well, I'm still worried about Tetsuzō.

O'NAO: I'm not—especially. You may be his father, but you're not related by blood.

ISE: You're a wicked woman.

---

[18] Born 1719, died 1788. Named to Shōgun's Council in 1772 and served until 1787.

[19] Born 1758, died 1829. A member of the Shōgun's Council from 1787, and noted for reversing the administrative policies of Tanuma Okitsugu because they were held to be too unorthodox.

O'NAO: Tell me. What do you mean by that?

ISE: That feigned innocence is charming.

O'NAO: Oh? I'm asking because I really don't know.

ISE: If I'm to get involved with you, I'd have to look after Tetsuzō until he can stand on his own feet.

O'NAO: Do you happen to like the poems by the popular Shoku-sanjin?[20]

ISE: Why do you ask, all of a sudden?

O'NAO:

> In this world
> If women had never been born,
> How serene
> The hearts of men would be,
> Without the cares of love.[21]

. . . What does this poem mean?

ISE: Just what it says. How carefree men would be if there were no women in this world.

O'NAO: Then, I'd be in the way if I stayed with you.

ISE: Don't be nasty. Shokusanjin is saying women are that precious to men.

O'NAO: Women don't want to be treasured by men. If a woman is, then isn't she just an ornament set in an alcove?

ISE: Then, you want to be treated roughly?

O'NAO (*mischievously*): Hush!

(O'NAO *nods meekly and closes her eyes. She offers her lips.* ISE *tries to kiss her. Suddenly,* O'NAO *slaps* ISE's *cheek hard.*)

ISE: Ouch!

O'NAO: This is only the beginning. The beginning of the fun between a gentleman and me. (*She runs off.*)

ISE: I agree. I certainly agree . . . (*Rubbing his cheek.*) So, she thinks she's provoked me by doing that? Still, I've got to give Tetsuzō credit, though he's only my adopted son. He really understands my taste in women. (*Clapping his hands.*) Where's everybody? I have to leave for the palace soon. Get the mirror

---

[20] Ōta Nampō (1749–1823), a samurai best known for his novels and poetry.

[21] A parody on an earlier poem by Ariwara no Narihira (825–880) in book i, poem 53, of *Kokinshū* (A Collection of Ancient and Modern Poems) (905) in which the well-known poet uses the cherry blossoms for his main theme.

stand ready for me . . . That gold-lacquered one we finished this morning.

(*Suddenly,* TETSUZŌ *appears.*)

TETSUZŌ: I got carried away. Please give O'Nao back to me . . . (*Throws the money down on the ground.*)

ISE: O'Nao's gone . . .

TETSUZŌ: Where?

ISE: I don't know. But I'm pretty sure that she'll never go back to your place again.

TETSUZŌ: Here comes the thunder shower! I can't be bothered with pictures now! (*Shouting.*) O'Nao! O'Nao! I can't live without you—after all! (*He runs off.*)

ISE: That Tetsuzō's destroying himself.

The stage darkens.

Scene Two

Place: In front of Aidaya, a footwear shop in the Iida district in Edo.

Time: At dusk, about a month after Scene One.

(SASHICHI *is replacing a thong on a wooden clog. He still retains the manner of a samurai and appears too dignified and intellectual for a merchant. This young man of twenty-eight is to become known later as* KYOKUTEI BAKIN. *Nearby,* O'EI *is spinning a top. She is* TETSUZŌ's *fifteen-year-old daughter. Though she is about to blossom into womanhood,* O'EI's *behavior is quite open and boyish.*)

SASHICHI: Tetsuzō didn't come home last night, either, O'Ei?

O'EI: Dad's young and single. And you have to be open-minded about his night life.

SASHICHI: You're such a sensible daughter. I can't tell which of you is really the parent. But, O'Ei, you're certain to starve eventually if days like this continue.

O'EI: It'll work out somehow. I know it will because Dad says so.

SASHICHI: The world isn't such a carefree place. And Tetsuzō's pictures aren't worth selling yet. That's what a leading printer told me.

O'EI: I know you can't bear watching the way Dad lives. It looks so dangerous. Uncle Sashichi, a person like you first has to

save a lot of money, stabilize his daily existence, and then devote his life entirely to becoming a novelist.

SASHICHI: That's right. Your work invariably suffers if you're
writing for money.

O'EI: To be perfectly honest, I don't like your way of thinking. It's
no fun.

SASHICHI: I see.

O'EI: After all, Uncle Sashichi, weren't you born into a samurai
family?

SASHICHI: Yes. My father was a steward of Lord Matsudaira
Nobunari,[22] a retainer of the Shōgun. Still, we were poor.

O'EI: Nevertheless, you became the adopted son of a wealthy
footwear dealer with a house and property because you
wanted so badly to be a novelist. I think there's something
mercenary about that. Besides, isn't your wife three years
older than you?

SASHICHI: You've made a thorough check on me.

(O'HYAKU *emerges from the back.*)

O'HYAKU: If you're spinning a top, do it in the road—understand?
The floor will get dirty. Tell her to be careful, Sashichi.

SASHICHI (*cringes*): . . . Well . . . That is . . . You're right
but . . .

O'EI: Why should I? The shop is closed today. And the chief clerk
and the shop boys are off work.

O'HYAKU: They're certainly insolent for a father and daughter
who are living off our generosity.

O'EI: We pay our rent on time.

O'HYAKU: So far . . . Though you know very well you can't from
now on.

(O'HYAKU *retires to the back. Relieved,* SASHICHI *resumes his stern
expression.*)

O'EI: How could she be so stingy with a face so gentle that she
seems incapable of even killing a fly?

SASHICHI: People seem to become increasingly so as they pile up
money.

O'EI: But it's a little better than before. When O'Nao was here, it

---

[22] A member of a minor samurai family whom Bakin's forebears (i.e., grandfather and father) served, and also Bakin himself, in his early youth—exact dates
unknown.

was terrible. (*Mischievously.*) O'Hyaku was on edge everyday, worried O'Nao might snatch you away from her. Why are women so jealous?

SASHICHI: Mind your tongue! I'm not of such low character that I would take a friend's girl away from him.

O'EI: Of course not. Your wife simply got that into her head.

SASHICHI: Still, I wonder where O'Nao went?

O'EI: Dad is on a drunken spree. It must be because O'Nao's missing. Tell me, Uncle Sashichi, isn't a man quite heartbroken when he falls in love and gets jilted?

SASHICHI: You'll find out someday when you grow up.

O'EI: I will? But when I grow up, I'll still be a woman. I'll never understand a man's heart.

SASHICHI: That's right, O'Ei, you're a woman.

O'EI: You're terrible. You know, even I have a secret love.

(*Carrying a sake jug,* TETSUZŌ *appears with a hangover but in good spirits.*)

TETSUZŌ: Here, Sashichi, have a drink. Something great happened to me last night.

SASHICHI: What's that?

TETSUZŌ: I'll tell you, so stop working.

SASHICHI: I can't. I'm not running a footwear shop for a hobby. Suppose O'Ei were in the middle of a reading and writing lesson or busily doing the washing or the mending. Would you say to her: "Stop what you're doing because I've got something interesting to tell you?"

TETSUZŌ (*at a loss for an answer*): . . . Well . . . If it's washing and mending, I wouldn't tell her to stop. I'd be the one to suffer later.

SASHICHI: How about reading and writing?

TETSUZŌ: A woman doesn't need an education. Besides, when O'Ei was small, she hated studying so much she quit school on her own.

SASHICHI: Actually, she wanted to keep it up, but you were always so hard up for money. And in her childlike way, she felt guilty about wasting it.

TETSUZŌ: That's ridiculous. O'Ei, didn't you give up school because the rest of your friends did? Isn't that what you told me, then?

o'EI: Yes, I did.

TETSUZŌ: You see?

SASHICHI: O'Ei, tell him the truth.

o'EI: Never mind. It's all over and done with.

SASHICHI: O'Ei lied to you. She was the only one who quit. She thought it would spare the feelings of her hapless, poor father if she said everyone quit.

TETSUZŌ: Hmm. What a precocious and hateful child.

SASHICHI: O'Ei's former school chums are now all dressed up in their finery and are busily taking lessons in the various accomplishments. No wonder. They'll soon become of marriageable age. If you have time to drink, you've certainly got the time to, at least, teach her the fundamentals of drawing. I've heard O'Ei has artistic talent. Utamaro[23] was praising her.

TETSUZŌ: Hmm. You're practically preaching to me. A stranger might think you're my big brother since you look so sensible and proper doing it. Just remember, you're younger than I am.

(SASHICHI *continues working.*)

Well, anyway. Last night I went to see Kanō Yūsen, my teacher. You're free to think I went there to pay my respects to him after a long absence. With a conceited air, he was drawing a picture of a child trying to pick a persimmon from off a tree with a bamboo pole. (*To further explain,* TETSUZŌ *rises and begins behaving like the child in the picture.*) Let's say a branch with a persimmon is about—this high. But the tip of the pole the child is holding is much higher than the branch. Moreover, this child is on his tiptoes. It's strange, no matter how you look at it. It doesn't make sense unless the persimmon is on the farthest branch. Otherwise, there's no need to reach up for it. And when I pointed this out to him, Yūsen being a hothead, said then and there, I was expelled from his school. I might have made him still angrier since many of his pupils and admirers were there. (*Rather proudly.*) But they must have realized I was right.

o'EI: Wait, Dad.

TETSUZŌ: What is it?

o'EI: Mr. Yūsen, your teacher . . . (*Thinking deliberately.*) Maybe he wanted to draw an awkward child.

[23] A late Tokugawa *ukiyo-e* artist (1753–1806).

TETSUZŌ: What did you say?

O'EI: . . . Or maybe, draw childlike innocence . . . Aren't there various ways of drawing pictures? A picture drawn exactly according to scale isn't worth looking at.

TETSUZO (*sitting properly*): . . .

O'EI: Dad, you steal all the good ideas of the great artists and cleverly put them together in a faultless work. In other words, you can't draw pictures which are uniquely your own. That means they aren't original yet. That's why they don't sell.

TETSUZO (*becoming sober*): Well, you may be right. Damn it! The thunder shower is here again. I'm trying my best! I really am! O'Ei, I'm sorry. (*Gulps down a drink.*)

O'EI: Please don't drink, Dad.

SASHICHI (*stops working*): Tetsuzō!

TETSUZO: Are you going to taunt me, too?

SASHICHI: Yes—about being thrown out of the Kanō School.

TETSUZO: I know! I know! Kanō School has tremendous power. First, I'm shut out from the Katsukawa School, and now, again, from the Kanō School. You probably want to tell me no printer will buy my pictures now. (*Sneering.*) Don't make me laugh. I won't sell them a thing, even if they come begging.

SASHICHI: Quit bluffing!

TETSUZO: I'm not bluffing. You know, I'm going to sell my own pictures. I'll become a printer myself. And I'll snub those stingy printers like Tsutaya, Eijudō, and Tsuruya. And if you'd like, Sashichi, I'll print your chapbook stories and novels, too.

O'EI: Where's all that money coming from, Dad?

TETSUZO: It's somewhere! There *is*—if I say so!

O'EI: And there *isn't*—if I say so!

(NAKAJIMA ISE *enters, preoccupied. He is dressed in an unusually youthful fashion.*)

ISE (*offering a handful of coins to* O'EI): Get yourself something good to eat.

O'EI: So it's something a child shouldn't hear. I wonder?

ISE (*to* SASHICHI): I want you to leave us alone.

TETSUZO: Don't forget, this is Sashichi's house.

SASHICHI: Never mind. (*Casually,* SASHICHI *takes the tool box and retires to the back.*)

ISE (*timidly*): Please, tell me. Where did you hide O'Nao?

TETSUZŌ: That's what I'd like to know.

ISE: . . . I see. From that day, O'Nao came to my house every night. And we drank sake together. And there were times when we almost went to bed. But whenever we reached the crucial moment, she'd tease me and go home, leaving behind that mysterious laughter. When you're treated that way, even someone like me, who should be thoroughly familiar with the ways of the world—and of women, too—practically becomes a naive youngster. And I can't even tend to my business affairs. Perhaps she saw through my present state. She hasn't been around for the past three days. So, I'd like to ask you a favor. This is all very embarrassing, but . . .

TETSUZŌ: Father, aren't you using powder on your face?

ISE: I'm desperate!

TETSUZŌ: How wonderful that you stay so young! You must be faithfully drinking your daily brew of Korean carrots.[24]

ISE: The more I think about it, she's a strange woman.

TETSUZŌ: What's strange about her? She lives exactly as it suits her, and she doesn't put on airs. Damn it, O'Nao! Where has that wench gone? I did a real stupid thing. I feel the same way you do, Dad. I keep having fleeting vision of her white body that I've never actually seen. And sad to say, I'm now drawing only erotic pictures[25] of me raping her. But, ironically, these pictures are very popular among the experts. They claim they're the best among my works and may even survive into later generations. . . (*Laughs self-mockingly.*)

ISE: We're both involved with a difficult woman. (*Suddenly with a thought, his eyes brighten up.*) Can you sell me those erotic pictures? I'll pay you anything for them.

TETSUZŌ: No, I won't.

ISE: Because I'm the buyer?

TETSUZŌ: I won't sell them to anybody. After all, I still regard myself as an artist. And they're certainly not my idea of art. Those pictures of naked women I drew only show what my blind love for O'Nao has done to me. How can I make a public display of such a silly spectacle?

[24] *Chōsen ninjin,* reputed to be an aphrodisiac.
[25] *Shunga,* pornographic and unlawful in Tokugawa times.

ISE: But you said you showed them to the experts!

TETSUZŌ (*recalling*): That's right. So I did. Ahh! What a sloppy fellow I am. Now will you go! And I'll strike you dead if you start seeing O'Nao again!

(ISE *leaves meekly.* TETSUZŌ *sprawls on the* tatami[26] *floor. Wearing his outdoor clothes,* SASHICHI *emerges from the back, carrying a package.*)

SASHICHI: I'm going over to Tsutaya to deliver the footwear.

TETSUZŌ: Did you hear that talk between me and the Old Man?

SASHICHI (*nods*): . . .

TETSUZŌ: What do you think?

SASHICHI: I've no interest in that kind of argument and have no particular opinion.

TETSUZŌ: I guess that's true. Your wife is berating you from morning till night, so you probably don't even want to understand the torment of men losing their heads over women.

SASHICHI: Why don't you try illustrations, Tetsuzō? I realize they may not sell right away.

TETSUZŌ: Don't talk to me about drawing anymore.

SASHICHI: But, you know, whether in drawing or writing, even the unskilled has to work with his brush every day. Otherwise, he loses his touch. And no matter how brilliant an idea flashes through your mind, what finally gives it form is the movement in the fingertips of your right hand. I admit that I came to this house as an adopted son and promised never to lift a brush again. Nevertheless, when my wife starts snoring, I wake up and face the desk. Naturally, it's just picture stories, written in my spare time, and will never turn into a first-rate work. But I keep at it. As a matter of fact, delivering the summer present[27] to Tsutaya, the printer, is only an excuse. I'm actually going over there to have them look at a chapbook story I finished early this morning. (*Producing a volume bound in Japanese-style from the fold of his kimono.*) Here it is.

TETSUZŌ: This must be the love suicide[28] story that you mentioned once.

SASHICHI: Yes. The wife of a kimono dealer and the young chief

[26] Straw mats used as flooring in Japanese rooms.
[27] *Chūgen,* a midyear gift.
[28] *Shinjū,* in which a pair of lovers kill themselves.

clerk have an affair. They finally stab each other in Tozuka Field and leave for the next world. The story is familiar enough, but it still serves in a small way as a writing exercise.

(*Inspired by an idea,* TETSUZŌ *rises. He thumbs through the chapbook story.*)

TETSUZŌ: Let me illustrate this, Sashichi. I think I could draw if it's on this theme.

SASHICHI: I'm glad you're enthusiastic, but I've got to take this work over today.

TETSUZŌ: Let me try just one. (*Pointing toward the end of the chapbook story.*) You see, it'll be a picture about this part—showing the couple after their gallant suicide. I can do it right now.

SASHICHI: You're so enthusiastic. It's a bit eerie. (*Laughs.*)

(*Frantically,* TETSUZŌ *skims through the chapbook story and begins to mull over his plans.* O'HYAKU *comes in from the back. Her eyes fall suspiciously on the chapbook story.*)

SASHICHI (*to* TETSUZŌ, *feigning innocence*): Who wrote that story?

TETSUZŌ (*unaware of* O'HYAKU's *presence*): What are you talking about. It's your . . .

(TETSUZŌ *and* O'HYAKU's *eyes meet. She snatches the chapbook story from* TETSUZŌ *and begins tearing it, slowly.* SASHICHI *hangs his head, dejectedly.*)

O'HYAKU: Be sure to tell Tetsuzō what we talked over before. Understand? (*She retires to the back.*)

SASHICHI: I've heard of men turning pale and trembling at the mere sight of a crab crawling sideways. Though I'm a grown man, to me, O'Hyaku is like a crab. This won't do. I've lost all my power of discrimination. A crab has to crawl sideways. If it went straight ahead, it'd be a monster.

(*As if possessed,* TETSUZŌ *begins sketching.* O'NAO *enters and looks into the shop.*)

O'NAO (*cheerfully*): Tetsuzō?

TETSUZŌ (*speechless*): . . . (*He is about to rush outside.*)

O'NAO: I'm in a hurry. (*Restraining* TETSUZŌ.) So I'll make it short. Come to the Yokoami district in the Honjo area in about two hours.

TETSUZŌ: At the Old Man's place?

O'NAO (*nods*): . . .

TETSUZŌ: What for?

O'NAO: I'll be doing something interesting.

TETSUZŌ: . . . I get it. You're going to marry the Old Man. And you want me at the ceremony. How cruel you are!

O'NAO: It's sultry this evening. It's time to put up the wind-bell.

TETSUZŌ: You want to have your revenge?

O'NAO: How you go on! Come to that arbor in the garden where we once met. And come quietly. Don't forget! (*She quickly turns around and leaves.*)

TETSUZŌ: Damn it! What a shifty woman. She's like a snowflake dancing in the wind . . . (*Restraining himself, he puts up a brave front.*) Listen, Sashichi, they say: "Just lie and wait for good fortune to come."[29] Now, I can get enough money from the Old Man. And I can become a printer myself.

SASHICHI: Tetsuzō, I've known you for a long time. I can understand your feelings so well it almost hurts. Right now, isn't O'Nao the most important person in your life? Do you intend to abandon her or sell her?

TETSUZŌ: What are you talking about? She's just a woman. You may not understand what I'm about to say because you come from a samurai family. But as a small child, and still a farmer's son, I've seen with my own eyes parents selling their daughters as whores just to keep from starving. Look here, Sashichi, a *ukiyo-e* artist will never rise to the top in this society, no matter how hard he tries. Lately, during Lord Matsudaira's reform, the only ones persecuted were from our circle. The artists who put up a big front were all left alone. Besides, the authorities bought their lousy pictures for handsome fees. But which pictures are alive? Theirs or mine? Just ask Kumagorō, the fish dealer, Tatsukichi, the vegetable seller, or any other townsman. They'll tell you.

SASHICHI: You don't mean my pictures. You're talking about your own career. In the future, you might become a fine artist. But, on the other hand, maybe, never . . .

TETSUZŌ: Oh, shut up! I'll be damned if I ever draw for the government. I'm drawing to please the common man. Those guys you can find on any busy street.

[29] A Japanese saying.

SASHICHI: Don't be so flippant. You suffer and people dislike you because you say such things. You want both fame and women. But in this world you can't always have your own way. The balance swings toward fame or women depending on the day's weather.

TETSUZŌ (*becoming serious again*): You've struck home. You're really sharp. One day, you're sure to become a professional novelist. Isn't it about time you started calling yourself "So-and-so" Bakin?

SASHICHI: No. For the time being, I'll devote myself entirely to pleasing O'Hyaku.

TETSUZŌ: You've got a strong will. But with my admiration for you, I'd like to ask one question: What shall I do?

SASHICHI: First, you should quit your heavy drinking and gambling. And, needless to say, whoring. At least, you won't starve, then . . .

TETSUZŌ: Ahh! I couldn't stand that! It gives me the creeps. I'd rather choose love suicide than to live that way! (*He gazes at his half-finished drawing.*) Through love suicide you destroy the two physical bodies. And the souls are truly united. And I must discreetly, oh so discreetly, take up this theme. (*Picking up the brush, he carefully continues to draw.*)

(O'EI *returns.*)

O'EI: I'm back. I passed O'Nao on the way over. Did she come and see you, Dad?

TETSUZŌ: Be quiet!

(*Drawing near him,* O'EI *tries to take a look at the drawing.*)

Stay back there!

O'EI: That's funny. He's excited all by himself.

TETSUZŌ: Never mind! Come here! (*Continues to draw.*) O'Ei's not a child anymore. Besides, we're more like brother and sister rather than father and daughter . . . For some reason, I feel so anxious now . . .

O'EI (*viewing the picture*): It's a man and woman sleeping together . . . All very proper with dignified expressions on their faces. Even though they're out in an open field, they haven't laid out a straw mat. And they're neatly decked out in beautiful clothes . . . Oh, it's a love suicide!

TETSUZŌ: O'Ei, I'm scared. I think I might commit love suicide with O'Nao if I see her tonight. But I know I shouldn't because I've got a daughter. And . . . I realize that so well, but . . .

O'EI: Dad, if you go, it'll be the end of everything. Your soul is dancing in this picture.

TETSUZŌ: Really? Do you think so?

O'EI: Since your passion rises and falls so quickly, I thought you'd get eventually tired of her, too . . . This is dreadful . . . I guess serious devotion never brings much happiness.

TETSUZŌ: I beg you, O'Ei. Just for tonight, stay awake and keep watch over me.

O'EI: Yes. All right. It's no trouble at all.

TETSUZŌ: I was afraid I might go through with a love suicide with O'Nao. So, I thought I'd calm myself by spewing out that unsettling feeling still coiled up in my heart into that drawing. But as I was at it, O'Nao suddenly appeared as though she had read my mind. And she said to me with her eyes: "You're wonderful," and "Let's go some place."

O'EI: What an obedient daughter I am! I listen so patiently to my Father's love affair.

(O'HYAKU *comes in from the back.*)

O'HYAKU: Did you tell him?

SASHICHI: . . . No, not yet.

O'HYAKU (*to* SASHICHI): Why don't you speak out? Then, I'll tell them. (*To* TETSUZŌ.) I want both of you to clear out of this house within the next day or two. And Sashichi agrees with me.

TETSUZŌ: I can't be bothered with that now!

O'HYAKU: Well, that's a very stupid answer. O'Ei, you understand, don't you?

O'EI: Uh-huh.

O'HYAKU (*pointing to* TETSUZŌ): Sashichi can't tend to his business when an *ukiyo-e* artist like you is around. All he thinks about is his novel, and a novelist is worse than a Kabuki actor.

SASHICHI (*bowing to* O'EI *and* TETSUZŌ): I'm sorry.

O'HYAKU: Aren't you making a mistake? If you intend to apologize at all, shouldn't you do it to me?

SASHICHI (*with a package of footwear in his hand*): Well, I'm going.

O'HYAKU (*snatching the package*): We don't have to send a summer present to Tsutaya. It makes me so unhappy. I try my best to serve you, but all you want to do is go around calling yourself such outrageous names as Takizawa Bakin and Kyokutei Bakin and act dapper.

TETSUZŌ: It's done! (*He shows the drawing to* SASHICHI.)

SASHICHI: What's this, milling around the victims of the love suicide?

TETSUZŌ: It's a fox, a wild fox. In other words, those who take this way out are stupid fools. It's like being tricked by a fox. At least, that's what I've tried to tell myself.

O'EI: What a relief!

SASHICHI: Well, I don't agree. It may be fine for you, Tetsuzō, and everyone's entitled to his own opinion. But I wrote this chapbook story!

O'HYAKU: So, you've finally confessed!

SASHICHI: The man and the woman I wrote about willingly chose suicide. I don't want any fox to brazenly appear in the scene.

TETSUZŌ: I see what you mean. If I'm not mistaken, Sashichi, you willingly became an adopted son of a footwear dealer. (*Suddenly rising.*) It's no use. I'm tired of arguing! Sashichi, O'Ei, take care of yourselves! I'm going through with the love suicide! (*He runs out.*)

O'EI: Dad, you mustn't! You really mustn't! Uncle Sashichi, please do something!

(SASHICHI *rises.*)

O'HYAKU: Where are you going?

SASHICHI: I'm going to heat up the bath water. (*He leaves for the back.*)

(O'EI *stamps her feet in frustration but finally runs after* SASHICHI.)

O'HYAKU: Why doesn't everyone put in an honest day's work? Man can live decently without having pictures or books. Aren't they ashamed before Heaven? (*Begins cleaning up. After a while, sniffing hard.*) Oh, this is terrible! The potatoes are burning! (*Runs to the back.*)

The stage darkens.

Scene Three

Place: The same setting as Scene One.

Time: About two hours have passed, and the sun has completely set. Moonlight. Sound of temple bells.

(TETSUZŌ *enters, glancing about carefully.*)

TETSUZŌ (*whispering*): O'Nao, where are you? Eh, O'Nao! (*Sensing the approach of someone, he hides behind a tree.*)

(NAKAJIMA ISE *appears, looking exuberant; he is lightly rouged and smartly dressed.*)

ISE: O'Nao, O'Nao! Don't try to tease me. Come to me.

(TETSUZŌ *reveals himself.*)

What are you doing here?

TETSUZŌ: O'Nao told me to come.

ISE: That's strange. A messenger came a while ago and said she had to see me here . . .

(O'NAO's *muffled laughter is heard.*)

It's O'Nao! Where are you?

O'NAO's VOICE: Here I am, beside the pond!

(ISE *walks toward the voice. Shocked, he hastily averts his eyes.*)

TETSUZŌ: What happened?

ISE: What a cruel punishment! (*He has turned completely pale.*)

TETSUZŌ: Eh! What do you mean?

O'NAO's VOICE: It's all right. I don't mind.

(*With determination,* TETSUZŌ *approaches the voices.* O'NAO *and a young man are clinging to each other on the grass. In a panic, the young man breaks away from* O'NAO's *embrace, puts on his clothes, turns his back, and cowers.*)

TETSUZŌ: It's Gosuke!

ISE: You know him?

TETSUZŌ: He works at Sashichi's place . . .

ISE: That footwear shop?

GOSUKE: Please forgive me. O'Nao enticed me . . . And deliberately attacked me . . . I'm not to blame. (GOSUKE *scampers off.*)

ISE: Didn't you just want to tease us a little, O'Nao? I'm sure nothing happened between you and that errand boy. Lie, if you must, but don't say anything that might torment an old man. Please, I beg you on my knees.

(ISE *kneels on the ground. As* O'NAO *rises, her kimono suddenly slips down from her shoulders, revealing her white, supple body.* ISE *quickly averts his eyes.*)

O'NAO: Why don't you look at me? I haven't hanged myself, you know.

TETSUZŌ: Hanged yourself?

O'NAO: Though my father and mother got along well together, they hanged themselves.

TETSUZŌ: Why?

O'NAO: I don't know. And I don't care. Still, as small as I was, I remember clearly that I had seen it all.

ISE: O'Nao did you or did you not make love with him?

O'NAO: You can believe whatever you like. Either way, it makes little difference to me. I just wanted both of you to see.

TETSUZŌ: What for?

O'NAO: What for? Well, I didn't give that any thought. Why don't you decide for yourself, Tetsuzō? And when you do, you can tell me. Anyhow, I was so bored for the past four, five days. I thought if I did something amusing, it might provide me with a diversion. And so I did. As a result I'm quite cheerful again. Now, don't I look it? Haven't I a rosy complexion?

ISE: She's mad!

O'NAO: Who—me? Of course not. What a horrible thing to say! Whenever someone succeeds in doing what you can't do yourself, you immediately treat him like a madman. Then, I wonder if the heavenly angel[30] with the beautiful garment of feathers who can fly through the air—fluttering and dancing— is crazy, too? (*Her eyes are laughing.*)

ISE: Why are your eyes so clear? (*In a fit of frenzy,* ISE *caresses* O'NAO's *entire body and prostrates himself in front of her.*)

O'NAO: It tickles. Who's crazy now?

ISE: I forgive you. I forgive you for everything. So come live with me. I'll give you all I have. I don't want anything now—my reputation, position, and wealth!

O'NAO: Tetsuzō, this is the moment when I can feel it was really worth being alive.

---

[30] A reference to the celestial being who joyfully dances back to heaven, once her feathery garment is returned by the fisherman; a scene depicted in a famous Nō play, *Hagoromo* (Feathery Garment), by the renowned dramatist Zeami (Kanze Motokiyo) (1363–1443).

TETSUZŌ: Then, Dad is a dupe.

ISE: If you don't want to live with me, at least—just this once—grant me my desire!

O'NAO: No! I despise a desperate man. There's a raw smell about him.

ISE: . . . That's right. If you'd like, I'll help you become a ranking attendant[31] at the Shōgun's court.

O'NAO: What's that?

ISE: A concubine of Shōgun Ienari. I'm on the very best of terms with Lady Asukai, his highest ranking concubine. She's now the most influential person in the inner palace. That would be quite a rise in the world, O'Nao.

O'NAO: What is that to me?

ISE: Then, what do you want?

O'NAO: If I knew, I might lose all interest in living.

ISE: Say something, Tetsuzō! Help me!

O'NAO (*whispering*): Still, it might be interesting to give birth to the Shōgun's son.

ISE: Of course! And if that happens, power and glory will be immediately yours.

O'NAO: I don't care about that. But come to think of it, wouldn't it be amusing to become the Shōgun's concubine while already carrying someone else's child? And then act innocent and give birth to the baby as his real son? (*Her eyes are laughing.*)

TETSUZŌ: That's nonsense.

O'NAO: I think it'd be fun. Perhaps a child born to Tetsuzō and me will one day become the master of all Japan.

ISE: So, Tetsuzō . . You and O'Nao . . .

TETSUZŌ (*to* O'NAO): Stop this foolishness. Father is really suffering.

O'NAO: Don't act so self-righteous. After you made me pose in those odd positions and exploited me terribly. How can you draw a decent picture after all you've done!

TETSUZŌ (*at a loss for words*): . . . But you gladly twisted your body . . .

O'NAO: This is awful! Both of you look so serious. It's getting chilly. (O'NAO *casually begins to dress as though nothing had happened.*) Should I get out of Edo? The town is so crowded. And

[31] *Chūrō*, a middle rank female attendant at the Shōgun's court.

I'm bored with it. I'll raise onions and white radishes in the country.

ISE: Don't toy with me, you whore!

O'NAO: . . . I don't mind being called a whore, but I've never toyed with you . . .

ISE: I'm sorry . . . (*Pause.*) . . . Why don't you kill me, O'Nao?

O'NAO: I despise a man who has little regard for life. (*She suddenly turns around and disappears.*)

ISE (*laughing weakly*): I, Nakajima Ise, the official mirror polisher, am finally despised for the first time! (ISE *leaves.*)

TETSUZŌ (*in confusion*): O'Nao said earlier she didn't even know why she wanted us to see her in that compromising situation. And she asked me to come up with the reason. Well, let me think. Is it because she's a naturally loose woman? That's partly true, but that's not the whole story. She—she carries something frightening within her which is beyond my understanding . . . At least, I think she does. I don't exactly know what that frightening thing is. It may turn out to be quite trivial. But, even so, I'm convinced what I saw was frightening. Besides, it was the first time in my life I realized this frightening thing was prominent in my existence, too. I had a humble birth and upbringing . . . What am I trying to say? . . . Oh, yes . . . I couldn't stand being so humble. And I took advantage of that lowly state and traded on it, persuading myself I could justify doing anything . . . In order to become the best *ukiyo-e* artist in Japan. And I used women, money, and my *ukiyo-e* teachers if they could serve my purpose. I thought I was at the center of the world, and everyone else should naturally become my sacrificial victims. In other words, I was proud of myself, believing I alone led a self-consistent life. But what a surprise! There was another individual who also led a self-consistent life. That was O'Nao. And, what's more, she spends a carefree existence in an entirely different world than mine—though I don't know whether it's splendid or not. And my eyes hadn't yet penetrated into that separate world. Now I feel as if my eyes are finally opened. Yes, and as I look at the world through these awakened eyes, nature is now breathing properly. And light and shadows are nestled closely together—

not to mention mankind . . . Hmm . . . Hmm . . . Well, I've
struck an unexpected wall. I'll never brag again.

(SASHICHI *and* O'EI *rush in.*)

O'EI: O'Nao isn't here.

TETSUZŌ: Stop talking about O'Nao! I'm busy thinking.

O'EI (*speaking softly to* SASHICHI): He's quite broken up, after all.
Right around here . . . (*Rubs her chest.*)

SASHICHI: Tetsuzō!

TETSUZŌ: I've decided to quit drawing.

SASHICHI: Are you serious?

TETSUZŌ: Of course!

O'EI: You mustn't, Dad! If you give up drawing, there'll be nothing else left.

TETSUZŌ: Now, now, the both of you, don't try so hard to encourage me.

SASHICHI: I meant the very opposite. I think that's fine.

TETSUZŌ: Eh?

SASHICHI: It's better for you to return to being the plain Tetsuzō.

TETSUZŌ: You think so?

SASHICHI: Why don't you work with me? A proprietor of a footwear shop is just as good as an *ukiyo-e* artist.

TETSUZŌ: And when did you become so wise, Sashichi? O'Ei,
you've got my blood running through your veins. You must
become a great artist—in my place.

SASHICHI: Not "great"—just an ordinary one.

TETSUZŌ: Then, an ordinary one. And I'll become a clam peddler
or a spice peddler—just an ordinary one.

SASHICHI: That sounds a bit too simple, but why not?

TETSUZŌ: I'm going to bid farewell to my previous self. Only, give
me one break. It's about O'Nao. I can't give her up. But she's
disappeared. (*Suddenly bursting into tears.*)

O'EI: Dad's like a child. That's why I love him.

TETSUZŌ: Thank you, thank you. They tell me a child born early in
your life is brighter and has a big heart, Sashichi. That's certainly true.

GOSUKE'S VOICE: How horrible! Someone has hanged himself!

(O'EI' *and* SASHICHI *run off in the direction of the voice.*)

O'EI'S VOICE: Dad! . . . Grandpa's hanging from a pine tree!

TETSUZŌ (*desperately trying to control himself*): What a shabby way to kick off . . . (*Suddenly striking a pose. Then, he walks around comically, behaving like a spice peddler.*) Spice for sale! Spice for sale! Red-red-red-red pepper! Red-red-red-red pepper!

Curtain

Act Two
Scene One

(*On a raised platform on stage,* TETSUZŌ, *now* KATSUSHIKA HOKUSAI, *gazes intently at a small grain of rice he is holding between his thumb and forefinger. He resembles a watch repairman wearing his jewler's loupe and adjusting a small screw. Finally, he deliberately grasps a fine brush the size of a sewing needle and then glares proudly at the large crowd that has gathered around him.* O'EI *is in attendance.*)

In this act, time and place shift freely, but the opening scene is about ten years after Act One; hence, HOKUSAI *and* O'EI *are in their forties and twenties, respectively.* HOKUSAI *wears expensive clothes and behaves arrogantly while* O'EI *wears no makeup and appears casual in both dress and manner.*

(*To the musical accompaniment of a small band,* NAKAJIMA ISE *and* O'HYAKU, *now both deceased, appear on the stage.* O'HYAKU *carries a book. They have triangular patches of white cloth attached to their foreheads and are dressed entirely in white. In other words, they are in shrouds. The song used may be a popular tune from the early Taishō period* [32]—*for example:*)

> Life is short.
> Fall in love, young maiden,
> Before your ruby lips fade,
> Before your ardent blood chills.
> There are no more tomorrows. [33]

ISE: Yes, as you can see we are now dead. And as in real life there are characters in a play who have already finished their roles. Nevertheless, if we bow out meekly, we'd continue to be a little anxious about the fate of Tetsuzō, Sashichi, O'Nao, and O'Ei. So, we've boldly stepped out—like this. (*To* O'HYAKU.)

[32] (1912–1925).
[33] A tune popular in the 1920s.

Well, why don't you start reading from the celebrated, "On
the Edo Arts"?

O'HYAKU: Yes, indeed.

ISE: Hold on! When was it written?

O'HYAKU: At the beginning of Taishō . . . Way after our time.

ISE: I'm told it was a rather dismal and difficult period. Please
proceed.

O'HYAKU: "And, therefore, the main reason for the admiration of
Hokusai by Europeans lies in his great contribution to the
emergence of the Post-Impressionists. Claude Monet's preoc-
cupation with painting the same scenery and objects under
each of the four seasons and under the changing light is said
to be inspired by Hokusai's 'Hundred Views of Mount Fuji' [34]
and 'The Thirty-six Views of Mount Fuji.' " [35]

ISE: Who wrote that exaggerated account?

O'HYAKU: A gentleman called Nagai Kafū, [36] the well-known
writer.

ISE: Please continue.

O'HYAKU: Yes, indeed: (*Reads.*) "At the time, Degas and Tou-
louse-Lautrec were under the influence of the current literary
naturalism and tried to obtain their subjects from among
women workers, dancers, circus acrobats, and washer-
women—all from humble circumstances within the market
places of Paris rather than from history and mythology. 'Hokusai Sketchbooks' gave these artists additional moral support." [37]

ISE: What a joke!

O'HYAKU: I beg your pardon?

ISE: That's only Kafū's blind admiration for him. (*Glancing at*
HOKUSAI.) Don't let him hear. He'll get more conceited than
ever. Please continue.

O'HYAKU (*lowering her voice*): "Hokusai's art was exported to the
West and stimulated the newly emerging Post-Impressionists.
And, finally, by the time this new French art form, in turn,

[34] *Fugaku Hyakkei* (1834).

[35] *Fugaku Sanjūrokkei* (ca. 1823–1831), actually forty-six pictures in all.

[36] Born 1879, died 1959. An important modern writer.

[37] "Edo Geijitsu-ron" (On the Edo Arts), *Kafū Zenshū* (Complete Works of
Kafū), Shunyōdō, Tokyo, vol. I (1927), p. 440.

swept the Japanese art world, there was no longer anyone in his own country who remembered Hokusai."[38]

ISE: Is that true? Were the countrymen who came after him so lacking in humanity? Well, there's no need to exaggerate Tetsuzō's importance. But he surely deserves proper recognition. Now, let me have the book.

O'HYAKU: Yes, indeed.

ISE (reading): "Among the works of Hokusai, a majority of them have now left Japanese soil and are in the hands of the European connoisseurs. The most highly rated popular art of the Edo period is now virtually monopolized by foreigners as a treasure. Our bureaucratic, militarist government often advocates the pressing need for patriotism and martial spirit. The martial spirit is admirable. But I find it difficult to understand what they mean by patriotism."[39] Imagine that! Hokusai's been finally turned into a touchstone for patriotism. Hmm, hmm, hmm. I still find the younger Tetsuzō easier to get along with.

Scene Two

HOKUSAI (while drawing): My pictures for "The Illustrated Song of Itako"[40] is certainly popular today. But I, formerly Fusenkyo Hokusai, now Hokusai Shinsei, have already reached a point far beyond "The Illustrated Song of Itako." (Lays down his brush.) It's done. Please observe closely. On this very tiny grain of rice, two birds abide, pecking at their bait.

O'EI: The head of Echigoya Store[41] wants badly to buy that grain of rice. He's going to make it a family treasure. Look at this pile of shiny gold coins!

HOKUSAI (throws the gold coins on the floor): How despicable, O'Ei!

---

[38] Ibid.

[39] Ibid., p. 441.

[40] Itako Zekkushū (ca. 1802), a volume containing illustrations of beauties by Hokusai. The work is based on a popular song (Itako-bushi) current in the area of the present Ibaraki Prefecture which lies northeast of Tokyo. It also has parodies of the original lyrics in a Chinese-style poetry chüeh-chü (zekku), written in four-line stanzas. Shū indicates a collection, presumably of Hokusai's drawings.

[41] A kimono shop founded in 1673, later Mitsukoshi Department Store.

Does he think that this picture which I drew with all my heart
and soul can be bought for money?

O'EI: You can't mean that! Echigoya has the largest kimono store
in Edo. You'd be insulting him.

HOKUSAI: So, what if he's number one in Edo! I'm the celebrated
Hokusai Shinsei. Listen, just the other day, I was the only
ukiyo-e artist in town, along with the Japanese-style artist,
Tani Bonchō,[42] who was invited to an audience with his Lordship, Shōgun Ienari.[43] And I even gave His Lordship a work of
mine, free of charge.

O'EI: But why make a big thing out of painting two birds on a
grain of rice? Isn't it just a pastime for you? Actually, it's the
same thing you did in the garden of Gokokuji Temple[44] in
Otowa.[45] There, you spread out that enormous, thick piece of
paper . . . Must have been at least one hundred and twenty
mats.[46] And you dipped a straw broom instead of a brush into
a sixteen-gallon ink barrel[47] and ran about the top of the
paper. Then, Dad, you proudly told the spectators: "Well, everyone, climb up to the roof of the main building and look
down!" And they did. What they saw below was a huge picture of Bodidharma.[48] Everyone was flabbergasted. Aren't you
using the same trick? In other words, it's a bluff, a hoax. You
should, by all means, openly accept money and make profit on
such pictures.

HOKUSAI: You stupid fool! When did you start having a vulgar attitude like that? I draw all my pictures with total dedication.
But unless I draw them to suit popular taste, everyone gangs
up and says it's a bluff or a hoax. The same thing happened
when I studied Dutch copper engravings and went on to produce natural scenery on woodblocks. Everyone said they were
monkey-like works by an artist infatuated with the West. I'll

[42] A well-known painter (1765–1842) who mastered the Kanō style and the
Chinese-style but also studied the Western techniques.

[43] The eleventh Tokugawa Shōgun (1773–1841).

[44] One of the largest temples in Tokyo, founded in 1681.

[45] An area now in Bunkyō Ward, Tokyo.

[46] One mat equals approximately three feet by six feet; hence, the total surface
area of the paper would be over three hundred and sixty square yards.

[47] "Four *to*" in the text (one *to* equals 3.97 gallons).

[48] The semi-legendary figure who is said to have introduced Ch'an (Zen) Bud-
dhism to China in the sixth century.

be damned if I'm ever understood by those bunch of fools! Those who can't understand this Hokusai Shinsei's sentiment should go home! Go home!

Scene Three

ISE: Can you imagine such a thoroughly conceited attitude?

O'HYAKU: He's bluffing. He doesn't even have enough in the rice bin for tomorrow. Poor O'Ei—she'll have to start making trips to the pawnshop again. No matter how popular *ukiyo-e* prints are, they bring in so little. And Tetsuzō recklessly drives away that precious source of income. I'm told O'Ei has a job on the side making designs for toys[49] and kites children buy at the candy shops.

ISE: That's nothing! When Tetsuzō really gets hard up for money, he does the same thing on the sly, claiming they're O'Ei's.

O'HYAKU: I wonder what he's up to?

ISE: An upstart invariably gets cocky when he's suddenly treated like a teacher or a master. After all, he grew up without eating a decent bowl of polished rice. So he's all too aware of the value of money. And, for that very reason, he insists on making a public display of his low regard for it.

O'HYAKU: Then he's the very opposite of my Sashichi.

Scene Four

(*In his house,* BAKIN, *facing the desk, manipulates the abacus. The dialogue between* ISE *and* O'HYAKU *continues.*)

O'HYAKU: Sashichi is well known for his steadfast dedication to writing with his shutters tightly closed, even during daytime. But actually, though he's facing the desk, he spends most of the time with an abacus. He's reckoning how much he ought to receive when the *New Water Margin*[50] is translated. Or, how

[49] More precisely, *menko* in the text is a children's game using discs made of heavy paper, tin, or similar light material.

[50] *Shin-Suikoden*, based on a famous Chinese tale of the Ming period (1368–1644), *Shui-hu Chuan*, about a band of Robin Hood-like robbers during the twelfth century.

much of a raise he must get for his *Crescent Moon: The Adventures of Tametomo*[51] when he negotiates directly with Kadomaruya Printers. Just things like that. And to think he has a samurai background!

ISE: These days the samurai are all the same. That's why riots happen. But the rioters are shrewd. They demand contributions from even merchants like me with close governmental connections. So I think many people were quite distressed when I hanged myself. It's all absurd.

O'HYAKU: Oh, someone's knocking softly on the door. It's a woman. Must be O'Nao! I'm sure she's out to tempt Bakin. I'll find out what's going on.

(*Since she is a dead spirit,* O'HYAKU *is able to "pass through" the wall of Sashichi's room. A knock at the door. He opens it, and* O'EI *enters.*)

O'EI: I'm sorry it's so late, Mr. Kyokutei Bakin.

(*Relieved,* O'HYAKU *returns to* ISE's *side.*)

O'HYAKU: It was O'Ei.

ISE: How casually you go back to the world of the living! You must have an unappeased hatred.

BAKIN: O'Ei, don't call me "Mr. Kyokutei Bakin." I hate that. Call me Uncle Sashichi—as before.

O'EI: But I came to borrow money again. I wouldn't feel right if I spoke too familiarly.

BAKIN: Shall I give you the usual amount?

O'EI: Uh-huh.

BAKIN (*offers her small change*): This isn't a loan. I'm giving it to you.

O'EI: Eh?

BAKIN: I'd get angry if I thought I was actually lending it to Hokusai. Far from being grateful, he's telling everyone Kyokutei Bakin is a tightwad and antisocial.

O'EI: Dad imposes on you.

BAKIN: I don't mind that so much. Only, the more he talks badly of me, the more his own reputation goes down.

O'EI: And it's all due to your generosity that Dad is finally established. Otherwise, he might be peddling spice for the rest of his life—the way he used to.

[51] *Chinsetsu Yumiharizuki* (1807–1811), a novel by Kyokutei Bakin; concerns Minamoto Hachirō Tametomo, a brave warrior from the eleventh century.

[*Flashbacks (a), (b), and (c) in Act Two go back about ten years, to the time of Act One (1794); they take place on the same stage.*]

Flashback (a). A field in the outskirts of town at dusk.

(*Still carrying a huge wicker basket covered with paper and shaped like a red pepper pod on his back,* TETSUZŌ (*later* HOKUSAI) *is squatting on the shoulder of the road. Dressed in a spice peddler's costume, he appears completely exhausted.* O'EI *arrives.*)

O'EI: Dad, here you are! I've been looking all over for you.

TETSUZŌ (*in a gentle tone*): I dropped by an antique shop. There was something I needed. I'm sorry I went shopping when we're so poor. But it was cheap.

O'EI: And what did you get?

TETSUZŌ: Don't ask me that, O'Ei. But, you know, it's terrible, sweating away working. And at my age, I've finally found out. I thought it'd be simple to be a spice peddler. But why? Oh, why? First, my legs gave out. I wonder how far I walk each day? Next, it was my throat. "Spice for sale! Spice for sale! Red-red-red red pepper!" My voice became hoarse. Oh, where did that stray dog go? It kept following me until just a while ago . . . You know, it sneezed when I gave it a piece of pepper. (*Smiles forlornly.*) I'm sorry I did that to a stray dog. It was so attached to me. I feel the happiest these days when I'm talking to dogs and cats. See, I got this at a secondhand shop. (*He takes out a small figure of Saint Nichiren* [52] *from the fold of his kimono.*)

O'EI: It's Saint Nichiren!

TETSUZŌ: . . . (*Self-mockingly.*) Somehow, your Dad has lost his will to go on. And unless I hold onto something, I feel as though I'm finished . . .

O'EI: Dad, you've changed! You can finally let others see your own weakness.

TETSUZŌ (*praying to Saint Nichiren*): Namu Myōhōrengekyō,[53] Namu Myōhōrengekyō. Please help this Tetsuzō to become the best spice peddler in Japan.

[52] Born 1222, died 1282. The founder of the Nichiren Buddhist sect.
[53] "Honor to the Sutra of the Lotus Flower of the Wonderful Law." A familiar incantation used by the Nichiren sect.

Flashback (b). SASHICHI'S *house.*

(*Alone,* O'EI *should appear to be talking to* SASHICHI [*later* BAKIN].)

O'EI (*sobbing*): Uncle Sashichi, this is my final request. Please praise the pictures of the wretched spice peddler who is drawing, secretly. I don't care if they don't sell. It would be encouragement enough for Dad just to be praised by Uncle Sashichi.

Flashback (c).

(*Alone,* SASHICHI *should appear to be talking to Tsutaya Shigesaburō, the printer.*)

SASHICHI: Please, Mr. Tsutaya, I'm not asking you to buy Tetsuzō's pictures. I'll pay you for it, so just print them. You may laugh, thinking I'm trying to be a do-gooder, but keep this a secret from Tetsuzō and the rest. You must act as if you really liked his pictures and decided to print them. You know, Mr. Tsutaya, though I'm a novelist and Tetsuzō's an *ukiyo-e* artist, I still understand how he feels. Encouraging him may be simply a trick, but if he believes he's gained public recognition, he'll get self-confidence. Especially since Tetsuzō's such a show-off.

(SASHICHI *places a heavy package of money on the* tatami *floor.*)

[*End of flashbacks*]

The scene shifts back to the present at BAKIN'S *house.* O'EI *and* BAKIN.

O'EI: I'm sorry we haven't been able to repay you—though you've been so kind to us.

HOKUSAI'S VOICE: Are you in, Bakin? (HOKUSAI *comes in drunk. He wears a threadbare* yukata.[54])

O'EI: What are you doing here, Dad?

HOKUSAI: My "A Guide to Both Banks of the Sumida River"[55] is

[54] Unlined kimono—summer wear.
[55] *Sumidagawa Ryōgan Ikken* (1806).

in such demand now. So I'm going to invite some geisha and gather all together at the Sumida River and drink till morning on a river boat.

BAKIN: Thanks for the invitation. But I still have work to do.

HOKUSAI: I didn't come here for that. I only feel uncomfortable and get a stiff back when I go out with you. I want to borrow money. I need to at least get my clothes back from the pawnshop. Otherwise, this celebrated Katsushika Hokusai can't look his best. (*Thrusting his hands out.*)

BAKIN: I refuse.

HOKUSAI: Don't act so stuffy. I'm not living extravagantly for the fun of it! Don't you know that Kōrin[56] became a fine painter after his father left him an inheritance, and he squandered money like bath water?

BAKIN: And you want to be an Ogata Kōrin?

HOKUSAI: Don't be silly. Who cares about that kind of queer and stiff painting? That's decorative art—not real painting. And besides, his designs are too contrived. Take that picture of the peacock, for instance. Since he's proud as a peacock,[57] it was probably easy for him.

BAKIN: That's all very well, but what has a rich man's son from the Kyoto-Osaka area have to do with a son of an Edo . . .

HOKUSAI: Oh, I know. I was raised at the rock bottom of society. And that's why I can't catch up unless I live more lavishly than the others. You know, my spirit seems to leap mysteriously when I act like a rich man-about-town. And when I see the hangers-on fawning on me, I can thoroughly despise them as poor wretches. And I can measure mankind with a rather interesting yardstick. You've got to help me! (*Reaching out.*)

BAKIN: If you're so desperate for money, why did you give all of his inheritance to his mistress when Nakajima Ise died? He had cut ties with her long before.

HOKUSAI: There was a thunder shower, then.

BAKIN: I absolutely refuse. Ask some printer to give you an advance! You should have no difficulty with your present popularity.

---

[56] A famous painter of decorative art (1659–1716).

[57] A reference to Kōrin's aristocractic bearing as well as his selection of subjects for his works.

HOKUSAI: That's why I've already borrowed wherever I could. Come on!

BAKIN: Don't pester me.

HOKUSAI: Well, if that's how you feel, I've made up my mind, too. I won't have anything more to do with illustrating *New Water Margin*. Let me tell you something . . . That's selling because of my pictures—not your story. That's right, instead of me quitting, I'll have you dropped from further writing, and Takai Ranzan[58] can take your place. Kadomaruya Printers will listen to whatever I say.

BAKIN: Never mind. I quit.

HOKUSAI: What a bad sport! I saw someone exactly like O'Nao at the Matsubaya Tea House.

BAKIN: That's taking an unfair advantage! You think you can get away with anything by just mentioning O'Nao.

HOKUSAI: What was that?

BAKIN: You used O'Nao as an excuse to drive out all your wives. And you also tricked married women and innocent girls, a number of times. And forced many women to have abortions. Then, when you finally left them, Hokusai, you offered the same excuse: "Forgive me, I still can't forget O'Nao." . . . You might fool the rest of the world with that talk. They may think the arrogant Hokusai is, after all, only human. That he's a simple *ukiyo-e* artist who has the vision of only one woman locked in his heart for ever. But you can't fool me. You were only devoted to O'Nao up to the time you quit spice peddling. After that, you're merely using her as a stepping stone.

HOKUSAI: And what's wrong with that? A man has to forge ahead day by day. You know, today, my Old Man's . . . Nakajima Ise's hanging himself—despite his advanced age and mature judgment—doesn't seem like the act of a sane man . . .

BAKIN: "Out of sight, out of mind."[59]—so you're following exactly the familiar saying. How childish you are! But, Hokusai, thanks to O'Nao's dissolute way of living and Nakajima Ise's

---

[58] A popular novelist (1762–1838) who replaced Bakin in the writing of *New Water Margin*, beginning with volume XII.

[59] Equivalent to the sense of the Japanese saying: "Once it clears the throat, the hotness is forgotten."

ludicrous and obstinate infatuation, you were able to look
more closely at humanity.

HOKUSAI: Are you quibbling again? I'll lose an argument with
you since I'm not a good talker like you. But no matter what
you say, I'm still mad about O'Nao. At least, I'm certain of
that. Yet, my attraction to her has changed. Hmm . . . How
can an upright fellow like you ever understand my feelings!

BAKIN: Hokusai!

HOKUSAI: If you don't shut up, it's all over between us.

BAKIN: You've already cut yourself off from both Utamaro and
Toyokuni,[60] and Jippensha Ikku,[61] the novelist. And
now—me. You won't have any close friends left.

HOKUSAI: What are you getting at? Did O'Ei ask you to warn me?

O'EI: Dad won't listen to anyone.

HOKUSAI: I'm not playing around with woman for the fun of it.
Women are like natural scenery. They're each different. Scen-
eries may be similar, but each have their subtle differences.

BAKIN: You once told Utamaro and Toyokuni you couldn't understand anyone who drew beautiful women and actors. You said
beauties are to sleep with and actors are to watch.

HOKUSAI: We're finished, all finished! I don't care if I ever see you
again! There's still someone I can really count on.

BAKIN: You mean Saint Nichiren and "Namu Myōhōrengekyō"?

HOKUSAI: That's right.

BAKIN: I think Saint Nichiren gave up on you, long ago.

HOKUSAI: Is that so? Then, I'll cut ties with him, too. Now that
I'm a full-fledged artist, I don't need any god, either Shintō or
Buddhist. In fact, I've never thoroughly studied the Buddhist
scriptures. And I clung to Saint Nichiren only when I felt completely discouraged and helpless. (Laughs.)

BAKIN: When a man loses his sense of gratitude, it's the end.

O'EI: Dad, it's just as Uncle Sashichi says.

HOKUSAI: Why do you always side with him? So, it's "encouragement of virtue and the chastisement of vice"[62]—it crops in all
your novels. You rake up money because you're always work-

---

[60] A late Tokugawa *ukiyo-e* artist (1769–1825).

[61] A writer of "humorous stories" (1765–1831) and remembered especially for
his *Shank's Mare* (*Tōkaidōchū Hizakurige*) (1802–1809), an amusing tale about a pair
of travelers.

[62] *Kanzen chōaku*, an important moral notion often incorporated into writing of
the Tokugawa period.

ing where there's the least danger. But don't forget that your books sold, thanks to my illustrations. All right, hand over the money!

BAKIN: I refuse.

HOKUSAI: We'll see about that . . . (*Glancing around the room,* HOKUSAI *takes out a letter box from the closet and grabs a handful of gold coins.*)

O'EI: You mustn't, Dad! How could you be so rude to such a fine man!

HOKUSAI: Shut up! (*He pushes aside* O'EI.)

BAKIN: How disgraceful!

HOKUSAI: After throwing a lavish party tonight, I'll start on a trip tomorrow. I'm going to make the rounds of all the places where I can see Mount Fuji. And someday I'll draw one that'll astound everybody.

O'EI: Then, how do you expect me to live? A single woman with all this debt?

HOKUSAI: With a face like that, I guess you're not fit to be a first-class whore. Let Bakin take care of you.

BAKIN: You're totally alone now, Hokusai. Everyone despises you. Of course, it's your own fault. You deliberately scorn all sympathy or generosity.

O'EI: Please try to remember, Dad. Your luck changed for the better around the time you were selling spices. And you said then, as you looked at the beautiful printed pictures: "Saint Nichiren is wonderful. He always knew I wanted to become Japan's best *ukiyo-e* artist." And you sincerely—oh, so sincerely—put your hands together in prayer toward Saint Nichiren. Can't you go back to the Dad I knew then? Please try!

HOKUSAI: Don't be ridiculous. Those pictures were clumsy and worthless. How can I, Katsushika Hokusai, the greatest in the land, ever go back to those days when I was such an inept *ukiyo-e* artist?

O'EI: Then, Dad, let me tell you something.

BAKIN: Don't, O'Ei.!

O'EI: Dad, your pictures were printed because someone took over a pile of money to Tsutaya Printers.

HOKUSAI: Don't say anything you'll be sorry for. And who, exactly, provided this large sum?

O'EI (*looks at* BAKIN): . . . Who else, Dad?

BAKIN: It was O'Nao!

HOKUSAI: O'Nao?

O'EI: Uncle Sashichi!

BAKIN: O'Nao sent over the money secretly while she was on her travels. She may have somehow heard a rumor about your wretched circumstances.

HOKUSAI: My God! What an impudent thing for her to do! And where is she now?

BAKIN: I don't know.

HOKUSAI: She must want to be my wife. I'm sure that was her intention. How impertinent! (*He leaves.*)

O'EI: What shall we do?

BAKIN: Leave him alone. Listen, O'Ei, I feel rotten, now that you've brought up that old story.

O'EI: What do you mean?

BAKIN: I must be a hypocrite. I secretly gave the money to the printer to help out Hokusai . . . And now I tried to act virtuous by claiming it was O'Nao's doing . . . I have this rather contemptible way of making myself out to be so moral, just to gratify myself. It's an affectation. And that comes out in my novels, too. I must rewrite *Crescent Moon: The Adventures of Tametomo.*

O'EI: I'll do anything to make up for what I've done. I'll do whatever you ask.

BAKIN: That's wonderful! Then, I'll excuse myself and tidy up the bed.

O'EI (*appears stunned*): . . .

BAKIN (*skillfully begins making the bed*): You know, I'm slowly reaching forty, but I'm still in the prime of life. Don't you agree?

O'EI: Uh-huh.

BAKIN: And isn't it a pity that day after day I fritter away my manhood?

O'EI (*becoming increasingly tense*): . . . . Uh-huh.

BAKIN: As you grow older, you can't help losing your virility. And you must accomplish what you can't do later.

O'EI (*making up her mind*): I can well understand.

BAKIN: I'm glad O'Hyaku's dead. I honestly am.

(*Unconsciously,* O'EI *brings the fold of her kimono together—modestly.*)

O'EI: Of course, I don't mind . . . But won't people talk?

BAKIN: I know you're a discreet woman, O'Ei.

O'EI (*snuggling closer*): Uh-huh. Of course I am.

(*With his back toward* O'EI, BAKIN *takes off his topcoat*[63] *and begins folding it. Behind him,* O'EI *gazes desperately and rapturously, but finally with determination, she begins to undo her sash.*)

BAKIN: Those who buy my novels may think I work in a neatly arranged study, sitting properly, and busily writing with a brush. In fact, I'm sprawled out on a bed which is always left out and contemplating while pulling out hairs from my nostrils. Curiously, I can speak freely to you.

(O'EI *reties her sash.*)

Upsy-daisy. (BAKIN *crawls into his bed.*) Well, I guess I'll let you help me with my work. These days my eyes get blurry, and I can't write.

(*Appearing miffed,* O'EI *faces the desk.*)

"Crescent Moon: The Adventures of Tametomo: the continuation of Book Five in Part I . . ." —First, I'd like you to write that on the corner. "Suspicious and confused as to whether it was divine or human, when he walked over to the railing . . ." —Oh, use the simple syllabary[64] for the Chinese characters[65] you don't know. I'll write them in later. ". . . When he walked over to the railing, he saw a beautiful girl about sixteen dressed in a manner neither of the capital nor the country . . . She had charming crescent brows and slender willowy hips. She was like aronia blossoms blooming on a cherry branch suffused with the fragrance of lotus."[66] (BAKIN *has an ecstatic expression as if a beautiful girl was actually before his eyes.* O'EI *appears jealous.*) How old are you, O'Ei?

O'EI (*rather sharply*): I'm no longer a sweet sixteen, but an ugly duckling of twenty-four.

BAKIN: You'll soon have to find yourself a husband.

O'EI: I'm too old. No one will have me.

BAKIN: Now that you mention it, you've reached that age.

---

[63] *Haori,* an outdoor garment worn over the kimono.

[64] *Kana:* there are two types of Japanese syllabaries containing simple characters—*katakana* and *hiragana* (see footnote 84).

[65] *Kanji,* Chinese characters used in Japanese writing.

[66] Kyokutei Bakin, *Chinsetsu Yumiharizuki* (part I, book 5, ch. 12), in *Iwanami Koten Bungaku Taikei* (Collection of Classical Literature), vol. XL (1958), pp. 186–87.

O'EI: But Jippensha Ikku said I was in full bloom.

BAKIN: He would, being the author of the amusing *Shank's Mare*[67] . . .

O'EI (*looking dejected*): You should be the one to marry. You've already had the first-year memorial service for O'Hyaku. And isn't it hard for a man to live all by himself?

BAKIN: Not especially. Unlike Hokusai, I love cooking, washing, and housecleaning. There's something a bit effeminate about me.

O'EI (*dropping a hint*): It must be easy for a woman to be married to a man like that.

BAKIN: There are no decent women among those who marry for that reason.

O'EI (*desperately*): But, Uncle Sashichi, a woman likes to say things in a roundabout way . . .

BAKIN: I've got to go to the toilet. (*He leaves.*)

(*Unable to bear it any longer,* O'EI *begins to wail loudly like a small boy.*)

O'EI: I've loved you for such a long time . . . But I'll never bring it up again—ever. (*Wiping away her tears, she quickly gulps down the sake from a bottle at one corner of the room.*) That's funny. Who ever said women shouldn't drink!

BAKIN (*returns*): Nothing came out.

O'EI: I'm going to tell you the truth, Uncle Sashichi. I drew a third of Dad's pictures.

BAKIN: What?

O'EI: How can one living man draw so many pictures? But now I'm happy because he's so good that I can't imitate him anymore.

Scene Five

O'HYAKU: A warm breeze is beginning to blow.

ISE: A sure sign a dead acquaintance will be coming soon.

(*Accompanied by festive music,* O'NAO *arrives, glancing about curiously.*)

It's O'Nao!

O'NAO: Oh, it's been a while.

ISE: So, you've finally come. Now, you're just mine. Hokusai and

[67] See Jippensha Ikku (footnote 61).

Gosuke, the errand boy at the footwear shop, are still in the world of the living. Even a wanton like you can't find a new lover—once you're dead!

O'NAO: Are you sure you're all right?

ISE: O'Hyaku, everyone who's fresh from the world of the living thinks he's still alive.

O'HYAKU: That's right, that's right!

O'NAO: This is terrible. Even O'Hyaku is going along with this farce.

ISE: When you've settled down, you'll realize what's happened.

O'NAO: What are you talking about? Fortunately, the fact that O'Hyaku is beside me is the best proof I'm still alive.

O'HYAKU: Is that so? Explain it to me.

O'NAO: Don't act so innocent. A great scholar has written all about it in a book on this subject. (*Taking out a volume, she turns the pages and reads.*) "Since O'Hyaku, the wife of Kyokutei Bakin, was so suspicious and jealous about the relationship between O'Michi, the wife of her eldest son, Sōhaku, and Bakin, she died insane at the age of seventy-seven on the seventh day of the second moon in the twelfth year of Tempō."[68] But, O'Hyaku, you seem to be in the prime of life—no matter how you look at it.

O'HYAKU: After all, I died at thirty-five.

ISE: Since I made frequent visits to the inner palace, I was on very good terms with the great historians and scholars. As a matter of fact, these fellows were a gang of fakers. In short, take Tetsuzō, for example . . . That is—oops—now Katsushika Hokusai . . . The biographies of Hokusai are sloppily written. They're all based on Iijima Kyoshin's *The Biography of Katsushika Hokusai,*[69] published in 1893, and uncritically accept what he's written. Hence, once you cast doubt on his veracity, all the Hokusai biographies are in a shambles. For instance, O'Nao, you don't even appear in Professor Iijima's book.

O'NAO: That's strange.

ISE: As for O'Ei, Professor Iijima says she was the daughter of Hokusai's second wife. But if that's the case, O'Ei wasn't even born when I was still alive. Broadly speaking, *ukiyo-e* artists

[68] Twelfth year of Tempō (1841).
[69] (*Katsushika Hokusai-den*) (Tokyo: Renkukaku, 1893). Exact reference unavailable.

had no ties with the government and led meager lives as social outcasts. So they wouldn't be written up in history. For better or for worse, only those involved with the government are mentioned in them. (*To* O'HYAKU.) As proof, there's substantial material on your husband.

O'HYAKU: Nonetheless, that book is outrageous. It says Sashichi quit the footwear business after he established himself as a novelist, but . . . (*Gradually becoming excited.*) That's totally wrong. Actually, Sashichi was a poor businessman. He ruined my store, which, till then, had lasted for generations. And what's more, to have it said that he even gave money to Tetsuzō! That Sashichi was tormented all his life by my jealousy is a damn lie! The facts are just the opposite: my husband even made special temple visits to pray that I would go crazy and die! And when I did die, he promptly sold my house and property!

O'NAO: . . . Now I know. At that time when everything turned black in front of my eyes . . . And later, when I thought I'd revived, it was after I had actually been killed. Still, I don't blame him. Besides, you're not a real man unless you have the guts to kill your lover—if she happens to be unfaithful. My last man was a farmer with a powerful, sturdy build. I suppose that since he couldn't read, that share of his energy was passed over to the body.

ISE (*laughs hysterically*): Hee, hee, hee, hee!

O'NAO: What a funny laugh.

ISE: I'd like to kill myself again.

O'NAO: Now, if only Tetsuzō would come. Then it would get lively again.

ISE: Do you miss him?

O'NAO: Not in the least.

ISE: Well, he's not about to drop dead. He's too busy working on his "Sketchbooks."[70]

O'NAO: "Sketchbooks"? I've never heard of that.

ISE: His "Sketchbooks" are, in other words, memoranda. In them

---

[70] *Hokusai Manga*, "Hokusai Sketchbooks" (1814–1849). After the publication of the first volume in 1814, Hokusai completed twelve more works for this series during his lifetime, for a total of thirteen. The standard collection today contains two additional volumes printed posthumously. The term *"manga"* in the text, which has been translated "sketchbooks," carries a strong flavor of a carefree and unrestrained activity—most appropriately describing the entire life of Hokusai.

Hokusai draws, lightly and simply, subjects from all creation at random so that a complete picture may be drawn someday. In any case, since I'm dead, no one can stop me from acting pedantic, so allow me to elaborate. The foreigners, who came later on to our shores on the Black Ships,[71] were just astounded. Why? Well, in "Hokusai Sketchbooks," he carefully and accurately captured with simple lines how a man's muscles behaved when he's laughing or crying. And how the human body behaves when it's moving or at rest. You know, Westerners have clumsy fingers. And the word got around that a great genius was living on a tiny island in the Far East . . . Hokusai's an egotistic fellow but has an unusually sharp power of observation. And with those egoistic eyes, he carefully observed not only man but animals and landscapes. But for that very reason, he turned into a sort of man who could not become totally absorbed in anything.

o'NAO: But I was his one exception.

ISE: How lucky you are to be your usual optimistic self.

(*Again, the warm breeze begins to blow.*)

o'HYAKU: Oh, look. Another acquaintance has joined our ranks . . .

(*To the accompaniment of various national anthems, the aged* GOSUKE *appears.*)

GOSUKE: Oh, it's been a long time. I'm Gosuke.

o'NAO: Oh, Gosuke, are you dead, too?

GOSUKE: I'm so happy to join all of you. The present world of the living is too hectic. Dutch warships visited Nagasaki, followed shortly by American ships to Uraga.[72] But not to be outdone, warships from France and England also came . . . I wonder what'll happen to Japan . . . And it's a great relief to be spared such worries.

o'NAO: If you're dead maybe Tetsuzō is . . .

GOSUKE: Mr. Hokasai is quite unconcerned about the changing world and lives quietly in the Shōten district[73] in the Asakusa area.

o'HYAKU: You mean, he's moved again?

GOSUKE: I'm told it was his ninety-fourth move.

---

[71] *Kurobune*, popular Tokugawa term for Western ships.
[72] The port of entry for Edo, lying south of the capital city.
[73] The final residence and burial place of Hokusai in the Asakusa area.

ISE: He just can't stay put in one spot too long. And, as for his names, Tetsuzō has thirty-one. It started with Shunrō, and, you know, even when it's Hokusai, he combines it with other names which come either before or after it . . . Let me see . . . Hokusai Sōri, just plain Hokusai, Fusenkyo Hokusai, Hokusai Shinsei, Zen-Hokusai I'itsu—five of them.

GOSUKE: The Shōten district is quite near the Saruwaka district[74] where the three great Kabuki theaters are. Why don't we visit him on the way to a performance?

ISE: That's an excellent idea. But he may move away unless we hurry.

O'HYAKU: Is he moving again?

ISE: To his last destination.

O'HYAKU: Where?

ISE: This world, of course.

O'HYAKU: You mean the "other" world.

ISE: So, isn't it "this" world? Well, let's hurry! Let's hurry!

(Everyone marches off to modern music.)

Now, let me see. To get to Shōten district, we must get off either at Asakusa Station on the Tōbu Railway Line or at Kaminarimon Station on the subway. Then, walk leisurely the rest of the way.

GOSUKE: Yes, I understand it's the center for wholesale business now. Watch out for the auto exhaust! It can make you sick.

ISE: What are you talking about? This is 1848, the first year of Kaei. (Rather pleased with himself.) It's nearly half-way into the nineteenth century. And, Gosuke, do you know what happened this year? (Taking out a notebook.) First . . .

(Short pause.)

O'HYAKU: What is it?

ISE: Kyokutei Bakin died at eighty-two!

(All exit. Suddenly, from "Thirty-six Views of Mount Fuji" by HO-. KUSAI, "Red Fuji"[75] and other scenes are flashed on the screen. Examples from "Hokusai Sketchbooks" are also included.)

BAKIN'S VOICE: O'Ei, Tetsuzō has certainly become a loathsome fellow. But his pictures are becoming sharper than ever. Per-

---

[74] The name of that part of Edo in the outskirts of town where the main Kabuki theaters were relocated due to the Tempō Reform (see footnote 90).

[75] Gaifū Kaisei (Clear Day with a Southern Breeze), Print Thirty-three in "Thirty-six Views of Mount Fuji."

haps he was able to completely draw off the poisonous thing he carries within him into his daily life. That's the reason there's no poison or impurity in his pictures. They're fresh. It's as though Tetsuzō himself had plunged into the heart of both nature and man . . . And he's singing his own song.

O'EI'S VOICE: Hush! My eccentric Dad is sounding off again.

HOKUSAI'S VOICE: So, it's "Thirty-six Views of Mount Fuji." Hmm, it's nothing special. And there are only two or three out of that entire lot that seem halfway decent. Which are my favorites? Decide for yourself! As for the rest of them, as long as the printer has the Mount Fuji, they're bound to sell. They're all works I forced myself to draw because the printer begged me! That's why Mount Fuji is dead! However, the people and the scenery—apart from the mountain—are very much alive. So, if I were to give away my secret, I'm Mount Fuji! And I stand there conspicuously and gaze down aloofly at human existence! Well, my real challenge still lies ahead. This Hokusai is only eighty-nine!

Curtain

Act Three
Scene One

Place: Inside HOKUSAI'*s quarters at a tenement house within the compound of Henshō-in Temple in the Shōten district in the Asakusa area.*[76] *In Iijima Kyoshin's* The Biography of Katsushika Hokusai *(1893), his room is described as follows: "The interior of the room is in total disrepair. On the spruce door is pasted a piece of paper with these words: 'All Requests for Souvenir Drawings Strictly Refused. Signed: Miuraya Hachiemon.' An empty orange box nailed high on a post enshrines a statue of Saint Nichiren. A sack of charcoal from Sakura,*[77] *a gift basket of bean paste cakes,*[78] *and* sushi[79] *wrappers are*

[76] The largest center of entertainment in Edo, which was west of the Sumida River; now part of Taitō Ward. Its rapid growth occurred after 1657 when Shin-Yoshiwara, a new pleasure quarters, was built in an area north of the Kannon Temple. The original Yoshiwara Pleasure Quarters was destroyed earlier that same year in a great fire which consumed a large part of the city (see footnote 98).

[77] A fine grade of charcoal from a region now in eastern Chiba Prefecture.

[78] *Sakura-mochi*, more exactly, a bean paste rice cake wrapped in a cherry leaf.

[79] Small cakes of boiled rice flavored with vinegar and often topped with raw fillet of fish or other marine delicacies.

*scattered about next to the charcoal brazier. It is like a combined tool
shed and rubbish heap.''*

Time: Winter morning in 1848.

(Hunched forward, HOKUSAI, *eighty-nine, is warming himself at the
charcoal brazier and dozing with his back toward the audience. A few
dozen miniature dolls are strewn about the* tatami *floor. They repre-
sent the product of* O'EI's *part-time work. Accompanied by* O'NAO,
who is dressed like a typical daughter of a poor peasant family, O'EI
noisily opens the door and enters. O'EI *is now seventy.)*

O'EI: It's urgent, Dad! Please wake up!

HOKUSAI *(remains asleep):* . . .

O'EI: A little earlier, I went to the employment office, looking for
a girl to paint the miniature dolls I do as a sideline. And, to
my surprise, this child was standing inside!

O'NAO: Please don't tug at my arm so hard and listen to my story.
If I'll do, use me. I came here all scared from the country. My
village was completely ruined by the recent big famine. And
there was no work. Luckily, I heard that a man I once knew in
the village was successful in the employment business in
Edo's Asakusa area. Dad was a poor peasant . . . That's the
whole story. Can you really hire someone like me?

O'EI: Don't act so innocent, O'Nao!

O'NAO: Oh, how did you know my name?

O'EI: . . . O'Nao . . . Please . . . Wait a minute. *(Gazing at herself in the mirror.)*

O'NAO: I'm so glad I can work at Mr. Katsushika Hokusai's place.
His pictures are popular in my village, too. They're carefully
stored in the landowner's storehouse. Please take me to Mr.
Hokusai's house at once.

O'EI: . . . If O'Nao's still alive, she should be much older than I
am.

HOKUSAI: Has someone been calling O'Nao's name? *(Rising,*
HOKUSAI *stares at* O'NAO. *Finally, he approaches her on all fours.)*
Oh, it's you, O'Nao. I've wanted so badly to see you.

*(*HOKUSAI *clings to her.* O'NAO *thrusts him back, and he falls down
awkwardly.)*

O'NAO: Stop it, you lecherous old man!

O'EI: Even the efforts of the great Hokusai are in vain.

O'NAO (*shocked*): You can't mean he's . . .

HOKUSAI: What's happened, O'Nao? You must be crazy, treating me this way!

O'EI: If O'Nao's still alive, she should be much older than I am.

HOKUSAI: I've heard that line before.

O'EI: If you understand what I'm trying to say, Dad, why do you carry on this way? . . .

HOKUSAI (*whispering, rather mischievously*): I'd be to my advantage to believe she's the other O'Nao. (*To* O'NAO.) O'Nao, have you really forgotten this Tetsuzō?

O'NAO: You see? His name is Tetsuzō, after all. Mr. Hokusai wouldn't live in such a messy and dirty tenement.

BAKIN'S VOICE: Hello. (BAKIN *appears, leaning on a cane. He is eighty-two and dressed tastefully.*)

HOKUSAI: You came at the right time. Tell her my name.

BAKIN: Miuraya Hachiemon.

HOKUSAI: That's what I use now, but what do people usually call me?

BAKIN: Gakyōjin, "The Mad Artist."

HOKUSAI: You're exasperating!

BAKIN: Fusenkyo I'itsu.

HOKUSAI: You bastard, I'll knock you down!

BAKIN: Then, have you thought of another outlandish name for yourself, Hokusai?

HOKUSAI (*sighing, deliberately*): Finally, it's out.

O'NAO (*convinced*): I'm sorry. I now realize that even great men become feeble-minded with age.

HOKUSAI: Bakin, doesn't she look like O'Nao?

BAKIN: O'Nao? Who's that? I forget.

HOKUSAI: Say, O'Ei, dress her up in pretty clothes and turn this child into a perfect likeness of the old O'Nao.

O'EI: We've no money.

HOKUSAI: Damn it! Say, Bakin, lend me some money. I hear you always carry your entire fortune around with you.

BAKIN: I refuse. When you grow old, there's nothing else you can depend on except money.

HOKUSAI: Doesn't one of your nephews—whatever his name is—want to become my pupil?

BAKIN: What about it?

HOKUSAI: Well, I'll sell him my Hokusai name. Then you should have no objection.

BAKIN: And what will you do?

HOKUSAI: I might call myself Manji Rōjin, "Old Man Fylfot."

(*Reluctantly,* BAKIN *gives money to* O'EI.)

O'EI: It's too late complaining now, but all my life I've had to put up with Dad's stupid and useless ways—living in his shadow. (*Drinking sake from a large cup. To* O'NAO.) Come along.

(O'EI *and* O'NAO *leave.* HOKUSAI *has an ecstatic expression on his face.*)

BAKIN: What happened?

HOKUSAI (*grinning foolishly*): Bakin, I'm in love.

BAKIN (*seriously*): I see. As a matter of fact, I am, too.

HOKUSAI: We're like-minded, after all. (HOKUSAI *slaps* BAKIN *on the back.*)

BAKIN: However, I'm not in love with a girl. It's the natural scenery of this world . . . (*Begins narrating.*) ". . . And thus spring passed in vain, and though it was the beginning of the fourth moon, there was no word from Mochimitsu and Tadashige. As the world became warmer, in the distant open sea and on the island of many sorrows where the whales roar, fair weather prevailed. And the wind and the waves were still calm. Having been advised that the islanders may become troublesome if they are bored and restless, he allowed the fishing boats to set sail. Although somewhat late for the cherry seabream,[80] it was the start of the run of the bonito . . ."[81]

HOKUSAI: I know. That's enough. I get the chills whenever I'm forced to listen to your tales, told in that story-teller fashion.

BAKIN: You know, I'm in love with the spring sea.

HOKUSAI: You must be patient a little longer. Winter is hard on every old person—not just you.

BAKIN: Have you heard that I went blind in my right eye about five years ago?

HOKUSAI (*failing to listen to him*): That's right, since O'Nao's

---

[80] *Sakuradai,* a fish so named because the best season for its catch occurs in spring after the cherry blossoms have appeared.

[81] *Chinsetsu Yumiharizuki* (part II, book 2, ch. 20), in *Iwanami Koten Bungaku Taikei,* vol. XL, p. 290.

young, I must have become young, too. (*Straightening out his shoulders, he tries to act haughty.*)

BAKIN: And my left eye has finally failed me. I'll be totally blind before spring.

HOKUSAI (*completely preoccupied with himself*): It seems like yesterday that I left O'Nao, though it's been fifty years.

BAKIN (*oblivious to* HOKUSAI'*s words*): How's your pissing these days? I'm having a terrible time.

HOKUSAI: Come to think of it, I've got to express my deep gratitude to O'Nao. I'm a better judge of women because she left me. Hiroshige's[82] suppose to be popular now, but his beauties are worthless. He can only draw them superficially. And you can't catch the true character of women by puny, feeble efforts.

BAKIN: How's your stomach, Hokusai? I get gripping pains as soon as I overeat a little rice.

HOKUSAI: . . . When it comes to that, my "Thirty-six Views of Mount Fuji," "Hokusai Sketchbooks," and "Waterfalls throughout the Country"[83] are all magnificent works. Hmm, they certainly are!

BAKIN: I'm about to go crazy when I think of the day I'll be completely blind. As you know, there are many Chinese characters in my novels, and only a handful know as many as I do. If I let one of my pupils take down my words, he's bound to use the simple syllabary.[84] And my passages will lose their force. I get scared when I worry over such things.

HOKUSAI: This is fantastic! I've got a hard-on, after all these years!

BAKIN: Come to think of it, why am I here?

HOKUSAI (*places one hand on his belly*): It's no use. I've lost it.

BAKIN: Yes, I remember now. I had a confidential report from the Kitamachi Magistrate.[85] You've done a wonderful thing. (*Shouting.*) What are you fussing about—at your age!

HOKUSAI: Did you say something?

BAKIN (*taking out a volume of pictures bound in Japanese-style*): Lord

[82] Born 1797, died 1858. *Ukiyo-e* artist.

[83] *Shokoku Takimawari* (1833).

[84] *Hiragana*, one of the two Japanese syllabaries containing its simple characters. This particular form was commonly used in popular fiction.

[85] *Kitamachi bugyō,* one of the two chief magistrates of Edo.

Saemon-no-jō,[86] the Kitamachi Magistrate, looked through the "Complete Colored Book,"[87] which you published recently, and . . .

o'EI (*enters hurriedly, full of excitement*): I'm back. They certainly must take us for fools!

HOKUSAI: What happened to O'Nao?

o'EI: She's being fitted. Will be back soon.

HOKUSAI: Did you find her a kimono?

o'EI: I chose the most expensive one at Iseyoshi's.

BAKIN: What are you so upset about, O'Ei?

o'EI: Even I know that the present government has handed down a stupid edict which bans cosmetics and wearing of attractive, delicate silks and scarlet silk crepes. But try explaining what happened to me, just now! As we were walking down the street, a dirty-minded police detective was stopping all the girls . . . Now listen to this. He says: "You must be wearing silk undergarments or a bodice of scarlet silk crepe." And orders: "Tuck up your hem. Still higher, I can't see . . ." (o'EI *fidgets with the hem of her kimono.*)

BAKIN: And you got the same treatment?

o'EI: No, I was the only exception . . . Though all the rest of the girls had to submit. And that makes me even madder. The detectives these days are too damn playful. I'd like to start an uprising in Edo, like the one led lately by Ōshio Heihachirō[88] in the Kyoto-Osaka area!

BAKIN: There, there. That's exactly what Lord Tōyama is concerned about. There are signs that the young people nowadays—and the old women, too—are collecting swords and guns in a disturbing fashion for an insurrection. And this stems entirely from the improper method of discipline used by the schoolmasters in teaching children. Well, this is how Lord Tōyama views the situation . . .

[86] Another name of Tōyama Kinshirō (?–1855), who had served as a Kitamachi magistrate in the 1840s. He is celebrated in ballads and stories as the folk hero "Tōyama no Kin-san," who bears a magnificent tattoo with cherry blossoms on his arms and shoulders and is admired for his integrity.

[87] *Ehon Saishiki-tsū* (1848), a textbook for painting.

[88] A Confucian scholar (1793–1837). Remembered as a leader of a short-lived insurrection in 1837 that attempted to help the starving populace.

HOKUSAI (*yawning*): . . . Though he was once even punished with a tattoo mark[89] as a young man for his wayward, flamboyant behavior, that Lord Tōyama has turned out to be a worthless wretch.

BAKIN: And at such a critical time, he was quite impressed by your "Complete Colored Book." He regards it as a helpful picture book for children with a very noble purpose and wants to commend you for it. (*Turning the page.*) You say: "It's sole purpose is to teach those things which will be easily learned by children who love pictures." I must bow down to you. It's so carefully worked out. And it proceeds to teach by taking the child virtually by the hand. You begin with the difference between red and pink, and blue and green. And you show how the behavior of water varies. A large river flows majestically, a rapid one flows swiftly, and the lake water lies flat and motionless. And along with landscapes, birds, animals, insects, and fish, you also show the appearance of dress, man's muscular development, the condition of wind and rain, and the phases of the moon. They're all clearly pictured in detail. As Lord Tōyama declares, by enjoying this "Complete Colored Book," the children will unconsciously learn the value of education and how perseverance and self-control are so necessary in the business of living.

HOKUSAI: Such a great purpose never crossed my mind.

BAKIN: I was worried that the career of Hokusai had come to a standstill after you had changed your name to Miuraya Hachiemon. And you could no longer draw. But I'm so happy you could dedicate yourself to this extent to a work meant merely for children.

HOKUSAI: I don't like it. I didn't have the slightest intention of pleasing the government when I drew them.

O'EI: He's right. Dad didn't draw them for the government or the children. Because Dad returned to his childhood innocence, that frank and innocent feeling turned directly into the pictures.

BAKIN: Then, you refuse the commendation, Tetsuzō? That means you'd be mocking the government. And you might be

[89] See footnote 86.

censured in some way. Listen to me, the Tempō Reform [90] may
have run its course, but it's no time to let down your guard.
Wasn't it just recently that the sentimental stories [91] of Tame-
naga Shunsui [92] and Ryūtei Tanehiko [93] were proscribed by an
edict to reform public morals? [94] They were put in chains and
their woodblocks burned. And Tanehiko was even driven to
suicide. Naturally, I don't approve of their sentimental stories.
They only capture the intimate conversations of lovesick play-
boys and geisha in a sensual way and urge wealthy men to
take on as many wives as they please. These writers indeed
have low aspirations. But they hadn't done anything so despicable that they deserve to be treated as common criminals.

HOKUSAI (*again, yawns*): . . .

BAKIN: Don't forget! When we were still young, Utamaro was put
in chains for merely drawing pictures of beauties who happened to be the concubines of Toyotomi Hideyoshi. [95] And
Utamaro was arrested on the absurd charge that he had carica-
tured the Shōgun and his inner court. Remember, Tetsuzō,
these are times when even Danjūrō [96] and Kikugorō [97] can't
perform on the Kabuki stage.

HOKUSAI (*sniffing his runny nose and wiping away his tears*): You
mean Utamaro? I'm glad you reminded me.

BAKIN: You finally seem to get my point. But you needn't cry.

HOKUSAI: These days my tear ducts are weak. In fact, I even get
tearful when I'm able to move my bowels easily. O'Ei, get me
a paper handkerchief. It's not for me. Bakin has mucus in his
eyes.

BAKIN (*finally, looking offended*): Now, Tetsuzō, it's important for
a man to pursue his own particular goal throughout life. For

[90] A series of sweeping political measures attempted between 1840 and 1842
with the intention of producing a radically different moral, social, and economic
climate in Japan. They were instituted by Mizuno Tadakuni (see footnote 113).

[91] *Ninjōbon.*

[92] Tokugawa writer (1790–1843).

[93] Tokugawa writer (1783–1842).

[94] More precisely, the Custom Reform Edict, a part of the Tempō Reform (see
footnote 90) directed toward townspeople's clothing, food, cosmetics, etc.

[95] "Taikō Hideyoshi" (1538–1596) in the text; a noted military dictator and pre-
decessor of Tokugawa Ieyasu (1542–1616), who founded the regime named after
him.

[96] Ichikawa Danjūrō VII, (1791–1859), Kabuki actor.

[97] Onoe Kikugorō III (1784–1849), Kabuki actor.

me, it's the novel and for you—*ukiyo-e*. And, therefore, it's important to achieve a certain status which allows us to continue working freely until the very end. And you'd only be the loser by fighting with the government, especially at a time like this. Aren't you being too casual about politics?

HOKUSAI: You don't make any sense at all.

O'EI: Dad doesn't give a damn about politics. And it's the same with money. In fact, he thinks he can rent this entire house for the price of a single white radish. Moreover, he thinks that the present Shōgun is still Lord Ienari.

BAKIN: Then, explain this to me. (*Turning the pages.*) It says here: "The reason for the modest appearance of this book is to make it cheap and easily available." Isn't the fact that this book is so inexpensive proof he wanted to enlighten society?

O'EI (*laughing*): Oh, I wrote that for him, thinking a cheap book would sell better. As you can see, we are a poor family.

HOKUSAI: Hey, that reminds me. Does money go with the commendation from the government?

BAKIN: Naturally.

HOKUSAI: Then, I'll gladly have them commend me. I want to take O'Nao to Yaozen Restaurant in Sanya[98] and treat her to seabream soup.[99]

BAKIN (*relieved*): I'm glad.

HOKUSAI: Once it's mine, I can do with it as I please. Then I'll start immediately on erotic pictures . . . Since that lively, young O'Nao has come back to me.

BAKIN: . . . It must be the "spirit of rebellion."[100]

HOKUSAI: What does that mean?

BAKIN: Going against the times. I'm through talking.

HOKUSAI (*improvising a tune*): La, di, da, di, da . . .

> In love and longing
> For this futile evening—
> When we meet
> It's all a waste of time.

[98] A region north of the Asakusa area; the principal pleasure quarters of Edo was in its immediate vicinity (see footnote 76).

[99] *Ushio,* regarded as one of the finest soup dishes in traditional Japanese cooking.

[100] *Hankotsu seishin.*

. . . Right, Sashichi? (*Laughs.*)

O'EI: Stay away from erotic pictures, Dad. It'll ruin your reputation.

HOKUSAI: What was that phrase again?

BAKIN: "Spirit of rebellion."

HOKUSAI: Spirit of rebellion! What a splendid phrase!

O'EI: Dad, you're so stubborn!

HOKUSAI: So what! O'Nao's certainly late. I feel so impatient, I'm about to faint.

BAKIN: I didn't want to tell you this, but I recommend you to Lord Tōyama.

HOKUSAI: I can't work up any tears of gratitude. (*Putting his hands together prayerfully in front of the statue of Saint Nichiren,* HOKUSAI *begins his meditation.*) Namu Myōhōrengekyō, Namu Myōhōrengekyō. Please help me draw good erotic pictures. Please make sure Bakin never writes a garish and deceitful work like *Satomi and the Eight "Dogs"* [101] again.

BAKIN (*forcing a smile*): . . . Suit yourself.

O'EI: I'm sorry, Uncle Sashichi. (*Bowing.*) I really understand your generous heart.

BAKIN: O'Ei, I'm so tired now.

O'EI: You and I understand each other. But Dad always sat firmly between us. And I just had to take his side. It's been very trying for me.

HOKUSAI: Well, I must get down to work.

BAKIN: . . . How I envy you. Though I'm so eager to get started, when I try holding my brush like this—between my thumb, forefinger, and the middle finger—I can't write a single character. O'Ei, it's snowing.

O'EI: Eh? (*Looking outside.*) No, it's not!

BAKIN: No—black, powdery snow is blowing wildly before my eyes. And within my heart, I see such black and fluffy snowflakes . . . (*Groping with his hands,* BAKIN *locates the cane and leaves with faltering steps—like a blind man.*)

O'NAO'S VOICE: Oh, be careful!

BAKIN'S VOICE: Thank you, young lady. Judging by your voice,

[101] *Satomi Hakkenden* (abbreviated title for *Nansō Satomi Hakkenden*) (1814–1841), written by Kyokutei Bakin.

you must be very beautiful. But my eyes are blurred as though
there was a mist . . . Please excuse me.

(O'NAO *walks in backwards as though seeing* BAKIN *off.* GOSUKE, *the
errand boy of Iseyoshi, follows.* HOKUSAI *has been anxiously waiting
for* O'NAO.)

HOKUSAI: O'Nao!

(O'NAO *turns around. She is now fully dressed like a girl from the
downtown area of Edo and looks beautiful.*)

O'NAO: I'm back. (*To* GOSUKE.) Thank you. Why don't you drop
by again?

HOKUSAI: Hmmmm . . . (*He is excited.*) I can draw! At this age, I
can finally draw the essence of womanhood! (*Gazing steadily at*
O'NAO.)

O'EI: Work hard, Dad! Don't worry about money because I'll earn
it. (O'EI *drinks sake from a large cup and begins her sideline of
painting miniature dolls.*)

O'NAO: What's the matter? You're embarrassing me, Mr. Hokusai.

HOKUSAI: O'Nao, please become my bride!

O'NAO: Oh, dear!

HOKUSAI: Those eyes, Ah, they're laughing.

(*Taking out a brush,* HOKUSAI *begins to draw.* GOSUKE *is thoroughly
fascinated by* O'NAO.)

The stage darkens.

Scene Two

At dusk, a few weeks later at HOKUSAI's *place.*

(*As usual,* O'EI *is painting miniature dolls.* O'NAO, *in her finery, sits
comfortably nearby.*)

O'EI: Then, you absolutely refuse?

O'NAO: But it feels strange being all naked.

O'EI: Even after Dad's been bowing like that and begging you,
time and time again?

O'NAO: I certainly don't mind that.

O'EI: O'Nao, you keep telling us this house is like paradise, and
you're living in a dream. Who do you think is responsible for
all this?

O'NAO: Of course, it's Mr. Hokusai. Can I help it if he's crazy about me? I didn't ask to stay. Rather, tell me, which restaurant are you taking me this evening?

O'EI: The noodle vendor will be around soon. You might try eating, standing up.

O'NAO: Penny pincher!

O'EI: Then, let Dad draw you in the nude.

O'NAO: No!

O'EI: If you're so stubborn, he'll soon lose his patience, and you'll get a thrashing.

O'NAO (*undaunted*): Mr. Hokusai wouldn't do that. Absolutely not!

O'EI: And why not?

O'NAO: He loves me. And love forgives everything.

O'EI: Even Ikku's humorous stories don't have so ridiculously stupid a line that it sets a person's teeth on edge. Oh, it gives me the shivers.

O'NAO: I'm the one who should get the shivers. Imagine a woman who had never slept with a man in all of her sixty-nine years! You give me the creeps.

O'EI: How dare you! You bitch! I can say in all modesty that men trying to possess me were as many as the grains of sand on the seashore.

O'NAO: That's hard to believe.

O'EI: But I didn't feel like getting married. Besides, how could I ever leave the house and abandon Dad, who knows nothing about the ways of the world?

O'NAO: How you go on. Probably Mr. Hokusai's three marriages ended in divorces because of your unwanted presence.

(*Hokusai returns. Again, according to Iijima Kyoshin's* The Biography of Katsushika Hokusai, *"He wears a thick, hand woven cotton kimono with blue stripes and above it a sleeveless jacket of persimmon color. For a cane, he uses a wooden pole over six feet long. Even in the winter rain, he refuses to wear clogs and goes out in slippers with linen soles."—And this evening, he carries a fish basket home. Squirming inside are two octopuses.*)

O'NAO (*putting on airs*): We are pleased to have you return.

HOKUSAI: Yeah. (*Looking annoyed.*) I tried so hard to place an order. But the guy at the fish shop had the gall to tell me the sea was rough and never brought over the giant octopuses I ordered before.

O'EI: Our bills are long overdue.

HOKUSAI: Then, why don't you settle the account, once and for all?

O'EI: Where's the money? Doesn't all our income go into O'Nao's clothes, and accessories, and meals?

HOKUSAI: That can't be helped. (*Gazing at the octopuses.*) I'll just have to settle for these smaller fellows. Unless I hurry, the pictures forming in my mind will disappear. (*To* O'NAO.) All right, off with your clothes! Be quick about it!

O'NAO (*glancing at* O'EI, *whispers*): He's completely senile. And he's already forgotten though I refused him so firmly before he left the house.

O'EI: It can't be helped. It's for Dad's sake. I'll take mine off.

HOKUSAI (*gravely earnest*): I'm not drawing a ghost. It's an erotic picture. It shows a big and a small octopus clinging to a naked woman and raping her.

O'NAO: Now, that sounds like an interesting picture.

HOKUSAI: Of course, it is. Now listen, it's on a seashore and takes place behind a rock. A woman diver is laying on her back—totally exhausted. (*Selecting the largest of the miniature dolls,* HO-KUSAI *lays it on its back.*) Let's call this the woman diver. And close to her lips a small octopus is . . . (*He busily takes out the small octopus from the fish basket and forces it to cling close to the doll's lips.*) And the big fellow is near the woman's hips while she has her legs outspread—like this. (*Forcing the other octopus to cling to the doll.*) Good. The small octopus is squirming and the woman squirms along with it. The big fellow buries itself completely between her thighs. One of its arms furtively stretches out and jiggles her breast. The woman's pained expression gradually—oh, so gradually—turns into one of ecstasy . . .

O'NAO: Let me try!

HOKUSAI: I knew it! O'Nao was that kind of woman! She was demonic. Every human has a demonic streak. But O'Nao, I was crazy about you because you never slyly concealed that demonic streak in a pretentious, ornamental box.

O'NAO: Who knows? That O'Nao and I may be directly related.

(*In the meantime,* O'NAO *has assumed the same pose as the miniature doll.* HOKUSAI *in a frenzy, forces the octopuses to cling to* O'NAO's *lips and thighs.*)

Oh, it tickles! And they're so slimy . . .

HOKUSAI: O'Nao would never say that! She was more serious. This is bad. It's phoney! I can't draw this. Listen carefully, when a woman is aroused, she clinches all her toes together.

O'NAO: . . . Like this? (*Bending her toes.*)

HOKUSAI: More! Till they're numb. Till the muscles in the calves are taut.

O'NAO: It's hard!

HOKUSAI: Good! That's fine. You see, the octopuses are chatting . . . (*The following lines should be delivered as if* HOKUSAI *has assumed the role of the octopuses—in a tone both farcical and grotesque.*) "We've been finally rewarded for our patient stalking and caught her—today of all days! Oh, what a nice and plump snatch. Well, well, I'll suck and suck and suck away to my heart's content. And then I had better take her to the palace of the Sea King . . ." (*Frenzied, sucking noises.*)

O'NAO (*suppressing her laughter*): This is awful!

HOKUSAI: What are you laughing at, you stupid fool! Now it's your turn to do the talking. (*In the following lines,* HOKUSAI *imitates* O'NAO's *voice.*) "Oh, what a detestable creature!" (*Snickering.*) "Since it's sucking on my little pot, I'm running out of breath." . . . O'Nao, twist your body more. You're supposed to be out of breath! . . .

(*Obeying,* O'NAO *pants heavily.*)

Now, you've got it! (*Still in* O'NAO's *role.*) "Ahh, let me see . . . I'd rather try its suckers." (*Panting.*) "That's the way! . . . Oh, dear! What are you trying to do? . . . Oh, no! That's too much! . . . But do it once again . . . And again!" The big octopus speaks: "Till now . . ." (*Sucking and smacking noises.*) ". . . Till now, people merely treated us as octopuses, but . . ." (*More frenzied sucking and smacking noises.*) ". . . How do you like the feel of these eight arms grabbing you at once! Tell me, tell me!"

O'NAO: It's heavenly! Simply heavenly!

HOKUSAI (*still in the role of the big octopus*): "Oh, my God! Her insides are swelling up, and, ahh, her hot, slimy, passion juice is gushing out! . . ."

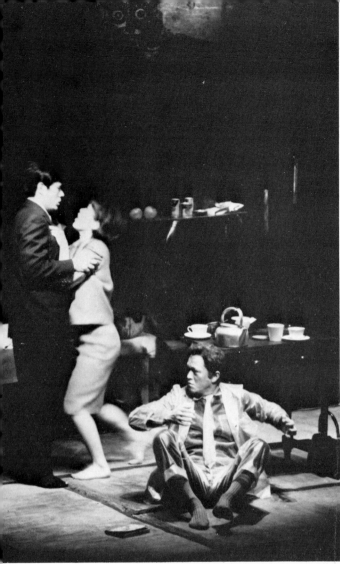

You, Too, Are Guilty,
Scene Three. Left, MAN
(Gō Katō); middle,
WOMAN (Katsue Nitta);
right, DEAD BODY
(Tadashi Fukuro).
From the original pro-
duction in 1965
at Haiyūza.

Courtesy of Shinchōsha, Tokyo

Courtesy of TEATRO Magazine, Tokyo

You, Too, Are Guilty,
Scene Four.
From left to
right, DEAD BODY
(Tadashi Fukuro);
MAN (Gō Katō);
WOMAN (Katsue
Nitta); MAN NEXT
DOOR (Eijirō Tōno).
From the
original production
in 1965 at Haiyūza.

Courtesy of TEATRO Magazine, Tokyo

From *Yoroboshi*, where TOSHINORI makes his stage entrance.
From left to right, TOSHINORI (Kiichi Suwa); SAKURAMA SHINAKO
(Kyōko Kishida); MRS. TAKAYASU (Sachiko Kōtsuki); TAKAYASU
(Yūsuke Minami). From the 1976 revival at National Theater.

Courtesy of Seiichi Yashiro

Hokusai Sketchbooks, Act One, Scene Two. Left,
o'ei (Kazuko Imai); middle, TETSUZŌ—later HOKUSAI (Ken Ogata);
right, SASHICHI—later BAKIN (Hideo Kanze).

Courtesy of Seiichi Yashiro

Hokusai Sketchbooks, Act Two, Scene One. From
left to right, O'EI (Kazuko Imai); HOKUSAI (Ken Ogata); O'HYAKU
(Hiroko Seki); NAKAJIMA ISE (Eitarō Ozawa).

Courtesy of Seiichi Yashiro

Hokusai Sketchbooks, Act Three, Scene Four.
Left, HOKUSAI (Ken Ogata); right, O'EI (Kazuko Imai).

The Boat Is a Sailboat, Act One. Left, SATOMI (Asao Koike); right, TATSUNO HIROSHI (Munenori Oyamada)

Courtesy of TEATRO Magazine, Tokyo

Courtesy of TEATRO Magazine, Tokyo

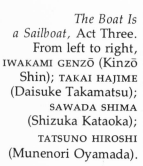

The Boat Is a Sailboat, Act Three. From left to right, IWAKAMI GENZŌ (Kinzō Shin); TAKAI HAJIME (Daisuke Takamatsu); SAWADA SHIMA (Shizuka Kataoka); TATSUNO HIROSHI (Munenori Oyamada).

Courtesy of TEATRO Magazine, Tokyo

The Move, Scene One. From left to right, FATHER
(Nobuo Nakamura); MAN (Taketoshi Naitō); WOMAN (Yūko
Kusunoki); MOTHER (Sachiko Murase).

Courtesy of TEATRO Magazine, Tokyo

The Move, Scene Four. From left to right,
WIFE—Billposter's Wife (Sumie Sasaki); HUSBAND—Billposter
(Dai Kanai); MAN (Taketoshi Naitō); WOMAN (Yūko Kusunoki);
MOTHER (Sachiko Murase).

O'NAO: Will you stop now!

HOKUSAI: No, your body's still dead! Let's give the small octopus its chance: "When the boss finishes up, I'll take over and use these suckers on her. I'll keep sucking until I do a complete job . . ." (*More sucking noises.*)

O'NAO: I see, if that's the case, don't let me stop you. What a sweet and adorable creature you are!

HOKUSAI: Precisely! Now, you've got it. You're coming alive. Your body is graceful. But your face . . . It still needs to be worked on. Look more scornful . . . And yet ecstatic. Be quick about it! (*Frantically,* HOKUSAI *approaches* O'NAO *and personally assuming the role of an octopus, he grabs the hem of* O'NAO's *kimono and disarranges it. He also spreads open the fold of her kimono, exposing her breasts. Again, he begins drawing.*) I don't want to draw a picture of an octopus raping a woman. It's got to be one of a woman amusing herself with an octopus. Can you understand? Eh, O'Ei?

O'EI (*nodding vaguely*): . . .

HOKUSAI: Like in this picture, a woman—I mean a human being—is such a frightening creature. But, in another way, he's so comical. Do you understand? And I want to draw faithfully this frightening yet comical spirit of man. What if the public decides it's a suggestive picture [102] or an erotic picture. I don't give a damn! (*He lays down his brush.*) Just remember this, O'Ei. Katsushika Hokusai's masterpiece won't be the likes of the "Red Fuji" in "Thirty-six Views of Mount Fuji." It'll be the ever-changing face of a demonic woman I'll be drawing from now on. You can count on it because it's me doing the talking. When was it? Years ago, I once saw a suggestive picture by Utamaro. A young girl was being raped by a palanquin bearer in a desolate spot in the mountains. It was so stupid I burst out laughing. The man had such a wild expression on his face, and the girl was so beautiful in a sweet and pathetic sort of way. A contemptible work, solely for vulgar tastes. Utamaro must have been really hard up in those days. Now, if I were drawing the same picture . . . (*He pinions* O'NAO's *arms in back of her.*)

O'NAO: You're hurting me.

[102] *Abuna-e*, a work barely within the law in Tokugawa times.

HOKUSAI: I'd draw the palanquin bearer as an extremely simple fellow. And the girl's face will, naturally, look more or less pathetic . . . On the other hand, the lines of her body would be burning with ecstasy. (*Panting,* HOKUSAI *falls back on his haunches.*) Damn it! I want to be young again!

O'NAO: I'll massage you.

(O'NAO *begins rubbing* HOKUSAI's *shoulders. Hence it turns into a peaceful, innocent scene of an old man and his grandchild. A children's song is heard.* HOKUSAI *begins singing, absent-mindedly. Now totally blind,* BAKIN *gropes his way in. He also sings, leaning on a post.* HOKUSAI, *recognizing* BAKIN, *laughs happily. Though facing entirely in the wrong direction,* BAKIN *responds, laughing, thinking he faces* HOKUSAI.)

BAKIN: Everyone was once a child. And a child doesn't know boredom. That's what I envy in them.

HOKUSAI: Have you gone completely blind?

BAKIN: How can you tell?

HOKUSAI: I'm not over there. I'm here. "I say, Mr. Goblin, come this way. Where I'm clapping . . ." [103] I should be calling to you.

BAKIN: Right! Right! No cheating now, Tetsuzō. I'll catch you.

(*With unsteady gait,* BAKIN *tries to catch* HOKUSAI. *He fails.* HOKUSAI *purposely makes it easier for* BAKIN *to grab him.*)
See, I've got you!

HOKUSAI: Good! Good! You've done a fine job of catching me. (*Pretending to cry.*)

BAKIN: You got caught on purpose. Isn't that true?

HOKUSAI: That's right, Sashichi. I don't want to lie to you.

BAKIN: . . . I see. Thank you. I'm glad I came, after all.

O'EI: How nice of you to come all this way, in spite of your poor eyes . . .

BAKIN: No trouble. The palanquin brought me to the front of your house.

O'EI (*to* O'NAO): Then give the bearers some tea . . .

BAKIN: I've sent them away. I don't expect to ever go home again.

O'EI: That's a strange thing to say.

BAKIN (*quite plainly*): Not at all. I'm tired of living now. So, since

[103] A familiar phrase used in a game similar to blindman's buff.

I was born a samurai, I'm thinking of committing *seppuku*. After I went blind, my mind and spirit are in total darkness. Not a single line or a single word occurs to me. In such a state, I'm not Kyokutei Bakin or Takizawa Bakin: I'm simply a feeble and worthless old man. I've always been proud of my own industry and talent. And I've even had respect for myself. But now I can't. There's nothing to do except end my own life.

HOKUSAI: That's splendid! I could never do it. The very thought of dying is so frightening to me. See? I'm trembling already. But if you intend to commit *seppuku*, Bakin, do it some place where I can't see you.

BAKIN (*angrily*): Then, you're not going to bear witness to my final moments? I was counting on that.

HOKUSAI (*angrily*): Don't impose on me. O'Ei, throw him out and sprinkle salt on the ground.[104] If I look at his face, it'll shorten my life. All right, God of Death, off with you! I still have mountains of work to do.

BAKIN: I won't go!

HOKUSAI: What did you say?

(*The two grab hold of each other but are soon exhausted.*)

BAKIN: I quit! I quit! My arms are numb. I won't have any strength left when I try to commit *seppuku*. O'Ei, rub my arms.

(O'EI *massages* BAKIN's *arms.*)

Oh, that feels good.

HOKUSAI: Don't you see? Everything is possible if you're alive. Oh-oh! I can't move my fingers, either. (*He tries to pick up a brush, but it slips from between his fingers.*) This is terrible! I can't draw anymore.

O'NAO: Aren't you going to cry?

HOKUSAI: There's no room for crying when you're really unhappy. O'Ei, O'Ei, do something! Fix me up right away! Your massage is the best in Japan. Aren't you my one and only daughter? Forget about Sashichi!

O'EI: Dad, just look at Uncle Sashichi. Doesn't he look contented? I'm showing him now that it's better to live a wretched life then to die gallantly. (*Massaging carefully.*) Be patient for a while.

[104] An old custom to ward off evil.

HOKUSAI: Damn it! Now I know. You're in love with Bakin. Isn't that so? That's why you've stayed single until sixty-nine. Well, don't hold yourself back. Hurry and have your affair.

O'EI: Don't try to bring disgrace upon your aged daughter, Dad.

HOKUSAI: I was feeling sorry for you, having spent your entire life looking after me. But now, finally, the truth is out. Ah, Bakin is certainly far more manly than I am. This fellow has lived his whole life, planning it out systematically. When he was still young, he made money by becoming an adopted son of a footwear dealer. Then, after he made enough, he devoted his life exclusively to writing. And when he was a half decent writer, he tormented his jealous wife to death. By forty, he became a full-fledged writer, so he started on *The Crescent Moon: The Adventures of Tametomo.* By fifty, he built a magnificent mansion and hired a pretty young maid, who was actually his mistress. He was writing about karma and "encouragement of virtue and the chastisement of vice" in his moralistic novels, and if the public found out, his popularity would have dropped. By sixty, he was the foremost novelist in Japan. And at seventy, he started writing his world-famous masterpiece—*Satomi and the Eight "Dogs."* See how everything has worked out according to his own plans? He's got a strong will. And I admire him for that. But somehow, he hadn't planned on going blind. It serves him right.

BAKIN (*quietly*): O'Ei, is what Tetsuzō said about you true?

O'EI: I suppose so, Uncle Sashichi. Just as Dad decided that O'Nao was his one true love, you were the only one for me. It's—like father, like daughter.

BAKIN: I didn't realize there was such a wonderful person right before me . . . My entire life was simply going back and forth between my desk and the publishers . . . I admit I had relations with the maid, but that was merely physical. My heart was always dedicated to writing novels.

HOKUSAI: Get out, both of you! We're no longer father and daughter. I've got O'Nao!

O'EI: Dad, are you serious?

HOKUSAI: Damned right! I don't want to see your face again!

(HOKUSAI *draws* O'NAO *close to him. As though waiting for this very moment,* O'NAO *relents.* O'EI *helps* BAKIN *to stand.*)

O'EI: Take hold of my hand, Uncle Sashichi.

BAKIN: Don't bother.

O'EI: At our age, there's no more physical charm or desire. But if I'm with you, you won't have to commit *seppuku*.

(*Led by* O'EI, BAKIN *slowly and falteringly takes two, three steps.*)

HOKUSAI (*bursts out laughing*): What a pair! It's a sight to even outdo Jippensha Ikku.

BAKIN: Are you sure, Tetsuzō? You're letting a big fish get away. O'Ei has unselfishly devoted herself to you. Self-sacrifice hardly describes all she's denied herself for your sake . . .

HOKUSAI: Oh, shut up!

BAKIN: Then, I'll take her with me. And I'll make her into a fine *ukiyo-e* artist—if it's the last thing I do. Ever since she was young, O'Ei's talent was recognized by the *ukiyo-e* artists—by men like Kitagawa Utamaro, Tōshūsai Sharaku,[105] and Ichirissai Hiroshige . . . And you should know best of all. But being so selfish, you've neglected to develop her talent. In fact, you've even plucked it in the bud. All her life you've forced O'Ei to do sketches for your pictures. To be perfectly frank, you've turned her into an imitator, who works behind the scene.

HOKUSAI: What of it? O'Ei was perfectly satisfied with that!

BAKIN: I'm sorry to say that's true. O'Ei loved the great Katsushika Hokusai more than herself.

O'EI: Why go on?

BAKIN: After all I've said to you, Tetsuzō, you won't try to stop her?

O'EI: He won't.

BAKIN: Why not?

O'EI: Dad wants to live alone with O'Nao. That was his lifelong dream. We've lived as father and daughter for sixty-nine years. I *really* understand him. Let's go! Let's go!

(O'EI *and* BAKIN *start leaving.* HOKUSAI *is actually bluffing. Finally he can bear it no longer.*)

HOKUSAI: Hey, O'Ei!

O'EI: What is it, Dad?

HOKUSAI: Nothing. Go away.

O'EI: O'Nao, I'm depending on you.

---

[105] *Ukiyo-e* artist (fl. late eighteenth century).

O'NAO (*she is looking the other way*): . . .

HOKUSAI (*calls again*): Hey, O'Ei!

O'EI: Dad!

HOKUSAI: Shit!

BAKIN: Did I hear you say, "Hey?"[106] (*Sarcastically.*) Then, let's make O'Ei's professional name, Hey.

HOKUSAI: Suit yourself!

(HOKUSAI *retires to the back followed by* O'NAO.)

O'EI: Let me take you home.

BAKIN: Don't bother.

O'EI: But you actually want me to see you home, don't you?

BAKIN: Of course I do.

O'EI: You know, I'm the kind of person who feels compelled to carry out the wishes of others.

BAKIN: And Tetsuzō kept imposing on your good nature.

O'EI: When I was very young, I used to despise Dad's selfishness. Later on, after thinking it over, I still made up my mind to devote my whole life to him. And that was really for my own sake, not his.

BAKIN: For your own sake? Why?

O'EI: I can't explain it too well. To tell you the truth, I have a kind of disgusting sludge within my heart. And I get the irresistible urge to do what others despise. For example, I want to take your hand and say, "This is a shortcut" and then deliberately push you into the river and try to drown you. This sort of cruel feeling reveals my true motive. When Dad was still an unknown and Utamaro was at the height of his popularity, I even dreamed I had secretly told the authorities about Utamaro's erotic pictures and had him jailed. I can leave Dad now because I'm hoping that if I'm not there, he'll become a plaything for O'Nao's youthful body and die of exhaustion.

BAKIN: . . . Is that so?

O'EI: Since I have such a sludge-like heart, I must try even harder to help others. Or else, it would be dangerous—for me.

---

[106] In Japanese, "$\overline{O}$-i!" is equivalent to "Hey!" or "I say!" Here a pun is intended involving O'Ei's professional name, which was Katsushika $\overline{O}$i. Since the sounds of "$\overline{O}$i" are found in the Chinese characters for her name, which mean "to respond" and "to perform," Bakin's sarcastic remark rebukes Hokusai for constantly exploiting the tireless devotion of his own daughter. O'ei was actually Hokusai's third daughter; facts about her life are scant.

BAKIN: There's something I want you to do for me.

O'EI: Just ask me anything.

BAKIN: . . . Kiss me.

O'EI: You're so gentle, Uncle Sashichi. (*Sniffling.*)

(*Groping with his hands,* BAKIN *embraces* O'EI. *By bringing their cheeks close together, they kiss lightly like* HOKUSAI'S *two small birds on a rice grain.* HOKUSAI *comes in from the back. He looks at* BAKIN *and* O'EI *incredulously and rubs his eyes.*)

HOKUSAI (*whispers inadvertently*): What a beautiful scene. Hmm, it certainly is.

(BAKIN *and* O'EI *remain frozen.*)

It'll make a fine picture. I'm glad to be alive because I can see so many things. But this scene won't make my kind of erotic picture. Mine has to be . . . How can I put it . . . Well . . . Something more penetrating and refreshing . . . In other words, it's not like the meeting of lovers after a long absence in some fairy tale[107] . . . And it can't be purely fanciful . . . It has to be down-to-earth, human lovers, who care for each other . . . (*Shouting.*) That's enough! Break it up! Don't be impertinent! Get out of here!

(BAKIN *and* O'EI *leave.*)

Well, O'Nao, let's go out. I hope there's something you'd like to eat.

O'NAO'S VOICE: I'd like some bean paste candy[108] from Funabashiya Store. But it's too far to Fukagawa[109] if we start out now.

(O'NAO *emerges from the back.*)

HOKUSAI: What of it? A palanquin will gladly take us there if I tip generously. But it's just like a young girl to crave sweets instead of supper. (*Laughs.*)

O'NAO: But it's impossible. O'Ei said there was no money this morning.

HOKUSAI: Don't worry about that. Suppose I draw erotic pictures for the first time on a regular basis . . . They should bring

---

[107] "Meeting of Kengyū and Shokujo on Tanabata" in the text; Kengyū (Ox-leader Plowman) and Shokujo (Heavenly Weaver) are husband and wife who are destined to meet only on the seventh day of the seventh moon according to the lunar calendar (on Tanabata), when Kengyū can cross the Milky Way.

[108] *Neriyōkan.*

[109] A leading center of entertainment along with Ryōgoku; east of the Sumida River (see footnote 3).

in—this much—without any trouble . . . (*Traces a figure on his left palm with his finger.*)

O'NAO (*peering at it*): Wow, you mean *that* much? We can live securely from now on, even if we spend lavishly.

HOKUSAI: If I just give him the word, the printer will gladly give me an advance.

O'NAO: I've changed my opinion about you. Frankly, Mr. Hokusai, I thought you were just a lecherous old man, but if you're really serious, I'll work hard. (*Enthusiastically,* O'NAO *unties her sash.*) Now, let's get down to business right away!

HOKUSAI: She's so mercenary. (*Laughing.*) And that makes her adorable. But my fingers . . .

O'NAO (*kissing his fingers*): My magic words will take care of that— abracadabra.

HOKUSAI (*fearfully moving his fingers*): Oh, marvel of marvels! It's well again!

O'NAO (*clinging to* HOKUSAI): Listen, Mr. Hokusai. Draw at least one picture every three days and keep it up for a year. Then I'll marry you!

HOKUSAI: That's wonderful, O'Nao, but it poses a problem. You know, I've had a change of heart. If my present existence becomes more comfortable, I'll want to give up erotic pictures. And I'll want to draw pictures that will purify my feelings as I do them. . . . Like the European ones of sacred figures and their disciples which Shiba Kōkan [110] once showed me at his place . . .

O'NAO: No! No! Except for erotic pictures, the rest of the *ukiyo-e* won't bring in much money, even if they're popular. If you want to purify your feelings, pray to Saint Nichiren. That should do for now.

The stage darkens.

---

[110] Born 1747, died 1818. A versatile individual of the late Takugawa period noted for his literary and artistic accomplishments; he painted pictures that indicated some Western influence.

Scene Three

"The Octopuses and the Woman Diver" [111] *from the erotic picture book, "Big Brother of the Little Pine Tree,"* [112] *is flashed on the screen.*

(O'NAO, *the model for the naked woman diver, sits modestly nearby.*)

VOICE OF PRINTER A: This is so devastating, I'm overwhelmed!

VOICE OF PRINTER B: The idea is daring and fantastic!

VOICE OF PRINTER C: Her rinsed hair flowing down to her waist in that fashion is elegant beyond words!

VOICE OF PRINTER D: Hee, hee, hee. When I'm reborn, I'd like to be Mr. Octopus!

O'NAO: Well, may I address all of the distinguished gentlemen of the printing trade who have assembled here? Please start taking your places in this area.

(*The voices of the printers subside, momentarily.*)

Quiet please. Needless to say, since the Tempō Reform of Lord Mizuno Tadakuni,[113] the works of this sort have been strictly forbidden. Therefore, the name and seal of the artist is attributed to Shishiki Gankō. In fact, they are original drawings by a famous *ukiyo-e* artist whom you all know.

VOICE OF PRINTER A: "Shishiki Gankō"—that's quite sophisticated. That means an exceptionally fine, male "you know what"—dyed in purple!

(*Laughter.*)

VOICE OF PRINTER B: Mr. Hokusai has been completely rejuvenated!

VOICE OF PRINTER C: And why not, embracing that young supple creature every night!

(*Laughter.*)

O'NAO: If you please, gentlemen . . .

(*The printers offer their bids. Their voices gradually grow louder, and the price rapidly soars.* O'NAO *looks charming.*)

Then this picture goes to Mr. Eirakudō. Now, let me show you the next original drawing.

[111] According to the playwright, Yashiro Seiichi, the dialogue in *Scene Two* was taken directly from the written passages appearing in the background of this Hokusai *shunga,* now part of a private collection.

[112] *Kinoe no Komatsu,* a three-volume *shunga* collection by Hokusai. *Kinoe* means older brother, while *komatsu,* a small pine tree, is probably a phallic reference (dates unavailable).

[113] Born 1794, died 1851 (see footnote 90).

(*Preoccupied,* GOSUKE *enters.*)
Who are you? I don't remember you. Are you the errand boy from Izumiya Store?

GOSUKE: . . . No, from Iseyoshi . . .

O'NAO: Oh, the young man from the kimono shop who saw me home once.

GOSUKE: Since you told me to drop over . . . I decided to come . . . I felt sorry for you—living with Mr. Hokusai.

O'NAO: Why?

GOSUKE: . . . Because you're being kept by that old man.

O'NAO: You find me attractive, don't you?

GOSUKE (*nodding*): . . .

O'NAO: Then, will you do anything I ask?

GOSUKE (*nods*): . . .

(*The voices of the printers are demanding: "What's happening?" and "Where's the next picture?"*)

O'NAO: I'm glad I was born beautiful. (*Smiling.*) Each picture is selling so fast . . . As if it had wings. And all the receipts will be mine. Later on, I'll treat you to a meal. (GOSUKE *leaves with an unsteady gait.*)

The stage darkens.

Scene Four

A spring night in 1849 at HOKUSAI's *rented house. The bed is made, and the lantern glows enticingly.*

(O'NAO *is changing into her night clothes. Apparently, overcome by fear,* GOSUKE *is tense and virtually hugs the wall.* O'NAO *secures the doors.*)

O'NAO: Now, we're ready. (*She quickly gets into bed.*) Gosuke, come over here.

GOSUKE: How can you say that? . . . (*Pointing toward the back.*) Isn't Mr. Hokusai in there?

O'NAO: Of course he is. Haven't you any spunk? If you don't want to, that's all right with me.

GOSUKE: Damn it! (*Takes off his clothes roughly and half undressed, crawls into bed and awkwardly embraces* O'NAO.)

O'NAO: No! No! Don't get so excited!

GOSUKE: But I'm so nervous, wondering when Mr. Hokusai will come in from the other room.

O'NAO: Then, let's simply invite him in. Won't that settle you down?

GOSUKE: That's crazy, O'Nao! That's why I tried so hard to get you to go somewhere like a cozy teahouse and really make love . . .

O'NAO: I don't want to. Mr. Hokusai, can you come here a moment?

(*Flustered,* GOSUKE *tries to slip out of the room. This time,* O'NAO *clings tightly to* GOSUKE *and refuses to let go.* HOKUSAI *enters slowly from the back room. He appears completely wasted. He fails to react to the sight of the pair who are squirming in bed—before him.*)

Doesn't Grandpa like to make everything look true to life? So, I thought I'd let you draw the real thing.

(O'NAO *peels off the covers. The two bodies are clinging to each other.*)

HOKUSAI (*shaking his head*): . . .

O'NAO: You aren't drawing?

HOKUSAI (*again, shaking his head*): . . .

O'NAO: I see. Suit yourself. You know, I've fallen for this young man.

HOKUSAI: . . .

O'NAO: Aren't you jealous?

HOKUSAI (*shaking his head*): . . .

O'NAO: You certainly are disappointing.

HOKUSAI: Take your time. (*He places his hand on the sliding door.*)

O'NAO: Hold on for a minute!

HOKUSAI (*turning around*): . . .

O'NAO: Mr. Hokusai, I've been unfaithful to you—with this young man. And you've caught us red-handed! I'm leaving this house because I'm sorry about that!

HOKUSAI: If you don't mind, do just that. (*He retires to the back.*)

O'NAO: Somehow, I feel strange it happened so quickly. But, anyway, everything has turned out exactly as I planned it. That's good! (*Rising.*) Now hurry up and put on your clothes.

(GOSUKE *dresses frantically.*)

GOSUKE: I don't understand. Mr. Hokusai looks quite weak.

O'NAO: After Mr. Bakin died at the end of last year, he suddenly lost his strength. His fingers keep trembling and he gets out of breath, just holding a brush—especially within the last four, five days. It's too pathetic. So, I've decided to get away from this house. I'd hate to take care of his bedpan.

GOSUKE: That's why you drew me into your scheme. To force Mr. Hokusai to cut ties with you!

O'NAO: I suppose that's true. But Grandpa was so big-hearted. And there was no need for such an elaborate farce. Here, help me.

(O'NAO *opens the wall closet. The wicker trunk and other bundles have been readied.*)

GOSUKE: The getaway was planned much earlier.

O'NAO: Help me carry these.

GOSUKE: Are we eloping? (*He carries the wicker trunk on his back and grabs the bundles in both hands.*)

O'NAO: We're going to Uraga. There, we go our separate ways. That's all there is to it. We have to be clear about that.

GOSUKE: And what happens after you get there?

O'NAO: I want to take a Black Ship and go beyond the sea.

GOSUKE: Eh!

O'NAO: There's nothing on the farm even if I go back there. So, I want to travel around freely in strange lands. I've saved plenty of money. Maybe I'll meet a wonderful, young man. Who knows?

GOSUKE: I'm young, too, you know!

O'NAO: I don't care for Japanese men. The Frenchman I once saw near Sakuradamon had blond hair, blue eyes, and such long legs . . . He was just too much. (*Grasping* GOSUKE's *hand,* O'NAO *gently touches her breast.*) Agreed?

GOSUKE: I don't want to walk my legs off.

O'NAO: I won't let you sleep outdoors.

HOKUSAI: Hey, O'Ei!

O'NAO: I can't get over it. He thinks he's calling *me*. Y-e-s! I'll be right over!

(*Placing her forefinger to her lips,* O'NAO *signals* GOSUKE *to be quiet and sneaks out, followed by* GOSUKE. *After the two have left,* HOKU-SAI *staggers in, carrying a few long strips of paper for writing poems.* [114])

[114] "Narrow strips of paper used for writing poems": *Tanzaku.*

HOKUSAI: "Released from the cares of the world, I am a doll re-turning to water and clay."—it's a lousy farewell poem. That Bakin remained quaintly pompous to the very end. When it comes to that, my farewell poem . . . Listen to this. It just occurred to me. (*Sitting properly,* HOKUSAI *reverently holds up a strip of paper in front of him.*) Here it goes: "Even as a ghost I will blithely wander the summer field."[115] (*Proudly sticking out his chest.*) "Summer field"—that's the clincher. I've decided to die in the summer of my hundred and first year. I'm exactly ninety now, so it's a good time to start. I'm through with erotic pictures. I don't have time to play around with young girls forever. Well, now I'll have to review my study of Western drawing. I must use a compass and a ruler . . . What was that called? Oh, yes—"perspective drawing." I'll spend the next five years mastering that . . . And, then, between ninety-five and ninety-nine, I'll put the finishing touches to my study of art. And when I reach a hundred . . . Yes, by then I may finally be able to draw a picture I'm satisfied with. I'm so eager for that moment, my heart is pounding! Oh, that reminds me. O'Ei, bring out that erotic picture. The one with a young widow grabbing the balls of a mendicant priest, I finished the other day. I'm going to tear that up to rouse myself to turn over a new leaf. Hey, O'Ei! What happened? Where's she gone? (*With no other recourse,* HOKUSAI *slowly stands up.*) I'm sure that picture is here. (*He opens the wall closet but finds it empty. He crawls inside. He nonchalantly comes out.*) . . . (*Inclining his head as if puzzled.*) It's empty. Hmm, that's odd. Hey, O'Ei! (*Laughing.*) Are you playing hide-and-seek? All right! (*Pulling out the hand towel hanging from his waist, he blindfolds himself.*) Mr. Goblin is here! Where's O'Ei? (*Becoming absorbed in this game,* HOKUSAI *walks comically around the room. He slips off the edge of the* tatami *floor to the dirt floor. Striking his head hard,* HOKUSAI *is unable to move. In a faint voice.*) Hey, O'Ei!

(O'EI *comes in.*)

O'EI: Dad! (*Embracing him.*)

HOKUSAI: Hey, O'Ei! (*He is limp.*)

O'EI: . . . You're filthy. Your clothes are in tatters. You can't do

[115] "Even as a ghost I will . . . the summer field": Hokusai's farewell poem.

anything unless I'm around. (*Gazing steadily at him.*) See, it serves you right—I came back to tell you that. (*Glancing around the room.*) O'Nao must have run off. Uncle Sashichi left for that other world, Dad. But he provided enough money for me to live out my life and to even pay for our funerals and headstones.

(*Festive music is carried over by the wind. Blankly opening his eyes,* HOKUSAI *raises himself.*)

You know, at my age, I can finally appreciate being able to rely on others.

HOKUSAI: They're getting ready for the festivals. The one at the Torigoe Shrine will be soon. And the other at the Kannon Temple, too. I'm glad I came to Asakusa. I was a brat of a poor dirt farmer in Katsushika[116] where the grass grew tall, and we lived in its shade. That's why for me, it was a lifelong dream to live in one of the busiest parts of Edo. And it must have been the dream of those like my long-dead father to mingle with the beautifully dressed women and attend the Kabuki theaters. Dad-Mom, they say Danjūrō's been pardoned and back in Edo.[117] Saruwaka district is right in front of us. They're doing Namboku's[118] *Ghost Story of Yotsuya.*[119] I'd like to take you there.

O'EI: . . . I've never seen my Mom's face. And now I don't even have a child who'll someday remember me.

HOKUSAI: Who is it? . . . Someone's calling me. (*He glances about slowly. Suddenly, he sees the Nichiren statue.*) Namu Myō-hōrengekyō, Namu Myōhōrengekyō. You've been such help to me, Saint Nichiren. You'll always watch over me as long as I'm faithful. I believed that. So, I've kept my faith no matter what others had said.

[116] Katsushika: the northeastern area of Tokyo contiguous to the present Chiba Prefecture.

[117] "Danjūrō's been pardoned and is back in Edo." Danjūrō VII was banned from performing on the Edo stage in 1842 for his extravagance, which violated Mizuno Tadakuni's Custom Reform Edict (see footnote 90); moreover, he was forced to temporarily go down to the Kyoto-Osaka area. He was pardoned and returned to Edo in 1849.

[118] Tsuruya Namboku IV (1755–1829). He was especially recognized for his brilliant, realistic Kabuki plays, among them *The Ghost Story of Yotsuya.*

[119] *The Ghost Story of Yotsuya: Tōkaidō Yotsuya Kaidan* was first performed in 1825 and is one of the greatest Kabuki plays ever written.

O'EI: He's a sly one. He hasn't even offered a single stick of incense for the last few years.

HOKUSAI: I've tried hard to accomplish what I wanted to do . . . I
must have been forty then. I was completely under your spell,
Saint Nichiren. I forgot all about drawing. I carried a hand
drum—like this—in the middle of winter, on nights when
even the stars seemed frozen. And I went *bong-bong, bong-
bong-bong——bong-bong, bong-bong-bong,*[120] wending my way
throughout all of Edo until daybreak. I added Fusenkyo to my
name and called myself Fusenkyo Hokusai. That was stretch-
ing it a bit. But it was a good name. Fusenkyo: "dyed, yet undyed"; "undyed, yet dyed"; "of this world, yet untainted."
You know, Saint Nichiren, to be perfectly frank, did I sincerely believe in you? I wonder? In fact, after I became a little
famous, I neglected you. Your statue was covered with dust
and unattended for years and years. But I never took you to
the pawnshop, no matter how poor I became. (*Forced laughter.*)
Still, when you weren't beside me, I simply couldn't settle
down—like this. Namu Myōhōrengekyō. (*He inadvertently
touches* O'EI'*s hand, and his hand travels to the elbow and to the
nape. Finally, he realizes there is a woman close by.*) Oh, it's
O'Nao! Thank you for returning her to me.

O'EI: There—you should sleep now.

HOKUSAI: Of course, O'Nao. But Saint Nichiren, I'd rather have
you return O'Ei. I want to take a trip on O'Ei's back. That's
right! Somewhere, nature is sure to be waiting for me. And for
a small woman, O'Ei has amazing strength.

O'EI: Do you still plan to overwork your daughter, after she's
turned seventy?

HOKUSAI: Oh, damn it! I'm becoming like Sashichi! My eyes are
blurry, and the scenery suddenly flies far, far away . . . It's
the law of perspective![121]

O'EI: Are you trying to be clever?

HOKUSAI: This is terrible! It's because I got carried away and
wrote my epitaph too soon. If I left one at all, I should have

[120] *"Bong-bong, bong-bong-bong"*: A familiar pattern of drum beats used by the
Nichiren pilgrims as they strike their hand drums.

[121] Law of perspective: *Enkinpō*, a remark intended to suggest that Hokusai's
dimming vision makes the scenery appear more distant than it actually is, and
that must be the effect of the "law."

drawn it, instead. What a bad blunder! (*Gathering his final strength,* HOKUSAI *uses both of his arms fully to draw a ghost in mid-air. Gradually, he begins to behave like a ghost.*) Boom-boom-boom-boom-boom-boom, boom-boom-boom![122] . . . In the summer field a withered human spirit amuses itself by behaving comically—this way—gently floating and sauntering along . . . This'll sell! I can buy a hairpin for O'Ei. O'Nao, a brush! Bring me a brush! (HOKUSAI *sees* O'EI. *Finally, recognizing her.*) O'Ei, it's you. O'Ei, you've made a terrible blunder, too! Had you married young you'd be surrounded by adorable grandchildren by now and taking life easy.

O'EI (*provides him with a brush and paper*): . . .

HOKUSAI (*grasps the paper and brush but immediately drops them*): . . . Heaven, if thou wouldst grant me ten more years of life . . . No, five will do . . . Heaven, if thou wouldst grant me five more years of life, I would become a true artist. (*Dies.*)

O'EI (*laconically*): Everyone leaves behind a clever remark when he dies.

(O'EI *gently lays down* HOKUSAI *on the* tatami *floor, forms his hands into a prayerful attitude, and closes his eyes. Putting her own hands together reverently,* O'EI *offers a silent prayer.*)

Curtain

[122] "*Boom-boom-boom-boom-boom-boom, boom-boom-boom*": A sound made by a large drum at a Kabuki performance indicating the entry of ghosts, etc.

The Boat Is a Sailboat
A Play in Three Acts and an Epilogue

MASAKAZU YAMAZAKI

Originally published in Japanese as
Fune wa Hobune yo
(Tokyo: Shinchōsha)
Copyright © 1971 Masakazu Yamazaki
All rights reserved

This play was first performed at Kinokuniya Hall (Tokyo) on January 20, 1973. The performance was directed by Toshifumi Sueki.

CHARACTERS
(in order of their appearance)

TATSUNO HIROSHI, thirty-seven or thirty-eight
AMANO YUMI, a girl of eighteen or nineteen
SATOMI, about forty, TATSUNO's section chief at work
THE MOVER and his assistants
SAWADA SHIMA, a woman, of about thirty
THE CLEANER and his assistant
NISHIKI HEIGO, nearly fifty
THE WOMAN'S VOICE, in her twenties
THE MAN, resembling TATSUNO
TAKAI HAJIME, about twenty
IWAKAMI GENZŌ, about seventy
THE SECONDHAND DEALER and his assistants

Act One

As the curtain rises, we see the rooms of a small apartment.

There is an absence of any furniture as if the occupant had just moved out. The apartment shows little sign of wear and tear. The color of the walls and the interior design indicate a bright, contemporary style.

The apartment is a fairly large "One-D-K." [1] *The large room is a ten-mat* [2] *room with a wooden floor and a kitchen area. At stage left is a smaller Japanese-style bedroom with a* tatami [3] *floor. Upstage, toward stage right, at the very rear of the left-hand wall of the large room, shelves, sink, and other facilities are provided for cooking. On the same wall, adjacent to the kitchen area, further down stage, there is a second door, this one leading to the hallway.*

A part of the hallway just wide enough for two or three persons to stand talking can be seen, suggesting that the apartment is probably at the end of the hallway.

The above setting should be thoroughly realistic to its smallest detail.

It is a clear April morning, around ten o'clock.

The brilliant rays of the sun fill each window located centrally on the back wall of the two rooms and also pour down from the direction of stage left onto the tatami *floor of the bedroom. Tree tops and roofs are seen outside of the windows and behind these, the pale spring sky.*

The faint melody of "The Boat Is a Sailboat," an old primary school song, is played on a harpsichord or a guitar. Briefly, after the curtain rises, the stage remains empty.

Upon closer examination, these empty rooms reveal various typical signs of recent habitation. On the wall, the slightly discolored traces of a recently removed picture remain.

A plastic coat hanger is on one of the nails hammered into the post.

---

[1] An apartment consisting of a room provided with kitchen facilities and a smaller room for sleeping.

[2] One mat is about three by six feet; hence, a ten-mat room is approximately one hundred and eighty square feet in area.

[3] Mats covering the floor of Japanese-style rooms.

At the rear of the tatami *room, the sliding panel covering the wall
closet is open and reveals empty beer bottles and cardboard boxes. The
electric cord hanging from the ceiling is gathered with a ribbon, possibly from a candy box, and the long string attached to the light socket
hangs all the way down to the* tatami *floor. The kitchen shelves are
lined conspicuously with empty cans and beer bottles; at the end of
the shelves are tacked several pieces of paper—possibly memos.*

*The former tenant was apparently a bachelor, for there is a large
nude calendar hanging in a prominent place in the kitchen area. It
still shows March. For some reason, two panes of the windows in this
large room are covered with black cloth tacked onto the frames.
In this apartment, which appears much larger because of the absence
of furniture, just the telephone on its stand creates an eerie impression.*

*(The music of the harpsichord gradually becomes louder, and as it
swiftly comes to an end, a middle-aged man with a large travel bag
appears in the hallway.)*

TATSUNO: I see. So this is my apartment.

(He is TATSUNO HIROSHI. *Although actually dressed quite properly,
there is a rather aimless, nonchalant air about him. He seems to have
the habit of making a slightly comical expression below his dry and
loose hair. A young girl of eighteen or nineteen, wearing a sweater
and a pair of sandals, and a man about forty dressed meticulously in a
business suit appear behind* TATSUNO. AMANO YUMI, *the girl, is the
eldest daughter of the apartment manager; the man,* SATOMI, *the section chief, is a friend of* TATSUNO *at work.)*

YUMI *(leading the way, unlocks the door and enters the apartment)*:
I'm sorry. The room hasn't been cleaned up too well. We had
such short notice . . . I'll help you later.

TATSUNO: Oh, don't worry about it. I can take care of it myself.
(As he enters the room and looks around.) Well, I'd say it looks
just fine. Besides, the apartment is much better than I expected. This is the kitchen area . . . And that's the *tatami*
room?

YUMI: And here's the bathroom and the toilet.

TATSUNO *(peeks through the door* YUMI *opens)*: This is great! Imagine finding an apartment for rent so fast. Especially in Tokyo,
these days. I was really lucky. Right, Satomi?

SATOMI: Yeah, I suppose so. *(Looking unimpressed,* SATOMI *cuts
across the room and peers out of the window.)*

YUMI (*after giving the keys to* TATSUNO, *opens a window*): You certainly were. The former tenant left suddenly just five days ago. And you came by before our rental agent could put out a notice . . . You're quite different aren't you? . . . Let me see. Was it "Mr. Tatsuno"?

TATSUNO: Yes, I'm Tatsuno Hiroshi. Oh? Am I so different?

YUMI: After all, you decided on renting the apartment without even taking a look. Father was surprised.

TATSUNO: I'm used to apartment hunting. I can usually get the general picture by talking to the rental agent. Also, I was being transferred by my company, and that kept me busy. So far, I haven't had any bad experiences renting. This place will probably do.

YUMI: Are you transferred often?

TATSUNO: I guess so. I've been to Kyūshū [4] and to San'in. [5] And I must have moved twice in Hokkaidō. [6]

YUMI: Will you move out of here soon?

TATSUNO: Well, I'm not sure. How about it, Satomi? You're my section chief.

SATOMI (*while still facing the window*): It's up to you, Tatsuno. It's all up to you.

TATSUNO (*emitting a low, forced laugh as he stands in front of the calendar*): That reminds me. Did you say the former tenant was a bachelor, too?

YUMI: Yes—a Mr. Murai. He stayed here about a year, but he also had to move a lot.

TATSUNO: What kind of a person was he? Young?

YUMI: Well, I guess he was about the same age as you, Mr. Tatsuno. Lean and tall. A terrible sleepyhead and always woke up past noon.

TATSUNO: What a lucky guy. I wonder what he did for a living?

YUMI: I heard he handled stocks or was in sales . . . I don't know that much about him.

TATSUNO: You weren't that interested in him?

YUMI: But there was such an age difference between Mr. Murai and me . . . Oh, Mr. Tatsuno, you're terrible!

[4] The southern most among the main islands of Japan.
[5] The southwest prefectures on the main island of Honshū bordering on the Japan Sea.
[6] The northern most among the main Japanese islands.

TATSUNO: Ha, ha, ha. You should be the one to talk. Let's see. You're Yumi, aren't you? I'm glad to know you. (*He bows in a half-joking manner to* YUMI, *who blushes with embarrassment.*)

YUMI: I'm Amano Yumi. I'm likewise pleased to meet you. As a matter of fact, this time, we'd already decided on refusing single people, but I said I'd make an exception in your case. You've a fine job. And aren't you a section chief at work?

TATSUNO: By the way, did you have trouble with Mr. Murai?

YUMI: Not especially. I'm a bit worried, though . . .

TATSUNO: Worried?

YUMI: Yes. Mr. Murai told us quite suddenly that he was leaving and disappeared without giving us his forwarding address.

TATSUNO: Disappeared? Is he missing?

YUMI: Well . . . He paid up all his bills . . . We still have problems, though. We need to forward his letters. And it's embarrassing to say we don't know his new address whenever anyone asks about him.

SATOMI (*suddenly he begins listening attentively to* YUMI's *words; then he slowly approaches the phone and picks up the receiver*): This phone still works?

YUMI: Yes, Mr. Murai had it installed. We took it over when he left. Didn't the rental agent tell you?

TATSUNO: Yes. So I decided to take it over myself . . . Since it's so convenient. That's strange, not telling the manager his forwarding address . . . (*He looks at* SATOMI.)

SATOMI: And you didn't bother to ask him, Yumi?

YUMI: He suddenly packed his things into a Rent-A-Car early in the morning and left with a friend. He said he'd drop by soon. We waited, but that was the last time we saw him.

SATOMI: A Rent-A-Car? (*Perhaps naturally or as a result of his position as the section chief,* SATOMI's *voice sounds unusually grave.*)

YUMI (*suddenly appears worried and lowers her voice*): Ah . . . You don't think Mr. Murai's done something wrong?

TATSUNO: Of course not . . .

SATOMI (*interrupts* TATSUNO, *who starts laughing*): Did you have something particular in mind, Yumi?

YUMI (*flustered and shaking her head*): No, not exactly . . . But I'm kind of scared.

(*For an instant,* TATSUNO *and* SATOMI *exchange glances. Then, with cheerful voices,* THE MOVER *and his assistants appear in the hallway, carrying a heavy load.*)

THE MOVER: Ah . . . Mr. Tatsuno? This was all your baggage? Where shall we put them?

(*They carry in a bedding bag, a small footlocker, and a very old, sturdy rocking chair.*)

TATSUNO: Oh, anywhere. Put them over there. There's still cleaning to be done.

THE MOVER: Yes, sir. But it was such an easy job. You didn't need a mover for this.

TATSUNO: Now, don't say that. And please remember me. I may need your services sooner than you think.

THE MOVER: Oh? Do you like moving?

(*Next to* SATOMI, TATSUNO *forces a smile.*)

SATOMI: He rather seems to enjoy it. That's the trouble.

THE MOVER: Then why not borrow a Rent-A-Car, and do it yourself? They say it's the latest thing. Besides, if you're in a jam, you can make a getaway at night. You can forget the monthly installments and the rest . . .

(TATSUNO's *forced smile intensifies; he tips* THE MOVER, *who has finished work.*)

Thank you very much. Goodby. Please call us again.

(*He leaves in good spirits with his assistants.*)

TATSUNO: I'm glad that's over with. What a terrible fellow.

YUMI (*looking anxious, addresses* TATSUNO, *who sits in the rocking chair*): Ah . . . Is this really all the baggage you have?

TATSUNO: Yes, that's it.

YUMI: Didn't you have a tea cabinet or a desk? You mean, you got along without such things at the other place?

TATSUNO: I gave them to my neighbors or sold them before I left. I'll eventually find something cheap around here.

YUMI: I'm surprised! Do you always do that when you move?

TATSUNO: Sure. Since I was a child, I've moved around dozens of times, and it's become a habit with me. As soon as I settle down in one place, I start thinking about the next move. After a long while I found out this was the easiest method to follow.

YUMI: And you aren't lonely? Without your own furniture and things?

TATSUNO (*slowly shaking his head*): When you take good care of something, you miss it when you lose it. I was still small when I lost some furniture for the first time. The whole town was burned out in an air raid, and only this chair survived out of our whole house. Since then I've bought furniture, but every-time I moved something would always turn up missing. And that would make me feel miserable. Finally, I began to think it was best not to have things of my own. That way I'd never lose anything again.

YUMI: Is this chair really old?

TATSUNO: Yes. It was Grandfather's. He was a sailor and came home just four or five times a year. He felt really at home only after he sat in this chair. I can't quite understand that feeling today.

(Gazing at TATSUNO, YUMI remains silent for a while.)

YUMI: All the same, Mr. Tatsuno, there's something different about you.

TATSUNO: You think so? . . . Then, I'm a bit of a chatterbox. (Suddenly realizing her concern, he starts laughing.) Don't worry. I've this ferocious section chief at work, and when I move, I promise to give you my forwarding address.

YUMI: Yes, please do. If you disappear, it'll certainly make it dif-ficult for us. Well, is there anything else?

TATSUNO (rising): No, thanks. If there's something I need to ask, I'll drop in.

YUMI: Yes, if Father's not downstairs, I'm sure to be there. (She hesitates for a moment.) But you know . . . It's about Mr. Murai. Please don't tell anyone I said anything. If the apart-ment gets a bad name, Father will be furious with me.

TATSUNO: I understand.

YUMI: Thank you, Goodby. (She trots down the hallway.)

SATOMI (glancing around the room): I wonder what it's all about?

TATSUNO: Me too. (While agreeing with SATOMI, he does not seem especially concerned and casually begins to check around the dresser in the kitchen area.) Hmm. There's some handy informa-tion written here. "Takara Market—closed Monday, Taishōken Chinese Restaurant and Meigetsu Noodle Shop—closed Tues-day." And . . . ha, ha, ha, ha. The former tenant must have loved public baths—"Kumano Bathhouse—closed Thursday."

That's great! I love it, too. I go sometimes, even when I have my own bath. Let me see: "Collection of noncombustible garbage—sixth, sixteenth, and twenty-sixth of each month. Makita Cleaners—collection Monday, delivery Saturday." He was a very meticulous fellow.

SATOMI (*meanwhile, goes out into the hallway, tears off the name card on the door, and reads*): Hey, I found his name card. It says Murai . . . Toyojirō. But no mention of his position or place of employment.

TATSUNO: Toyojirō? . . . It's rather old fashioned.

SATOMI: All the same, his behavior doesn't seem to fit the name.

TATSUNO: He can't be such a bad sort, though. At least, he's not the type to do something bad and then vanishes. . . . Hey, see what I found! (*From the shelf, he takes an unopened can with a white memo paper pasted on it.*) "High quality canned salmon. Bought on special but the content is guaranteed safe. Please help yourself. April 10. From the previous tenant." Ha, ha. What a delightful fellow!

SATOMO (*with both hands, he catches the can thrown by* TATSUNO *and reads the label intently*): Hmm. His handwriting isn't particularly good, but not that unpleasant either.

TATSUNO: So it's handwriting analysis this time? Forget about it! Rather, help me clean up this place a bit before lunch. Hey, give me a hand!

SATOMI: I wonder if we should? Suppose this character is in trouble. We might destroy some important evidence by cleaning up this apartment.

TATSUNO: That's silly. Do you really believe that, Satomi? . . . Well, here I go.

(*As soon as he takes off his jacket,* TATSUNO *promptly goes to work. He pulls out a cardboard box from the closet and skillfully puts away the empty cans and beer bottles. He unties the ribbon gathering the electric cord and throws it into the box along with the newspapers; in no time at all, he stores his own bedding bag and footlocker in the closet. Next, he takes out a nail puller from his pocket and quickly removes the thumb tacks and nails in the apartment, throwing them into the box. He pauses for a moment in front of the two pieces of black cloth covering the window panes.*)

What's this all about?

(*For an instant, he tilts his head to one side, looking puzzled.*)

Well, why not!

(*He removes the pieces of cloth along with the thumb tacks and thrusts them down to the bottom of the box. Finally, carried away by his own enthusiasm,* TATSUNO *tears off the nude calendar. He discovers a drawing of a nude winking and sticking out her tongue. He bursts out laughing.*)

Hey, I found it! I found it, Satomi! Here's the reason for his disappearance. How about that? He's quite an artist.

(*While silently seated in a chair,* SATOMI *gazes blankly at the nude drawing.*)

Well, see what's on the back of the calendar. Hasn't he got a good sense of humor?

SATOMI; I see. So that's how it is.

TATSUNO: What about it?

SATOMI: Well, it suddenly occurred to me that bachelors go home and carry on this way. Imagine a fully grown man drawing such pictures at night, all alone. I think it's rather weird.

TATSUNO (*in amazement*): What a nasty thing to say! (*He takes out a so-called chemically treated dust cloth from another pocket and skillfully wipes—here and there—around the room.*)

SATOMI: What's that for?

TATSUNO: Don't you know? It's what they call "No Water Dust Cloth." You must have seen it on TV.

SATOMI (*for a while, he gazes silently but finally draws a deep, deliberate sigh*): You're certainly good at it. You're so neat. How long has it been since you've started living like this?

TATSUNO: Never mind. Take these and wipe the windows. Isn't that what you came here for? (*He pulls a small can and a rag out of his pocket and throws them to* SATOMI.)

SATOMI: You've got more? What's this?

TATSUNO: Glass cleaner. Push the button on top, Satomi.

(*When* SATOMI *does, the liquid glass cleaner spurts out as a mist. After slowly spraying it two, three times in the air, he abruptly throws down the can on the floor and rises.*)

SATOMI: You know, Tatsuno, I just don't like this apartment. I get a funny feeling that there are ghosts and evil spirits wandering around here!

TATSUNO (*stunned by* SATOMI's *sudden outburst*): What did you say? Ghosts?

SATOMI: That's right. It's written with those complicated Chinese characters. I can't do it myself. Looking at this room, that word I'd forgotten for years, suddenly came back to me. The air in this room is bad for you. And I just don't like this Murai character. He left something evil behind. Now, Tatsuno, why don't you simply forget about renting this apartment?

TATSUNO: You must be joking, Satomi.

SATOMI: No, I'm serious. I really mean it.

TATSUNO: And what's wrong with this apartment?

SATOMI: Oh, everything . . . Rather, I just don't like your style of living.

(TATSUNO *throws aside the rag as he leans against the edge of the dresser and faces* SATOMI. *Walking around the room,* SATOMI *continues.*)

I admit this apartment is pretty attractive. And you'll probably be satisfied living this way. But to tell you the truth, the very idea seems close-fisted. Naturally, it's fine when you're still young. And if you're a writer or an artist, you might do it for the rest of your life. But for a mature officer worker, it looks a bit shabby to be living this way—year after year.

TATSUNO: So that's it. You're back on last night's sermon.

SATOMI: No. I might have been a bit disagreeable then because I was drunk. And when I'm drinking I'm actually a little jealous of the way you live. But now I'm quite sober. And though I may put it rather bluntly, when I see it in the morning in broad daylight, this is a miserable way to live.

TATSUNO: That's okay. Say all you want to . . . How about a drink? (*He gropes around the bottom of the travel bag and takes out a silver flask and a cup; after pouring one for himself, he passes them on to* SATOMI.)

SATOMI: You're always prepared, aren't you?

TATSUNO: Maybe it's because I'm a bachelor.

SATOMI (*forcing a smile, sits down, and takes a drink*): It's been ten years since we lived in New York together. In those days, we took turns washing the dishes and cleaning the apartment. You were pretty clumsy . . . Always breaking dishes and cutting your fingers.

TATSUNO: That was fun.

SATOMI: Yeah. That was great. But your present performance . . . When I see you ten years later, still cleaning . . . How can I put it? It's now strangely professional. That bothers me. You're like a professional widower.

TATSUNO: Ha, ha, ha. What a malicious fellow!

SATOMI: And you've become used to it. What's more, in a disgusting sort of way. A man shouldn't get so used to taking care of his various personal things.

TATSUNO: What can I say? I don't do this for the love of it.

SATOMI (*drains the cup of whiskey in a single swallow*): I know I've asked you time and time again, but why don't you get married?

TATSUNO: Don't get me wrong. I haven't especially decided against marriage. After all, I'm no homo. (*He casually gets up, goes to the window, and picks up a small paper box on the window sill. When he shakes it, there is a light, hollow rattle.*) I wonder what it is?

SATOMI: Hey, Tatsuno, listen to me seriously!

TATSUNO: I'm listening. Say, what are these? They look like pieces of chopsticks. (*Picking them up, he shows* SATOMI.)

SATOMI: Let me see. Wooden pegs? Or, plugs for something?

TATSUNO: Plugs? For what?

(*While* TATSUNO *fingers the small wooden pieces in the box, he sits down on the window ledge and whistles softly. It is a refrain from "The Boat Is a Sailboat."* SATOMI *listens patiently but finally speaks.*)

SATOMI: Now that you've returned to Tokyo, Tatsuno, I want to clear up something, once and for all . . . You haven't forgotten, have you? Why did you break off with that girl in such a cruel fashion?

TATSUNO (*looks up in surprise, but after a momentary silence, he blurts out*): Is that still bothering you?

SATOMI (*rather abruptly*): I'm not holding a grudge. And I'm not bringing it up again because I promoted the match. This time I want to find out what kind of a man you really are . . . I thought it was a perfect match. You were so enthusiastic. You even went with her for nearly a year. But then you suddenly broke it off with a single phone call and literally ran off to the

Kyūshū branch office on a new assignment. Why? It's been two years since then. Isn't it about time you gave me an explanation?

TATSUNO: I'm sorry, Satomi. That was certainly my fault.

SATOMI: I'm not asking for an apology. I really want to find out. That wasn't the first time, either. You meet a girl, date her a while, and when things are about to come to a head, you always break it off. Of course, that was the first time you broke off a relationship in such a brutal way.

TATSUNO: That girl . . . What's she doing now?

SATOMI: She's missing. Well, I guess you might call it that. She quit her old job. I was told she left her mother's place and went to live with a distant relative in the country. I've written her many times, but she hasn't answered at all. I don't know whether it's true or not, but I've also heard a more unpleasant rumor.

TATSUNO: Missing? I see. (*Suddenly, he sighs dejectedly. Then the telephone rings.* TATSUNO *starts to answer, but it stops.*) What's that about?

SATOMI: Hmm. That's strange. Well, it might be the manager's daughter, downstairs.

(*Again, the phone begins to ring.* TATSUNO *slowly picks up the receiver.*)

TATSUNO: Yes, hello . . .

(*After a few seconds, the voice of a woman desperately trying to suppress her emotion flows from the receiver. She is later identified as* SAWADA SHIMA. *While* SATOMI *is unable to hear, the audience can listen in on the conversation through the loudspeaker.*)

SHIMA: It's you . . . You were there, after all . . . Just as I expected . . .

TATSUNO: I beg your pardon?

SHIMA: I . . . I was so stupid. The other day, I said such cruel things and acted so childishly before I left . . . Since then, I went and stood below your apartment many times. But I just couldn't go in. As long as you were going to scold me, I thought it should be done over the phone. And then I wanted to see your cheerful face. I was terribly stupid . . .

TATSUNO (*though dumbfounded, he quickly recovers his composure*): Hello, would you mind telling me who you're trying to call?

I'm not Mr. Murai. I'm Tatsuno. Just moved in today . . .

(*A momentary pause. Then a scream.*)

SHIMA: Ahh!

TATSUNO: I'm sorry. I'm so very sorry. I didn't mean to let you talk on, but you caught me by surprise. Hello, hello, can you hear me? (*An abrupt sound of a disconnected receiver.* TATSUNO *replaces his receiver and sighs.*)

SATOMI: What happened? Who was it?

TATSUNO: Hmm. I think one of those ghosts or evil spirits you talked about has finally appeared.

SATOMI: Is it Murai?

TATSUNO: No. A woman!

TATSUNO: She must have had some kind of relationship with Murai. Sounded rather desperate . . . Well, what a surprise! (*Takes a drink.*)

SATOMI (*assuming a milder attitude*): Ha, ha, ha, ha. You've certainly moved into a strange place. How about it? Why don't you quit this kind of apartment living and decide, once and for all, to settle down. There's a place next to mine where you can stay for a while.

TATSUNO: Let me think it over. Still, I wonder what kind of a character Murai is?

SATOMI: He's either a playboy or a matrimonial swindler.

TATSUNO: In any case, he obviously disappeared on purpose. (*He suddenly rummages around in the cardboard box as if reminded and takes out a thin booklet and a few postcards.*) Now that you mention it, I found these. Take a look.

SATOMI: "U.F.O. Study Club: Announcement of Regular Meeting" . . . "Esperanto Study Club: Announcement of Spring Program" . . . He's definitely a strange character.

TATSUNO (*leafing through the booklet*): It's the "Membership List of the Keisei Senior High School Alumni Association." . . . Murai . . . "Murai" . . . Here's Murai Toyojirō. I see, he's from Class of 1950. 1950? . . .

SATOMI: What about 1950?

TATSUNO: Oh, nothing. Only, we'd be the same age if he went straight through school.

(*Brief silence. The phone rings.*)

Hello, this is Tatsuno.

(*The faltering voice of the earlier woman caller comes over the loud-speaker.*)

SHIMA: Ah . . . Ah . . . A while ago, I made such a rude phone call . . . I'm so embarrassed . . . I want to apologize.

TATSUNO: On the contrary, I owe *you* an apology . . . Please allow me.

SHIMA: Ah . . . then, I suppose . . . Murai has moved out completely from that apartment? Ah . . . by the way . . . do you happen to know his new address?

TATSUNO: I'm sorry. Actually, I just moved in. I haven't met Mr. Murai. Why don't you ask his friends or someone where he works?

SHIMA (*for a moment, her voice becomes firm*): He has no friends.

TATSUNO: Oh?

SHIMA: He quit his job, and he hasn't attended his club meetings for quite a while.

TATSUNO: I see. I have a few of the announcements right here . . . Some are rather recent.

(*A short pause.*)

SHIMA (*suddenly in a cheerful tone*): Then, there's mail for him?

TATSUNO: Yes, but . . .

SHIMA: Perhaps he'll come after it.

TATSUNO: Well, maybe . . . And there may be more coming.

SHIMA: Please. If he drops by, could you ask him for his new address and tell me?

TATSUNO: Well . . .

SHIMA: I know it's an imposition, and I'm terribly embarrassed about it. But I'm so worried about him. Maybe he's . . . Maybe he's . . . Please help me. Think of it as a way of doing him a favor and please give me his new address. I'll give you a call in about a week.

TATSUNO: Don't hang up yet. You said in a week, but . . .

SHIMA: Please help me. I . . . I'll never forget it for the rest of my life.

(*Finally, the voice seems muffled by sobbing, and the caller suddenly breaks off. For a while, after he replaces the receiver,* TATSUNO *is in a daze.*)

SATOMI (*slowly rising from his chair*): I don't know what it's all about, but it must be a complicated affair.

TATSUNO: I don't think so . . . Why should it be complicated?

SATOMI: That's fine, but . . . In any case, you should get out of this queer place as soon as possible. Aren't you convinced, now that you've got some idea about this guy Murai? . . . Well, forget it. I'm feeling kind of low today, so I'm going. One of these days, I'll let you tell me all about that earlier matter. (*He walks toward the door and sits on the door sill to put on his shoes.*)

TATSUNO: Hey! Satomi!

SATOMI: What is it?

TATSUNO: . . . I'll say this much. I didn't get tired of that girl.

(SATOMI *stops tying his shoes.*)

If I had, I think I could at least have made a clean break with her. So that wasn't it. I got this terribly strange feeling at the last moment. I don't know how to put it, but it's always the same. I start asking myself, must my marriage partner be this woman and no other? I don't especially dislike her. But out of the tens of thousands of women to choose from, does it have to be this one standing before me?

SATOMI: Don't talk childishly. Who in the world ever thinks that seriously before picking out a woman for his wife?

TATSUNO: You don't understand. It's the very opposite. I don't know very much about the qualities of an ideal woman. And if a woman marries a guy like me, *she* should be the one to be pitied. And when I think about it, I'm more than ever . . .

(*Standing in front of the door,* SATOMI *faces* TATSUNO.)

SATOMI (*in a rather low voice*): You know, Tatsuno, there's something I'm been wanting to tell you for a long time. There's a dark, gaping hole somewhere inside your chest. You may not realize it yourself. And I don't exactly know what kind of a hole it is, either. But beneath that seemingly happy exterior, there's an impossible hole with a cold, nasty wind, always blowing through.

TATSUNO: You're telling me I'm cold-blooded?

SATOMI: Not at all. You're a kind person. In fact, kind to everybody. You're just like this apartment. You're accommodating. And raise no problems. In other words, you basically lack any human warmth.

TATSUNO: . . . I see. Do I seem that way to you?

SATOMI: Look here, I'm not trying to be a matchmaker for the fun of it. But who knows? You might get over your sickness if you had a family and took on responsibilities like everyone else. No, you must get over it. Otherwise, your position in the company will be rather precarious. You know what I mean? That's why up to now you haven't become a section chief at the home office, and you've had to stick around in our branch offices in the outlying areas.

(*Silence. Outside, the wind is apparently beginning to blow. With his back toward* SATOMI, TATSUNO *stands before the rattling windows.*)

TATSUNO: It's the wind. They say the wind gets strong around here in the spring.

SATOMI: Listen, Tatsuno. I don't want to send you out in the sticks anymore. Maybe it's none of my business but think over carefully what I've told you. Okay?

TATSUNO: . . . Yeah. Thanks.

SATOMO: Ha, ha. Let's face it, this apartment is a bit run-down, even though it looks pretty sturdy. You'll get depressed if you listen to those rattling windows by yourself all day. Well, I'm going. Goodby.

TATSUNO: Goodby. I'll see you at work.

(*After* SATOMI *leaves,* TATSUNO *lies on his back on the* tatami *floor, resting his head on his arms. He whistles the melody from "The Boat Is a Sailboat." The wind rattles the windows still more, forcing him to get up and try to stop the noise, but as soon as he releases his hands, the windows rattle on persistently. He gives up and lies down once more but suddenly springs up again, shortly. He finds the small box he had found earlier, takes out the wooden pieces, and inserts them in the several cracks around the window frames. The windows become quiet, and* TATSUNO *chuckles softly to himself.*)

So, that was the set up.

(*This time, he lounges in the rocking chair and cheerfully whistles. Suddenly, brilliant lights shine through the windows in the kitchen area and strike the lower portion of the wall in the large room. When he stands up and peers out of the window, the lights strike his face, making him grimace.*)

I see . . . The cars turn that corner . . .

(*He takes two, three steps toward the chair but reminded, searches in the cardboard box. He pulls out the pieces of black cloth he had taken down before and covers the original spots with thumb tacks.*)

I get it. So, that's the way it works.

(*Suddenly, after vigorously rubbing his hands together,* TATSUNO *picks out the nails from the box and drives all of them into their original holes. He replaces the clothes hangers and hangs up his coat; he puts the nude calendar back in its original spot and tears off March— bringing it up to date. Finally, he takes out a small framed art reproduction from his bedding bag and carefully places it over the discolored area left by the previous picture.*)

Ha, ha, ha, ha. Well, Mr. Murai, this takes care of everything, doesn't it?

(*While* TATSUNO *is seated in a chair and begins contently to sip a cup of whiskey, a man carrying a suit on a clothes hanger appears in the hallway and knocks on the door.*)

THE CLEANER: Hello! It's the cleaners. Hello!

(TATSUNO *rises and opens the door.*)

Ah, I'm from the Makita Cleaners. I have, ah, a slight favor to ask you.

TATSUNO: I see. What is it?

THE CLEANER: It's very difficult for me. But this suit belongs to Mr. Murai, the former tenant. He must have moved away quite suddenly because he didn't pick it up . . . And we don't know what to do . . .

TATSUNO: I understand. In that case, he should be back for it eventually.

THE CLEANER: No. I mean . . . Due to circumstances, we're closing up and moving out to the country. We told Mr. Murai and urged him to receive the suit as quickly as possible. But for the last three weeks, whenever we came, he was always out. And finally he was simply gone.

TATSUNO: I see. And what do you expect me to do?

THE CLEANER: Yes, Sir . . . What we'd like to ask you is this . . . . It's an imposition, I know, but we'd like you to hold on to the suit for a while . . . (*Between pauses in his speech,* THE CLEANER *makes a hissing sound with his teeth.*)

TATSUNO: That's impossible! I'm not sure whether Mr. Murai will come back for it. Besides, I'm alone and usually out. Shouldn't you ask the housewife next door or the manager's daughter?

THE CLEANER: Well . . . There's no socializing in an apartment building like this. And we've hardly seen the faces of the tenants in the other apartments . . . And . . . Unfortunately, the manager and I aren't on speaking terms.

TATSUNO (*bursts out laughing*): You don't get along?
THE CLEANER: No, sir. We really can't ask him for favors . . .
    Moreover, Mr. Murai was never thought of too highly by him,
    either.
TATSUNO: But, see here. If that's the case, I've had far less to do
    with Mr. Murai.
THE CLEANER: Yes, we know that. But now, we don't have anyone
    else to ask. If we take the suit to the police, the chances are
    less likely of it reaching Mr. Murai . . . Please . . . Please do
    it as a favor to us . . .
TATSUNO: I don't know what to say.
(*At that moment, another man waits in the hallway. Although power-
fully built, there is something shabby about this fiftyish man.* TATSUNO
notices him.)
    Ah, are you looking for someone?
(*The man, later identified as* NISHIKI HEIGO, *bows in a very stiff, for-
mal manner.*)
NISHIKI: I wanted to ask you something. I can come back later if
    you're busy.
TATSUNO: No, not especially . . . (*To* THE CLEANER.) Mr. Cleaner,
    I just don't know.
THE CLEANER: We won't cause you any trouble. We won't charge
    you for it or ask for a receipt. You'd be a great help if you'd
    just keep it in the corner of your closet. (*He practically forces*
    TATSUNO *to take the suit.*)
TATSUNO: This is impossible!
THE CLEANER: Please understand that we're doing this as a service
    to our customer, and we'd like your cooperation . . .
TATSUNO: In that case, I'll keep it for you. But I won't be respon-
    sible.
THE CLEANER: Thank you. You've been a great help. Now we can
    close the shop without further worries and go back to the
    country. Thanks again.
TATSUNO: Still, where did Mr. Murai go, anyway? Have you any
    idea?
THE CLEANER: Well, I don't really know. Maybe he went back to
    his parents' place in the country. I've heard he's the eldest son
    of a landowner in the San'in area and has a fine house that's
    two hundred years old.
TATSUNO: Oh? Did he tell you that?

THE CLEANER: Yes, sir. He was a pleasant and cheerful customer. And he spoke often about his birthplace. There was a large dogwood on the estate, and even today you can catch eels— this large—in the back moat. He's living in town now because of circumstances. Someday soon, he plans to go back and take over the estate. He said a man shouldn't be a rootless plant. You won't be young forever. That's so true. Today, Tokyo is no place for humans . . . Oh! . . . I've talked too much . . . I must be going. Thank you very much. Goodby. (THE CLEANER *leaves after a businesslike bow.*)

TATSUNO (*addressing the middle-aged man who remains behind*): I'm sorry to keep you waiting. What can I do for you?

(*Once again,* NISHIKI *bows politely and presents his name card.*)

NISHIKI: How do you do. I live in the neighborhood. Here's my card.

TATSUNO: I see. You're Mr. Nishiki? I'm Tatsuno . . . Oh, you work at the art museum. And what is the "Security Section"?

NISHIKI: Yes, sir. I'm the watchman. I sit in the corner of the room all day and carry on a staring match with the old teacups and Buddhist statues.

TATSUNO: That's an unusual job. Please come in . . .

NISHIKI: Well, actually, having overheard your conversation, I don't seem to have any business now . . . (*Nevertheless, he nervously enters the room.*)

TATSUNO: You mean about Mr. Murai? Well, that's all right. I'm rather free today . . . Please sit down.

(NISHIKI *still appears nervous but sits down without any hesitation. Although he is extremely proper, his sluggish behavior can have a somewhat oppressive effect on those around him. As if deeply steeped in thought, he has a fixed, grim expression.* TATSUNO *hangs Murai's suit on a nail in the wall directly behind him and sits on his travel bag.*)

What do you want with Mr. Murai?

NISHIKI: Well, I simply must see him. Or my entire future might be in jeopardy . . . I thought if I came here, I might get a hint as to Mr. Murai's whereabouts . . .

TATSUNO: I wish I could help you . . . You seem to be quite disturbed.

NISHIKI: Yes . . . And it's such a strange incident . . .

TATSUNO: "Incident"?

NISHIKI: Yes. It concerns our museum.

TATSUNO: If you don't mind, could you explain the circumstances to me?

NISHIKI: Well, how shall I begin? . . . As a matter of fact, one of our statues of Buddha was stolen. Well . . . at least, it seems that way to me.

TATSUNO: I see.

NISHIKI: It may be difficult for you to understand, but there are forgers of artistic works.

TATSUNO: Yes, I suppose so.

NISHIKI: I strongly suspect that one of the statues of Buddha I guard every day was replaced by a fake.

TATSUNO: That's terrible! But how is that possible?

NISHIKI: Ours is a small, private museum, and we often loan out our works for various occasions. Recently, a statue of Buddha on loan was returned two weeks late. It was apparently loaned out to the home of a certain influential person—at his own request. When I saw the statue again, there was something definitely peculiar about it. It was no obvious forgery, and neither the museum director nor the board of experts have said anything. But unless my eyes have grown feeble with age, something happened to that statue within those two weeks.

TATSUNO: By "something," you mean . . .

NISHIKI: That statue is called the "Golden Bronze Buddha." It's made of an alloy. It would be quite simple to make a mold of the original and duplicate it. And if you add the patina and the tarnish, it would look exactly like the original. I strongly suspect that a copy was returned.

TATSUNO (*sighs deeply and rises*): That sounds fantastic. And have you proof?

NISHIKI (*for a while, stares silently; finally, in a low voice*): Mr. Tatsuno, I've been working at that art museum for eighteen years now. I had no special education and began working there at middle age. But I'm more familiar with that museum collection than anyone else. Or rather, I can safely say that my whole life was totally dedicated to gazing at those pieces on display. I've spent my life looking at that statue in the morning, in the afternoon, and even at night—under the beam of a flashlight. And these eyes tell me there's something strange about that statue.

TATSUNO: Have you already told the museum director about it?

(*Again, a short pause.*)

NISHIKI: I'm just the watchman. I have no special knowledge or authority.

TATSUNO: But isn't there a prescribed scientific investigation in cases like that?

NISHIKI: That would constitute a serious matter in itself. They'd have to call on a person from an outside research center. And that would put our director in a serious predicament. You must realize that I'd be accusing an influential person who also happens to be a patron of the museum. And if it turns out that the statue is genuine . . . I'd have to quit the job. And at my age, I still have a child in primary school.

TATSUNO: But suppose it's established as a fake?

NISHIKI (*with a terribly lonely smile*): I'd have to leave, anyway. The director and the staff of experts who've helped me would have to resign, stripped of their professional reputations.

(*Short pause.*)

TATSUNO: And, Mr. Nishiki, you have absolute confidence in your own judgment? Surely, you're not letting your imagination get the better of you.

NISHIKI (*suddenly rising, he shouts in a pitiful voice*): That's why I must see Mr. Murai! He's the only one who understands me. He said that the statue was suspicious, too.

TATSUNO: You mean to tell me Mr. Murai is an expert on such things?

NISHIKI (*sitting down*): Of course, he's an amateur. But he loved art and came often to the museum. He happened to live in the neighborhood, and we talked about everything. . . . And when I couldn't keep this to myself any longer, I consulted him. Mr. Murai said he wasn't sure, but he also agreed there was something quite strange about the statue.

(*Toward the end of his speech, NISHIKI suddenly breaks into a sob and covers his face with both hands. At that moment, a woman about thirty appears quietly in the hallway and stands waiting in front of TATSUNO's apartment. NISHIKI whispers.*)

Mr. Tatsuno, I'm afraid. I'm afraid of my own eyes. I want someone who would give me support and provide me with self-confidence.

(*At a loss,* TATSUNO *begins pacing around the room. After a few faltering efforts, the woman finally knocks on the door, having apparently made up her mind.*)

TATSUNO: Yes. Who is it?

(*When he opens the door abruptly without waiting for an answer, the woman backs away silently.*)

I'm Tatsuno. Who are you?

SHIMA: I'm . . . I'm . . . (*After stammering, the woman, who later identifies herself as* SAWADA SHIMA, *suddenly turns around and attempts to leave.*)

TATSUNO: Please wait! It's *you*, isn't it?

(*The woman stops short.* TATSUNO *goes out into the hallway and closes the door behind him.*)

It *is* you. Am I right?

SHIMA: I was beside myself and came all the way here. Earlier, when I was in the neighborhood and talked to you over the public phone . . . Afterwards, I got all confused . . . I'm sorry.

TATSUNO: Never mind. I was sure you'd be coming.

SHIMA: I'm Sawada Shima. I'm so ashamed, I can hardly bear looking at you. Please . . . I must leave.

TATSUNO: Please don't. There's something I want to show you. I have Mr. Murai's suit.

SHIMA: His suit?

TATSUNO: Yes. The cleaner left it a while ago. Can you take a look at it? Please come in . . .

(*As he leads the way,* SHIMA *follows as if she were being pulled in mysteriously and stands inside the door.*)

There it is.

(*When* SHIMA *sees the suit hanging, she utters a short cry and averts her eyes.*)

He apparently forgot and left it. Won't you take it with you?

SHIMA (*still averting her eyes, she murmurs*): He didn't forget. He left it behind.

TATSUNO: He did?

SHIMA: Rather, he thrust the suit back at me. After we got to know each other, that was the only gift I ever gave him. He simply hated getting anything. He finally took that suit, after I almost begged him. There's no reason why he should forget . . . If he left it behind, he'll . . . He'll never come back again.

NISHIKI (*suddenly, raising his head in surprise*): You mean, Mr. Murai?

SHIMA: Yes, he won't be back. I know it. He's disappeared for good.

NISHIKI: How could he be so heartless!

(NISHIKI *rises feebly. At that moment, the telephone begins to ring loudly. All three are startled. They instinctively draw closer to the phone but become momentarily confused as they try to yield the call among themselves. Finally, as* TATSUNO *decisively reaches out for the phone, it stops ringing. They sigh deeply and gaze at one another. After a momentary pause, a quick curtain.*)

Act Two

Early May about three weeks after Act One. It is late afternoon.

The setting is still TATSUNO'S *apartment. The windows, however, have curtains; plain chairs and a dining table are in the kitchen area; and the* tatami *room has a small tea table. The apartment has turned into a fairly lively dwelling.*

In the apartment, which looks generally quite tidy, the sliding screens are apparently being repapered and stand against the wall. Rolls of paper and a wooden paste bucket are scattered about the floor. And Murai's suit hangs prominently on the wall of the tatami *room.*

(*As the curtain rises to the same music played in Act One,* SATOMI, *who leans against the rocking chair at stage center, is smoking a cigarette while* AMANO YUMI *sits in a chair at the dining table near the entrance. Bottles of orange juice and whiskey along with glasses are on the dining table, and* TATSUNO *stands on its far side, talking on the phone.*)

TATSUNO: . . . I see. You say, it's 1,200 yen for a single column of fifteen letters? Then it's 3,600 yen per day for a three-line personal . . . I see. And that's only for the city edition. Yes, I understand. In any case, I'll think it over and drop in to see you. Thank you very much. (*He puts the receiver down and sits in a chair on the far side of the dining table.*) Well, Satomi, what do you think? Do these personals actually help?

SATOMI: You can forget about them. In the first place, isn't it quite unlikely that that Murai character is still in Tokyo? So, where do you want to run the ad?

YUMI: I agree with you. And even if Mr. Murai saw the ad, would he get in touch with a Mr. Tatsuno—someone he's never seen before?

SATOMI: Exactly. And what do you plan to say in such an ad? "Mr. Murai: I have your suit. Please contact me immediately." . . . Would a fellow who ran away deliberately pay attention to such a message?

YUMI: I'm more concerned about what the police had to say. Didn't you put in a "Missing Person's Report" recently?

TATSUNO: No, I decided not to. If he's involved in some complicated affair, we'd only make trouble for him by alerting the police.

YUMI: I'm surprised. You're very sympathetic toward him, aren't you? Do you want to cover up for Mr. Murai, even if he's done something wrong?

TATSUNO: I want to see him, that's all. I didn't start looking for him as a public service or from a sense of righteous indignation.

SATOMI: In fact, if you went to the police, you'll end up being laughed out of the station. Just imagine the number of more serious cases of missing persons occurring in Tokyo, each month.

TATSUNO: That's true. And when you really think about it, it won't be easy finding him.

YUMI (*sighs, deliberately*): You know, I just don't understand it. I realize I've asked you time and again, Mr. Tatsuno, but why do you have such an interest in Mr. Murai?

SATOMI: I feel the same way. You're too persistent, Tatsuno. It's been twenty days since you moved in, but every time we meet, it's the same old story.

YUMI (*laughs, recalling*): Like last Sunday. I heard Mr. Tatsuno ran all over Tokyo . . . He went around to some of the busiest areas in town and left messages on the blackboards at the train stations: "Mr. Murai: Please get in touch with me."

SATOMI (*with a gloomy expression, smokes a cigarette*): You shouldn't overdo it. You didn't come back to Tokyo just for that, did you?

TATSUNO: But how can I help it? At least two people desperately need his presence.

SATOMI: You mean a poor girl friend he dumped and a crazy museum watchman.

TATSUNO: He's not crazy!

SATOMI: It doesn't matter. That fact is, Murai is their problem, not yours. You're going a bit overboard if it's out of kindness.

TATSUNO: Well, you should see for yourself. It's quite serious.

SATOMI (*sharply*): Sure. You're a kind person, all right. You treat everyone kindly but you seem to be mocking them.

TATSUNO: Do you think I'm just playing a practical joke, Satomi?

SATOMI: Tell me, what are you planning to do with your own life? This is the most important period in your career. You should be concentrating your entire attention now on your own personal affairs.

(*An uneasy silence.*)

YUMI (*finally, rather naively*): If you ask me, I don't think Mr. Tatsuno is looking for Mr. Murai for the sake of those people. I don't exactly know how to put it, but I just can't help thinking that he has some special, personal interest in Mr. Murai.

TATSUNO (*forcing a smile*): Then, it must be due to the ghosts or evil spirits, after all.

YUMI: My guess is it's because Mr. Tatsuno resembles Mr. Murai in some way . . . Come to think of it, they have a great deal in common. Weren't they born in the same year, and don't they like to move a lot? Besides, they're cheerful, sociable, a bit talkative, and have no strong attachments to their personal possessions.

SATOMI (*this time, he forces a smile*): Ha, ha, ha. I'd say you've been thoroughly scrutinized.

TATSUNO: Well, it seems that way . . . But there's one important way in which we may differ. He has no strong attachment to his personal possessions. However, he apparently had one strong attachment—to his own birthplace. I understand he has

a fine house and property in the country and constantly talked
about them.

YUMI: Oh? I've never heard of that. You may be right, though.
Maybe he could move around so freely with only a suitcase
because he knew he had a home—somewhere.

TATSUNO: But unfortunately for me, I don't have one—anywhere.
The house where I was born happened to be in town and
burned down completely during the war. The temple, the
school, the town office, and even my birth certificate were destroyed. To make matters worse, the postwar mayor was a
very ambitious go-getter. He was totally sold on reconstruc-
tion. He built up an entirely different town out of the
bombed-out ruins. He filled in the river, leveled the hills, and
rerouted all the old roads. And the town I remember is entirely
gone. The street names and the house numbers have changed.
And, thanks to a merger, even the name of the town itself has
disappeared.

YUMI: But you must have former schoolmates or an alumni club
you belong to?

TATSUNO (*laughs rather happily*): After the primary school burned
down, the whole student body was dissolved and absorbed
into another school. As for the junior high school, they said
the educational system was being revamped. And it was dissolved while I was still going there. We moved a lot during my
senior high school days. I just don't know which is my alma
mater.

YUMI: No wonder you don't belong to an alumni club. Doesn't
that make you feel lonely at times?

TATSUNO: They often ask me that. The trouble is, I don't feel
lonely at all. To begin with, I've never had a home town or an
alma mater. And for some reason that doesn't bother me in the
least. Of course, my section chief often takes me to task. He
says that explains my strange personality.

SATOMI (*earnestly but with some reluctance*): You know, this fellow
has absolutely no feeling of loneliness, longing, affection, or
resentment. He's like a fish.

YUMI: Even Mr. Tatsuno must surely have someone whom he really loves or hates. Maybe a father or a mother?

TATSUNO: Naturally, I have parents. And I hope they live for a long time. But I have no business or estate to take over. Besides, we don't want to be mutually tied down, so no news means good news.

YUMI: I see. You're so free, Mr. Tatsuno. Since I'm the eldest daughter who must take over this apartment building, Father's always hounding me about a prospective husband and the like . . .

TATSUNO: You think so? I believe my case is a little different than having freedom. I don't feel particularly sad, but sometimes I get a strange feeling these days. The ground beneath me seems to give way, and I can't get enough brute strength to keep on living. I can, at least, notice that, as I grow older. Ha, ha, ha, ha. (*Suddenly, he laughs in a lonely way.*)

YUMI: I don't quite understand, but when I hear you say that, I'm convinced more than ever that you and Mr. Murai are alike . . .

TATSUNO: We basically differ. There aren't too many like me around.

YUMI: I still think you're attracted to Mr. Murai by something special. Finding someone who is only slightly different than yourself is like discovering a new facet within yourself. Perhaps a potentiality you haven't noticed before . . .(*She glances at her watch.*) Oh, dear! I must get back now. (*She picks up the envelope with the rent money from the dining table. There remains a large envelope placed there previously.*) Well, thank you for the rent. I'll leave the envelope with the receipt here. I'm sorry I was impertinent, Mr. Satomi.

(*Silently,* SATOMI *bows. Walking to the door,* YUMI *suddenly turns around.*)

That's right, I forgot. I've heard there's a huge American dogwood when you climb up Yakken Hill, farther on from here.

TATSUNO: American dogwood?

YUMI: Yes. It has large, pink flowers that bloom around April and is supposed to look something like a magnolia. Mr. Murai was crazy about it. Toward evening, he'd often take walks to the top of Yakken Hill.

TATSUNO: Oh? Was there such a large tree?

YUMI: I haven't seen it myself. But Father says many apartment houses are up there, and maybe Mr. Murai has moved there.

Come to think of it, he disappeared about the beginning of April. . . . Well, goodby.

TATSUNO: Goodby.

(*After she leaves,* TATSUNO *begins to skillfully repaper the sliding screens. He takes apart the four black frame pieces and peels off the old paper; he spreads out the new paper and dampens it with a brush. Then he takes the wet paper, covers the screen, and quickly strokes it with a dry brush. Next, he puts paste on the edge of the paper and attaches it to the screen. He skillfully continues this work in a happy mood.*)

SATOMI (*looking on nervously, finally unable to restrain himself*): Hey! Isn't it about time you told me? Frankly, what are you going to do?

TATSUNO: About what?

SATOMI: Oh, about everything . . . Concerning your Murai Toyojirō.

TATSUNO: I'm not trying to be secretive. I don't really know why I'm concerned with him, to tell you the truth. I just want to meet the guy. And talk to him. That's all.

SATOMI: Tatsuno!

TATSUNO (*laughs mischievously*): Maybe that girl is right in what she said about me.

SATOMI: Why don't you stop this! I'm trying to keep my temper. For God's sake! Answer me seriously!

TATSUNO (*continues to work*): I wouldn't tease you. Besides, I don't think I've bothered you, even if I did look around for Murai.

SATOMI: All right! Then let me ask you. What happens to this envelope? You should know. I came here today for this particular reason.

(*He picks up the large envelope and strikes the table.* TATSUNO *remains undisturbed and continues to paste.*)

TATSUNO: Isn't that the girl's picture? I said I'd take my time looking at it.

SATOMI (*briskly drains the whiskey glass*): You know, I must look pretty silly right now. There's nothing quite so ridiculous as playing a matchmaker with you as the prospect . . . Still, can't you see my side of it? While I'm talking dead seriously, you're intent on that stupid pasting job. Moreover, you detain Yumi and deliberately talk on about a personal ad. It's better to simply tell me to get out if you don't want to listen to what I say.

TATSUNO: I'm sorry. Did you say, "Deliberately"? I didn't intend it that way. (*Once again, innocently.*) Wasn't it better that I talked to that girl? The apartment area on top of Yakken Hill was fresh information. And the American dogwood. Remember? The suburbs of New York were full of them.

SATOMI (*shouts inadvertently*): Damn you! (*After a strained silence, speaking softly.*) You give me the creeps. When it comes to the important things in life, you can't get interested at all. On the other hand, if it's something trivial, you develop a mad curiosity. . . . Now, if that happens to be your natural attitude . . .

TATSUNO (*for the first time, he stops working and sits on the chair in front of the dining table—across from* SATOMI): Do I as a person . . . And my actions seem so strange to you?

SATOMI: You should be vaguely aware of it yourself. A while ago, didn't you admit it, in a way? You said you had a secret anxiety over this rootless existence.

TATSUNO: "Anxiety" is putting it rather strongly. Though I must admit these days I can't get excited over living. I don't have a clear notion of things I really want to do, or conversely things I really want to avoid. Especially, when it comes to what's five or six years ahead, I realize I don't get a strong urge to try becoming a success at it.

SATOMI: Isn't that "anxiety"?

TATSUNO: But this doesn't bother me. Besides, I don't feel like those young people who claim there's no satisfaction in human existence . . . To begin with, don't I work conscientiously?

SATOMI: . . . Like you were playing a game. You never get totally involved. You work so indifferently . . . As if it was all a joke. And yet you manage to do a perfect job. When I watch you work, I feel as if others around you are all being mocked.

TATSUNO: Maybe I'm strange, after all. (*Sighing, he starts pasting again.*)

SATOMI: When I see you pasting away like that, there's something a bit strange about it. You look so happy in your concentration. It's enough to give me the creeps. You said you made those shelves and curtains all by yourself . . . Naturally, there are guys in this world who are crazy about improving their own homes. But how about a guy who lives all alone and still beautifies an apartment that no one comes to see?

TATSUNO: Somehow, I can't settle down unless I do this.

SATOMI: And you do it every time you move?

TATSUNO: That's right.

SATOMI: Then, after going through all that trouble, you move and leave everything behind, after only a year or two.

TATSUNO: Sure. Perhaps that's why I want to do this sort of thing. A new apartment is like a total stranger. And this is the best way to become friends in the shortest possible time.

SATOMI: And just as you're finally about to become good friends, you move out again . . .

TATSUNO: It can't be helped.

SATOMI (*rises slowly*): I see. And that Murai Toyojirō . . . He also takes the same approach.

TATSUNO: What "approach"? What are you getting at?

SATOMI: It's not only the apartment. Even people are all total strangers to you. You treat everyone kindly, but you've no close friends with whom you're on familiar terms. No one treats you informally or sets about seeking your company. . . . Maybe you don't realize it, but you're actually anxious about that.

TATSUNO: I was born this way, so I really can't say . . . On the other hand, you may be right.

SATOMI: You may not feel lonely yourself. But your own "feelers," which are trained on people, are habitually searching. They're groping blindly and aimlessly just like those on a sea anemone. And sometimes they cling suddenly to an unexpected person.

TATSUNO (*stops working again and sits down; after taking a sip of whiskey*): Now that you mention it, sometime, I envy the old samurai who had to carry out a vendetta. This life would be so simple if you could thoroughly hate someone like that. Or, it might be great to fall madly in love like characters in a romantic story from a ladies' magazine. . . . Then, finding your self-image might become a simple matter. And you can accordingly choose your likes and dislikes and your course of action without getting confused.

SATOMI (*after a short silence, somewhat somberly*): Listen, Tatsuno. Why don't you try living an ordinary life, with a wife and children? There's nothing special about it, but I'm sure your self-image would become clear and simple. If your family barges in unannounced from somewhere, they'll force you to adopt a certain self-image. If you're served three lousy meals a day, you'll develop your likes and dislikes instantly. And if your kids keep pestering you on Sunday mornings, you'll know for sure what you don't want to do on your holidays.

(*Suddenly,* TATSUNO *bursts out laughing.*)

Now, I'm being serious, Tatsuno. Later on, you'll automatically have your home town and your relatives. And if you can stand your wife's idle talk, you'll gain your place in the ancestral grave and regain some of your childhood memories. After you get sick and tired of these things following you around, then you can run away again. By then, at least, you'll be able to cry and complain like the rest of us.

TATSUNO: Yes. Maybe you're right. And if that happens, I might get a little more brute strength to keep living.

(*As* SATOMI *is about to emphasize his point,* NISHIKI *appears in the hallway with noisy footsteps and knocks on the door.*)

NISHIKI: Hello! It's Nishiki. I won't take up much of your time . . .

(*When* TATSUNO *opens the door,* NISHIKI *virtually barges in.*)

I'm sorry. I know I'm intruding, but I had to see you for a moment . . .

TATSUNO: What happened, all of a sudden?

NISHIKI: Well, ah, I've been thinking a lot. And, finally, today, I've arranged to talk it over with the director . . .

TATSUNO: About that statue of Buddha, you mean?

NISHIKI: Yes. And . . . Oh, you have a guest. I'm terribly sorry . . .

(*When* TATSUNO *looks back with concern,* SATOMI *waves his hand, casually.*)

SATOMI: No, don't mind me. I was just leaving . . . Well, Tatsuno, this time think it over carefully. You don't have to give me a quick answer. But give it serious thought.

TATSUNO: Yes, I'll do that.

SATOMI: Well, I'm going. Goodby.

TATSUNO: Right. (*When* SATOMI *opens the door and is about to leave.*) Satomi!

SATOMI: What is it?

TATSUNO: . . . I appreciate all you're doing for me.

SATOMI: You idiot!

(*He leaves, slipping past* NISHIKI, *who is bowing courteously.*)

TATSUNO: Well, please come in. What happened?

NISHIKI: Yes, sir. That is . . . I . . . (*Walks in slowly and sits down.*) I can't make up my mind.

TATSUNO: You mean on how you should speak to the director?

NISHIKI: No. About whether I should even tell him that story.

TATSUNO: But, Mr. Nishiki, in that case . . .

NISHIKI: I'm scared, Mr. Tatsuno. I'm so scared. (*His expression suddenly becomes taut with concern.*) What I fear most is that a scientific investigation may not lead to a definite conclusion. Quite often a specialist will conduct a thorough analysis of the materials and fluoroscope the object and then make a final determination simply by using his own eyes.

TATSUNO: Well, I suppose that's true.

NISHIKI: But if that happens, Mr. Tatsuno, what becomes of me? From then on, the director, a specialist who thinks it's genuine, and I, the amateur who says it's a fake, must always remain enemies at the museum.

TATSUNO (*sighing*): I see what you mean.

NISHIKI: I'll be fifty soon. It's already too late for me to look for another job. And it's too long for the director and me to be glaring at each other for ten years, until my retirement. Feeling as I do, what can I say to the director if I see him?

TATSUNO: Why can't you be direct and honest? It's not your intention to expose the director, and you're not just being stubborn about you own theory. Why can't you say to him that it may be your own imagination, but you feel that the statue of Buddha looks strange? And you're telling him out of the goodness of your own heart?

NISHIKI (*suddenly becoming emphatic*): Mr. Tatsuno, my casting doubt on the authenticity of that statue is not done so frivolously as all that. I can assert it positively. That statue is an unquestionable fake!

TATSUNO: Well, you may be right. But men can make mistakes.

And, besides, if you're worried about the consequences, shouldn't you leave yourself an avenue of escape?

NISHIKI: If there was any room for doubt, I wouldn't have worried over it, from the beginning. I looked at that statue time and time again before I asked for a meeting with the director. And the more I looked at it, the more convinced I became that it was a fake. If it's only to say something clever, like what you suggested, I'd rather not see him at all.

TATSUNO (*somewhat miffed*): Well, if that's the way you feel about it, I certainly wouldn't encourage you to go. Then why not cancel the appointment?

NISHIKI (*emitting a painful cry*): Mr. Tatsuno! Are you suggesting that I should always remain in this emotional state? Are you telling me to keep silent when such a terrible crime is being committed right in front of my eyes?

TATSUNO (*inadvertently, becomes rude*): What should I say? . . . That you should be courageous in the defence of justice?

(*Short silence.*)

NISHIKI (*finally, timidly but in a somewhat forward manner*): You know, Mr. Murai offered to see the director himself. . . . He said he would tell him that he, rather than I, had discovered the fraud . . .

TATSUNO: That's crazy! Absolutely crazy! I couldn't do it. Besides, I've never seen the statue.

NISHIKI (*totally unconcerned, he replies*): As a matter of fact, Mr. Murai hadn't looked at it carefully, either. But he trusts me as a man . . .

TATSUNO: What an irresponsible person! . . . Absolutely irresponsible! That's impossible! I couldn't do that!

(*Silence.*)

NISHIKI (*whispering*): You're not trying to understand me. You don't realize how important to me that puny statue is. Mr. Tatsuno, I was an army officer during the war. I'm ashamed to say I graduated from officers' school with honors. And I was under a delusion that I could accomplish anything in the future. When the war was over, I was in the same boat with everyone. Everything was gone. Still, I tried my best to redirect my life. I went from one job to another, but none of them suited me. I wasn't a fast talker and couldn't get along too well with my fellow workers. This museum picked me up when I was at the end of my rope, and I've been working now at this job for eighteen years. At first, I liked this place because I didn't have to talk to anyone. But, Mr. Tatsuno, can you understand the feelings of a man who has gazed silently for eighteen years in the same room? No matter how often I look, nothing changes. And it's my job to make sure it doesn't. Now, listen! If you're a carpenter for eighteen years, you become a professional. You need only plane a single piece of wood to prove your qualifications. But what have I to show for my time spent? A watchman at a museum can't work as a guard in a department store. And I'd probably be treated as an unskilled worker if I went to another museum. I'm not an art specialist or a specialist on museums. I'm just a specialist on *that* museum.

TATSUNO (*weakly*): I see. So that's the way it is.

NISHIKI: Can you understand, Mr. Tatsuno? Why does a person like me exist in this world? . . . Well, to make sure that the display in the museum stays in the same way as it was the day before. Isn't that true?

TATSUNO (*nods, sighing*): I think I understand.

NISHIKI: I'm not complaining. At my age, I don't expect to lead a typical life led by others. . . . Still, I can't allow this to happen. I simply can't tolerate a rascal who tries to rob someone like me—who has so little to begin with. Am I so strange, Mr. Tatsuno? That statue being stolen in that way makes me as angry as the entire Japanese army being totally destroyed.

TATSUNO (*soberly*): No. I don't think it's strange. I think I can really understand.

NISHIKI (*suddenly shouting in a quaking voice*): My close friend committed *seppuku* on the evening of August 16, twenty-five years ago. I couldn't go through with it. I was a coward. Since then, I've lived on idly, and . . . This time, I'm still a coward.

(*With arms stiffly outstretched, he places both hands on his knees, as tears stream down his face. For a while,* TATSUNO *paces around the room.*)

TATSUNO: Give me time to think it over, Mr. Nishiki. I'll consider carefully whether I can do what Mr. Murai offered to do. In any case, why don't you go home for now and postpone your appointment with the director for a while? I'm sure it wouldn't work out for you if you see him in your present state of mind.

NISHIKI: Thank you. I appreciate your kindness. . . . These days my wife sometimes says to me that I must be losing my mind. I become so emotional that, at times, I can't control myself . . . I'm sorry to trouble you.

TATSUNO: Don't worry about it. I can't say, "Leave it up to me," but let's both think up a good plan. We may even find out Mr. Murai's whereabouts soon.

NISHIKI: Thank you. I'll go home and renew my determination. . . . Please forgive my rudeness . . . (*Rising slowly,* NISHIKI *is about to leave.*)

TATSUNO: Mr. Nishiki.

NISHIKI: Yes? (*As he glances back at* TATSUMO, *their eyes meet.*)

TATSUNO (*in a slightly muffled tone*): Having listened to your story, I . . . I envy you.

NISHIKI: Envy me?

TATSUNO: Yes I do. (*Interrupting* NISHIKI, *who is about to speak.*) No, never mind. It's just a personal reaction . . . Well, let me see you to the street corner.

(TATSUNO *leaves closely behind* NISHIKI. *In the empty apartment, the phone soon begins to ring. For a while, it rings on but stops before anyone answers. A few moments later,* SAWADA SHIMA *appears in the hallway. After glancing back a few times, to make sure, she quietly knocks on the door. When there is no answer, she casually touches the knob, and the door opens by itself.* SHIMA *whispers.*)

SHIMA: Excuse me, Mr. Tatsuno . . .

(*When she realizes it is vacant and is about to close the door, the phone begins to ring again.* SHIMA *becomes flustered, but since it rings on, she makes up her mind, goes into the apartment, and picks up the receiver.*)

Hello . . .

(*Over the speaker, a voice of a woman who conveys the impression of being dissipated.*)

THE WOMAN'S VOICE: I thought so. You were in, after all. I knew it all the time . . .

SHIMA: Ah . . . Hello.

THE WOMAN'S VOICE: Never mind! Call Kawahara to the phone. He's there, isn't he?

SHIMA: Ah . . . Haven't you made a mistake? There's no one here by that name . . .

THE WOMAN'S VOICE: Don't give me that. Tell Kawahara not to get scared and come to the phone.

SHIMA: Don't you have the wrong number? This is Tatsuno's phone. Or else, Murai . . .

THE WOMAN'S VOICE: Oh? Does he use so many aliases? . . . Well, what's the difference. And who are you?

SHIMA (*for a moment, remains speechless*): Who—me? I'm . . .

THE WOMAN'S VOICE (*emits a shrill laugh*): Never mind. Don't get so upset. Just tell him . . . He can do as he pleases, but I'll never give him up . . . Okay?

(*The phone cuts off.* SHIMA *sits in a nearby chair with a deeply disturbed expression and covers her face with both hands. A few seconds later,* TATSUNO *returns and cautiously peeks through the door, which had been left open so mysteriously.*)

TATSUNO: Hello. It was you, after all. I thought I caught a glimpse of you on the street, a while ago.

(*When he enters,* SHIMA *rises fearfully.*)

SHIMA: I'm sorry. I thought I'd wait out in the hallway, but the door was open. And the phone happened to ring . . .

TATSUNO: Oh, the phone? And was there a message for me?

SHIMA: No. It was the wrong number.

TATSUNO: Well, that was kind of you. How about a drink? Or, perhaps, tea? You probably prefer tea. (*Skillfully,* TATSUNO *cheerfully begins to prepare the tea.*) I'm sorry this place is in such a mess. If I'd known you were coming, I would have cleaned up a bit.

SHIMA: I don't mind.

(TATSUNO *continues to prepare the tea. After an uneasy silence,* SHIMA *speaks out, decisively.*)

Mr. Tatsuno, have you ever used the name of Kawahara?

TATSUNO: Kawahara? (*For an instant, he glances back with a stern expression but immediately returns to his innocent smiling face.*) Not that I know of. Ha, ha, ha. In the first place, do I look like the type that uses an alias? What happened?

SHIMA: That call was from a woman.

TATSUNO: A woman? And what did she say?

SHIMA: Nothing special. . . . Just that she'll never give you up.

TATSUNO (*suddenly laughs out loud*): Ha, ha, ha. That's a good one. Isn't that fantastic! (*Again, he becomes serious.*) Perhaps that call isn't for me.

SHIMA: Yes. . . . That's a strong possibility, isn't it? (*She sits down dejectedly.*)

(*Long silence.*)

TATSUNO: Have you had any new leads on Murai?

SHIMA: No, nothing.

TATSUNO: Of course. It's only been a week since our meeting at the steak house. What can you expect in a week?

SHIMA: I think it's hopeless now. I told you at the steak house that I didn't know anything about him . . . I'm more convinced than ever now.

TATSUNO: It's too early to give up. You get the most surprising news when you least expect it. (*He brings the teacups to the dining table.*) Have you heard that a magnificent American dogwood tree grows on the top of Yakken Hill?

SHIMA (*looks up startled*): No. Why?

TATSUNO: Mr. Murai really loved that tree and often took strolls up there to see it.

SHIMA (*replies rather firmly*): I wouldn't know. I really don't know anything about him.

TATSUNO: That tree rises high above all the other trees and is said to be quite beautiful. I've never seen it either, but I'd like to go and take a look.

SHIMA (*suddenly, rather loud and hysterically*): I wouldn't go!

TATSUNO: Why not? What happened?

SHIMA: Nothing. I simply don't want to.

TATSUNO (*serves tea, looking apologetic; then as if to mollify her*): You said you didn't know Mr. Murai too well, but wasn't he rather cheerful and talkative?

SHIMA: No—not in the least.

TATSUNO: That's strange. They say he was quite open and went into great detail about himself. And in that respect he was like me . . .

SHIMA: He was the very opposite. He was a poor talker and remained quiet and pensive in front of people . . . And he especially hated being talked about.

TATSUNO: Oh? How curious. Still, since you were closest to him, that might have been the real Mr. Murai.

SHIMA (*with increasing antagonism*): You call that being close?
TATSUNO: But wouldn't you say so?
SHIMA: May I have a drink?
(SHIMA *pours the whiskey into a glass on the dining table and drains it completely. Surprised,* TATSUNO *looks at her but silently pours her another.*)
There was a somewhat shocking aspect to our life together. We met for the first time last spring at a party and went to bed that very night. All we did was gaze at each other silently and angrily, and before I realized it, we were in bed together. (*She drinks up the glass.*) After we were up the following morning and drinking our coffee in the hotel room, he thrust his name card at me silently. Till then, I didn't even know his address.
TATSUNO: And that was the address for this apartment?
SHIMA: Yes. After that, I began visiting this place every Saturday night. Sometimes, when I came without bothering to call him, he was drunk and sound asleep. . . . I'd silently crawl under the covers. (*Suddenly, she laughs loudly.*) Ha, ha, ha. Just like a cave animal.
TATSUNO (*pours* SHIMA *another drink*): And that relationship went on for nearly a year . . . Until recently?
SHIMA: That's probably why it lasted so long . . . I'm . . . I'm a hopeless case. (*As she lifts the glass and gazes through it.*) You know how an ordinary girl talks about free, romantic love and all the rest. About how she wants to really talk things over, get to understand the other person, and then choose the right partner because of how she feels about him . . . That's impossible for me. I don't know what that means.
TATSUNO: You hate to talk?
SHIMA (*shaking her head, she laughs quietly*): No, it's not that. Is there anyone in this world that you can't understand if you really talk things over? I can understand all men, no matter how repulsive or wonderful they might be. Maybe I'm different. I can actually know them individually for what they really are. Since this always happens, how can I ever settle for a particular person? For me, to understand means I can no longer make a definite choice.
(*Surprised,* TATSUNO *looks at* SHIMA.)
I'm not complaining. If I could have someone, it doesn't matter who it is. And wouldn't mind living with him, either. But I

can't get all excited about thinking he might be the only one
for me.

(TATSUNO *slowly clutches the whiskey glass and drains it briskly. Then
he rises and walks nervously around the room. Finally, as if to shake
off his own confusion–*)

TATSUNO (*firmly*): You're different all right. Yes, quite different.
. . . And very unfortunate.

SHIMA: But aren't those men who are drawn to me much more
unfortunate? Or, are they fortunate?

TATSUNO: Fortunate?

SHIMA: Yes, especially if he's a typical autocratic husband who
doesn't care to talk with a mere woman. Come to think of it,
that could be my salvation. Sometimes I've thought how easy
it would be, if like the old days, you were simply handed over
to your husband by your parents. You didn't have to think
about yourself, at all. If only I could have been spirited away,
once and for all—in an ordinary, prescribed fashion . . .

TATSUNO (*in an obviously sarcastic manner*): You take yourself quite
seriously, don't you?

SHIMA (*quietly shaking her head*): I'm not exaggerating. I've never
been able to understand myself. . . . Don't misunderstand
me. I'm not speaking of self-sacrifice or self-renunciation. Ever
since I was born, there was never a need for that. My father
died early. Mother couldn't make up her mind about anything. So I made the decisions. I was never challenged, and
everyone waited for me to make the decisions. When such
freedom is forced upon a girl of twelve or thirteen, what kind
of self-determination can you expect her to develop? No one
had any authority over me, and I had no chance to rebel. And
since there was no need to, I never developed a personality
bent on asserting itself.

(SHIMA *laughs self-mockingly. While appearing to restrain himself,*
TATSUNO *silently pours a drink into* SHIMA's *glass and drinks up his
own.*)

You know, after my kid sister graduated from a women's college, she wanted to become a hostess in a third-rate cabaret in
the suburbs. My mother and I didn't try to restrain her. And
even if we had tried, it would have just turned into an argument. And there was no compelling reason to stop her . . .

My kid sister, who wasn't stopped from leaving home, left with a sad expression on her face. But as an older sister, I didn't feel the slightest impulse to make her stay.

TATSUNO: I understand. And, finally, according to your original desire, you met Murai. For he was the sort of man who didn't expect you to love him and took you against your will.

SHIMA (*laughing rather happily*): And this time, I was neatly abandoned against my will.

TATSUNO: By a man the complete opposite of someone like me, who loves to talk this way with women.

SHIMA (*suddenly becoming serious*): I still don't know anything about you.

TATSUNO: Yes. It's probably better that you don't.

SHIMA: Just like in Murai's case?

(TATSUNO *glances toward* SHIMA *but simply opens the window and begins to whistle a tune quietly as he sits down on the window ledge. The golden rays of the setting sun shine on his profile.* SHIMA *is startled by the melody.*)

What's that song?

TATSUNO: Don't you know? It's an old primary school song. (*He sings softly.*)

> The boat is a sailboat with three masts
> What is a mere thousand leagues of sea . . .

SHIMA: That's strange. I think I've heard it before. Murai sang it once.

TATSUNO: That's possible. This song never really had a chance to become too popular. When the prewar textbook was revised during the war, the song was included in the new edition. But when this textbook was again revised after two years, the song dropped completely from sight. So the only people who are familiar with it now are those who learned it during this very short period in primary school.

SHIMA: It's a fine song.

TATSUNO: This may be the only thing in common between Mr. Murai and me. (*Again, he hums the tune softly.*)

SHIMA: I . . . I was behaving very strangely today.

TATSUNO: Yes, you seemed a bit excited, didn't you? (*Stands in back of* SHIMA.)

SHIMA: Today I was really scared.

TATSUNO: What happened?

SHIMA: I bought a flatfish at the fish market this morning. Since it was fresh and still alive, I had them clean it and then I stored it in the refrigerator. When I opened it this noon, intending to cook the fish, it was, for some reason, alive and wiggling. I was so surprised. Just then, the young man from the greengrocer's came in, so I asked him to take care of the fish. He took a cleaver, cut off its head, and put it back in the refrigerator. But . .. but when I peeked in later, the headless flatfish had managed to jump down to the bottom shelf and was wiggling around. (*She covers her face.*) I . . . I flew out of the apartment and came straight over here.

(*A cry escapes from the depth of her throat. Gently,* TATSUNO *places his right hand on her shoulder. After a moment, her own left hand covers his. Then,* TATSUNO *grabs her around the waist and embraces her. A very long, tender kiss.*)

I'm scared. I'm really scared.

TATSUNO: You're . . . You're all alone, aren't you?

(*Then the two shift into the adjacent room, sinking to the floor. At that moment, a* MAN, *thirty-seven or thirty-eight, appears in the hallway. He is smartly dressed in a business suit and carries a Boston bag; in size and carriage he somehow resembles* TATSUNO. *He seems to have no particular purpose and stands, casually glancing around. As the curtain begins to fall slowly,* TATSUNO *whispers gently in a rather husky voice.*)

You poor thing . . . You poor thing . . .

Curtain

Act Three

A fall Sunday about five months after Act Two. It is late morning.
The curtain rises to the familiar music. In the apartment, the sliding screens between the two rooms are now closed.

(SHIMA *is still sleeping with the curtains drawn in the dark bedroom. In the bright, large room, the coffee is ready on the dining table, and* TATSUNO *is talking on the phone. Mindful of* SHIMA *in the next room, he is trying to hold down his voice but cannot suppress his agitation.*)

TATSUNO: Haven't I already told you that's impossible? I didn't check on the last owner when I got the phone. Besides, I'm at least the third owner, as far as this phone is concerned. I'm sorry. You're starting to get on my nerves. Can't you call the telephone office for that kind of information? Frankly, why bother me with these calls on Sunday morning? I'm sorry. I've got to hang up how. Goodby.

(*He slams the receiver down.* SHIMA *lazily sits up in bed and inquires through the sliding screens.*)

SHIMA: What's that all about? Who was it?

TATSUNO: Oh, did I wake you up? What a pest! He wants to know the whereabouts of the fellow who had this phone three years ago. He came in from the country expecting to look up his old friend. And when I said the guy wasn't here, he got all upset. He's phoned three times already.

SHIMA: I feel sorry for him.

TATSUNO: I'd say it was rather annoying. He just knows the phone number and hasn't even got the address. Country people are so easygoing.

SHIMA (*taking her time dressing, says coldly*): You think so?

TATSUNO: Well, isn't that true? It's absurd, depending on someone whose address you don't even know.

(*Having finished dressing,* SHIMA *rises quietly.*)

SHIMA: I . . . I know Murai's address.

(*Through the sliding screens,* TATSUNO *looks at her, sternly. While drawing the curtains open,* SHIMA *says casually*):

For nearly a year, to me, this room was Murai himself. If I came, he'd be here. Strange, isn't it?

(*Silently,* TATSUNO *pours the coffee. Pause.*)

TATSUNO: Hey, the coffee's ready. Come over here.

SHIMA: Fine, thanks. (*She carelessly folds the bedding and puts it away. As she gently holds down her hair with both hands,* SHIMA *enters the kitchen area.*) I hate telephones. They scare me.

TATSUNO: Scare you? (*He starts smiling but* SHIMA *remains serious.*)

SHIMA: Yes. It's like talking with someone who's lurking in the dark. Maybe he's not really the person you think he is.

TATSUNO: That's right. It may be an impersonation by some vicious scoundrel.

SHIMA: I didn't mean that kind of fear. Have you ever imagined that if you follow the telephone line far enough, maybe it suddenly ends without going any farther? Perhaps the voice you hear is from another star. Or, from beyond the grave.

TATSUNO: You're surprisingly romantic, aren't you?

SHIMA: I don't mind if you make fun of me. But you're the only one who hears the voice on the other end of the line even when someone is right next to you. And as you pick up the receiver, the person near you suddenly becomes distant. And the voice on the line is heard from far away . . . I never feel so lonely as when I'm talking over the phone.

TATSUNO: I see. There are no witnesses, and no evidence remains afterwards. And so nothing you hear sounds strange.

(*Short pause.*)

SHIMA (*sipping her coffee*): Come to think of it, from the very beginning my relationship was like a telephone conversation. Murai was definitely right before my eyes, but we had no witnesses. We had no mutual friends, and I never mentioned him to anyone. And now I'm not quite sure that he ever existed in this world.

TATSUNO (*smiles sardonically*): Like with me, for the last five months.

SHIMA: Oh? We didn't even talk seriously about anything. You and I only met . . .

TATSUNO (*quietly but sharply*): You said you didn't talk seriously with Murai, either. Have you forgotten?

SHIMA (*slightly confused*): Oh? Well, we didn't talk seriously about anything. Obviously, he wasn't that type. But he could open his mouth. Don't be silly. That's natural.

TATSUNO (*slowly drinks up the coffee and in a serious tone*): Did you discuss marriage?

SHIMA (*silently, she takes a cigarette from the table and lights it; while she quietly exhales the smoke*): Are we going into that, too?

TATSUNO (*deliberately rises in a comic fashion and as he pours coffee into their respective cups*): As a matter of fact, I was worried since morning that I'd have to prepare breakfast like this, even after we got married.

SHIMA (*coldly*): Oh? Were you really worried about that?

TATSUNO: Naturally. It's a terrible situation.

SHIMA: Don't you actually prefer a wife who lets her husband do the chores in the morning and rises graceful and beautiful?

TATSUNO: How about you? Do you want a husband who puts on an apron in the morning and stands in the kitchen?

SHIMA: I don't care.

TATSUNO: You may have to go out and do a full day's work.

SHIMA: I still hold down a job. I don't especially care for it, but I should be able to make enough to support the two of us.

TATSUNO: And suppose I don't like that?

SHIMA: It doesn't bother me. I frankly prefer housework. How about you?

TATSUNO: Unfortunately, I've never thought about it.

SHIMA: Then what do you think—watching me?

TATSUNO: Well, I could have it either way.

SHIMA: Actually, you haven't been watching me too closely.

TATSUNO: Is it something I could decide by watching—like this?

SHIMA: Of course, you can! But you never try to understand.

TATSUNO: Then how about you? What kind of a home would you like to have if I were your husband? Will you carry on as you are, or will you live decently, in a conventional fashion? How many children—just one, or ten?

SHIMA: I don't know. I've never thought of you in those terms.

TATSUNO: I see . . . But were you thinking of Murai in those terms?

SHIMA: Of course not! I didn't even discuss such matters with him.

TATSUNO (*suddenly, firmly*): Why not?

SHIMA: But, after all . . .

TATSUNO: Why not? You certainly aren't going to tell me he wasn't that type?

SHIMA (*mumbles*): I thought . . . I thought he should decide such things by himself. I was willing to follow him quietly.

TATSUNO: Then, suppose I've already made up my mind to marry you? Would you quietly follow me?

(*Long silence.*)

SHIMA (*nods firmly*): Yes.

TATSUNO: In other words, you're willing to marry me?

SHIMA: Yes.

TATSUNO (*suddenly cries out*): Liar!

SHIMA: Why? Why should I lie?

TATSUNO (*lighting a cigarette, he puffs roughly, two or three times*): Let's be honest with each other . . . Why do you avoid talking seriously with me?

SHIMA: Have I?

TATSUNO (*nods firmly*): Of course, I remember what you once said. You told me that when you're talking intimately with someone, you get confused about your own identity and your own feelings. You said that to live with a man, you didn't want to analyze your own feelings. Rather, you preferred to remain silent and be taken by force. Though I understood what you said, I thought they were just figures of speech. You weren't a schoolgirl anymore, so I thought you wanted to avoid such embarrassing topics as romance and love. But for the last five months, you've literally refused all conversations with me. We meet at the apartment, eat out, come back, and sleep together. We merely chat about the day's news or about a novel you've finished reading . . . Nothing else. When it came to things like finding out more about ourselves or planning our future together, you always cleverly avoided them, even when I brought them up.

SHIMA (*quietly shaking her head*): Well, you didn't really want to talk about them, either.

TATSUNO: I certainly tried. At least, two or three times. Have you forgotten?

SHIMA: No. But you did it knowing full well that I'd refuse to talk about them. You took comfort in that and brought them up as though you were joking . . .

TATSUNO: I did? Why?

SHIMA: Whenever you talked about such things, you always chose Murai as the topic of conversation. You'd ask: "What would Murai do?" or "What would Murai think?"—under similar circumstances.

TATSUNO: Well, that couldn't be helped.

SHIMA: Yes, I knew that you weren't doing that, just to be nasty. But why do you have such interest in Murai? Why do you show more concern for him than me? Why do you always want to know how Murai felt about me rather than to form your own opinion?

TATSUNO (*rising slowly, he walks back and forth across the room; then self-mockingly*): Probably because you treated me as if I were Murai's alter ego. . . . Though you claimed our personalities were the very opposite, you still tried living with me in exactly the same way you did with him before, as in some kind of farce. Isn't that true? You once laughed, saying the both of you lived like cave animals. But are we behaving any differently?

SHIMA: Dearest . . . Were you angry over that?

TATSUNO: No. Still, I'd like to know the reason why.

SHIMA: I can't live any other way with a man. I told you that at the beginning. I think it's sad, too . . . But . . . But you must force me to change my present course of behavior.

TATSUNO: I wonder? If that's the case, there's something unnatural about you. The other night you came here while I was sleeping and quietly crawled in under the covers. And I can distinctly recall what your action meant. When I woke up in surprise, didn't you raise your voice and laugh? I clearly realized, then. When Murai is present, I don't exist at all—for you. And you're repeatedly trying to make me feel that I don't exist. Ha, ha, ha, ha. If I were just an ordinary man, I guess I'd have been angry over the terrible humiliation.

SHIMA: Why aren't you?

(*Suddenly, her voice becomes high and piercing,* TATSUNO *turns around in surprise. As* SHIMA *tries to suppress her mounting emotion.*)

Well, why don't you get angry? Why don't you tell me, "I'm Tatsuno. Stop treating me like Murai"? Why didn't you force your thoughts and your desires on me, instead of making them all sound like a joke? You called it my farce. Well, why didn't you break up this farce and make me feel that you existed as a genuine person?

(*Wildly, she covers her face. Taken back,* TATSUNO *inadvertently places his hands on her shoulders.*)

TATSUNO: My dearest . . My dearest.

SHIMA: What do you really want to do? What kind of a woman do you want? Tell me what you're really like!

(*She suppresses her crying. Long pause.*)

TATSUNO (*finally, as he sits on the window ledge, speaks gently*): At least last night I thought I told you what were seriously on my mind. It wasn't much, but it was really what I wanted to do now. But you were against it. However, you gave me no reason. Ever since then, I've felt there was something strange about you. What happened?

SHIMA (*raising her head quietly*): You mean about quitting your present company and changing jobs?

TATSUNO: Right. It's not especially risky. I thought I'd like to set up my own business because I have certain contacts.

SHIMA (*quietly but decisively*): I don't like it. I just don't.

TATSUNO: But why not? I thought it would be more convenient if we planned to get married.

SHIMA: Is that the only reason?

TATSUNO: Not exactly. I'm bothered about settling down as a company man. I don't have any big plans, but I thought at this point I'd like to try something different.

SHIMA: You say you've already changed jobs?

TATSUNO: Yes, about three times.

SHIMA: Did something unpleasant happen?

TATSUNO: Nothing special. I simply lost the strong desire to stay on where I was working. I had no reason to quit. You might say I didn't find any reason to stay on.

SHIMA: Were you glad you changed?

TATSUNO: Not particularly. Though it kept me distracted for a while. You've got to get used to a new job. And you've clearly got a reason to stay on, at least, during that time.

(SHIMA *remains silent.*)

Look here. There's nothing for you to worry about. I may not be the ambitious type, but I don't have many failures, either.

SHIMA (*suddenly, she rises and takes the coffee cups, etc., to the drainboard*): I still don't like it. If you want my opinion, I'm absolutely against it.

TATSUNO: Hey, what's the matter? Are you leaving? Hey!

(*He begins to rise. At that moment,* NISHIKI *appears from the hallway in a flurry and opens the door without knocking. He is extremely excited, breathing heavily; his eyes are strangely set.*)

NISHIKI: Mr. Tatsuno! You didn't come, after all! Though you sounded so sincere, you finally broke your promise!

TATSUNO: Promise? What promise?

(*While he remains speechless,* NISHIKI *collapses into a nearby chair.*)

NISHIKI: Don't act innocent! Maybe this is half in fun for you, but to me it's a matter of life and death. Have you forgotten? Hadn't we decided this morning to have it out with my museum director?

TATSUNO: Have it out? You mean, about the statue of Buddha?

NISHIKI: What else? Thanks to you, I met the director by myself. I may be old, but I'm not a coward like you. I looked at him straight in the eyes and yelled at him. And as a result, beginning tomorrow I'm magnificently unemployed.

TATSUNO: Aren't you drunk, Mr. Nishiki?

NISHIKI: Of course not. I only had a sip. The director became very angry precisely because I was quite sober when I rebuked him.

TATSUNO: And how did it turn out?

NISHIKI (*laughs strangely*): Mr. Tatsuno, a totally evil person is amazingly clever. Listen to this. That statue was sent off to America yesterday and won't be back for six months.

TATSUNO: To America?

NISHIKI: It seems that there's a traveling exhibition over there. And only that piece was selected from our museum. Ha, ha, ha. What a neat trick! If in six months they find something peculiar about that statue, it would be impossible to determine when it happened.

TATSUNO: But Mr. Nishiki, did you have it out with the director without the actual statue in front of you?

NISHIKI: Why, of course! Nishiki Heigo is no coward. I may be fooled, but I won't easily compromise.

TATSUNO: And you bluntly told him it was a fake?

NISHIKI: Naturally. Moreover, I told him everything about the scheme I saw through—from the name of the powerful individual who stole the original to the technique of making a fake. Ha, ha, ha, ha, ha. By the time I finished, the director had turned completely pale.

TATSUNO: That's crazy, Mr. Nishiki!

NISHIKI: What's crazy about it? You'll never know how scared I was. I was so scared I was shaking like a leaf as I waited for you in front of the director's house. But I couldn't wait any longer. As soon as I stepped inside the gate, I charged ahead

like a steed with severed reins. Thanks to your cowardly behavior, this Nishiki Heigo won't have to feel ashamed anymore. Now I've fully redeemed myself before my old comrade
who committed suicide so gallantly—long ago.

(*He prayerfully closes his eyes. Anxiously,* SHIMA *gazes into* TA-
TSUNO's *face.*)

SHIMA: Did you really promise him?

TATSUNO: Well, I said I'd go with him to the director's house. But
we were supposed to talk it over once more before we went.

NISHIKI: Let's have no weak excuses. Young people nowadays are
all blabbermouthed cowards. You and that Murai, too.

SHIMA: Murai? (*Suddenly, showing interest.*)

NISHIKI: That's right. He was your lover, wasn't he? He was also
a big liar. He promised to go with me to see the director but
disappeared on that very day.

TATSUNO (*becoming attentive*): Is that true, Mr. Nishiki?

NISHIKI: I've a good memory. And I'll never forget that for the
rest of my life. I thought he was a superficial and disagreeable
man from the very beginning.

TATSUNO: But didn't you say he was a kind, altogether splendid
person?

NISHIKI: Hmm. He was a terrible flatterer. He said he envied me.

TATSUNO: Envied you? That's what I said . . .

NISHIKI: No, he definitely said that. I wouldn't forget. He said he
envied me because I had something which I could really get
involved in. He said he was sorry he was of the postwar generation and had nothing like that at all. Hmm. He hands you a
good line and mocks you . . .

TATSUNO: Perhaps he wasn't mocking you, after all.

NISHIKI (*curtly*): Then, why did he make such a promise, filling
me with false hope? And leave me high and dry? Isn't he just
toying with people to amuse himself?

TATSUNO: But I'm different. I really am. And even in Mr. Murai's·
case . . . (*Suddenly, he stops short and gazes at* SHIMA.) I don't
understand. What do you think? And how about Murai . . .

SHIMA (*avoiding his gaze, she lays her face down on the table and
weakly says*): I'm going now.

TATSUNO: Don't go! Shima, what kind of man was Murai, really?

SHIMA: I don't know. I told you that before.

TATSUNO: Don't go, Shima! . . . Mr. Nishiki, if you don't mind, could you please leave now? I'll drop over later, for sure, and explain about the promise . . .

NISHIKI (*suddenly, he collapses on the top of the table and begins groaning; in a feeble voice*): Please let me stay. Let me remain as I am . . . Where do you want me to go? I've no job anymore. How do you expect me to face my family?

(*Speechless,* TATSUNO *and* SHIMA *gaze at each other.*)

TATSUNO: This is just great! He's dead drunk.

SHIMA: Maybe he's sick.

TATSUNO: It can't be helped. Give me a hand . . . Now, Mr. Nishiki, why don't you take a rest over here for a while. You'll feel better after a nap. Here we go . . .

(*The two take hold of him and help* NISHIKI *up. As they lay him on the bedding, like a child, he no longer offers any resistance.* TATSUNO *and* SHIMA *return to the large room and sighing with relief look at each other.*)

SHIMA: I'm still going.

TATSUNO: Oh, don't go. I think we've finally reached a stage where we can talk seriously.

SHIMA: Perhaps you're right.

TATSUNO: We have to be clear on Murai. Otherwise, our relationship will never improve.

SHIMA: I agree . . . That's why I'm going. I'll phone you later.

TATSUNO: Have you something to think over seriously?

SHIMA: Yes. I have.

TATSUNO: Hold on! You're hiding something from me.

(*The two eye each other fiercely. At that moment, outside in the hallway, a young man, apparently a college student, and an old man past seventy, apparently a teacher, make their entrance and knock on the door.*)

Yes, who is it?

(*He opens the door and cautiously eyes the pair. The young man bows briskly.*)

TAKAI: Ah, I'm Takai Hajime. I'm in the Mountaineering Club of the Agricultural College.

IWAKAMI (*The man appearing to be a teacher presents his name card*): How do you do. I'm Iwakami Genzō, a retired schoolteacher.

TATSUNO: And . . . What brings you here?

TAKAI: We just met downstairs. We both wanted to see Mr. Murai . . . You do know Mr. Murai, don't you? We're looking for him.

TATSUNO: But he's not . . .

(*When he tries to push back* TAKAI, *who is half way through the door,* IWAKAMI *marches in.*)

IWAKAMI: Yes, we heard about that downstairs at the office. But we thought you might tell us something recent about Mr. Murai . . . Actually, he was a pupil of mine in junior high school. For the past ten years, I've been trying to locate him, for personal reasons. I finally thought I'd found his correct address, but I was too late in reaching him there. As I was feeling quite disappointed, I heard you were also trying to find him. And though I realize my impertinence, I decided to come up, hoping you would tell me all you know . . .

TATSUNO: I see. You were Mr. Murai's teacher.

TAKAI (*cheerfully*): I don't have any special reason. I happened to meet Mr. Murai in the mountains last fall. At that time, he told me to drop in and see him. When I asked someone about him recently, I found out he was apparently a very active mountaineer during his college days. And that suddenly stirred my interest and I came to visit him. It intrigued me more than ever when I heard he had disappeared.

TATSUNO (*annoyed*): Disappeared? We still don't know that.

TAKAI: From what they tell me, he's the type who might very well do that. And I became convinced of it when I heard this teacher's story. Isn't that right, sir?

IWAKAMI: Well, that's hard to say.

(*A few moments of silence.*)

TATSUNO (*suddenly has a thought*): I see. Then Mr. Iwakami must know a great deal about Mr. Murai!

IWAKAMI: No, not very much. He was a bit different. And he's strangely fixed in my memory.

TATSUNO: I understand. . . . In any case, Mr. Iwakami, it's rather awkward standing here. Won't you step in for a moment? By an odd coincidence, everyone here was involved with Mr. Murai. (*Curiously cheerful, he arranges the chairs around the table.*)

SHIMA: Hiroshi! (*She calls out* TATSUNO's *first name in a harsh, rebuking tone.*)

TATSUNO (*ignoring her, in a deliberately light-hearted manner*): Well, please sit down, Mr. Iwakami. I'm sure everyone will be delighted to hear your story.

(*With a fixed expression,* SHIMA *stands stiffly. In the adjacent* tatami *room,* NISHIKI *anxiously raises himself, slowly.*)

IWAKAMI (*becoming uneasy in this unsettled atmosphere*): I've dropped in so suddenly today. And I can see you're all busy. I'll come again . . .

TATSUNO: Not at all. This is Mr. Nishiki Heigo, an old friend of Mr. Murai's. He's had a little too much to drink today and is recovering. Well, Mr. Nishiki, do you mind?

(NISHIKI *bows meekly.*)

SHIMA: I'm leaving.

(*As she tries to slip by him,* TATSUNO *lays his hand on* SHIMA's *shoulder to restrain her.*)

TATSUNO: And this is Miss Sawada Shima. She was Mr. Murai's best friend. Though it may sound strange, in this group, I know the least about Mr. Murai. So please don't stand on ceremony. Shima, do you mind preparing the tea?

(*A few uneasy moments.* IWAKAMI *looks at both* SHIMA *and* NISHIKI *with a troubled expression. Finally,* SHIMA, *apparently resigned, gently brushes aside* TATSUNO's *hand and stands in front of the drainboard.*)

TAKAI: Mr. Iwakami, why don't you try reading that composition? I thought it was rather interesting that such a cheerful and talkative person had understood himself so well, even in his days in junior high school.

(*While speaking,* TAKAI *prods* IWAKAMI *from the back, and the pair enter the room and take their places.*)

IWAKAMI: Well, we'll only stay briefly . . .

TATSUNO (*referring to* TAKAI's *previous statement*): Did you just say that Mr. Murai was cheerful and talkative? Are you sure?

TAKAI: Yes, of course. You rarely find someone who talks that much about himself. We had only met for the first time. As we hiked in the mountains, he talked all day long about work, about women, and so on. Besides, he was very good at it.

(*Short pause.*)

TATSUNO: I see. So it was true, after all.

(*He quietly looks toward* SHIMA. *With her back toward him, she stops preparing tea and remains frozen. Finally,* TATSUNO *turns around, facing* IWAKAMI.)

And what about the composition?

IWAKAMI: Yes. I kept about fifty interesting papers written by students while I was teaching. After my retirement, I got the idea of traveling leisurely around Japan to find out how my former students had all turned out. It's been about five years now. When you meet them again, in this way, you realize that human existence is a sad thing. The former students who best recalled their junior high school days and showed the greatest fondness for me were the very ones who had not achieved what you might call success. Apparently, those who are the most insecure in their present existence and have failed to firmly establish themselves are more likely to seek their roots in memories of bygone days in junior high school. (*Forced, lonely smile.*) I'd want to carry on this pilgrimage especially for these students. Still, this Murai has been a problem. I've already made the rounds of five apartments and places of employment. But each time, I've been too late.

TATSUNO: And how was he regarded at these places?

IWAKAMI: Well, he had a very good reputation wherever I went. And as Takai just said, he was apparently a friendly and considerate fellow. He also talked a great deal about his own person and career. Of course, there were points on which I couldn't quite agree.

TATSUNO: You couldn't agree? . . . For example?

IWAKAMI: Well, they're rather minor. And they concern mostly his hometown and childhood.

TATSUNO (*sighing deeply*): That he had an old house in the San'in area and that he would eventually take over his father's work and look after the estate . . .

IWAKAMI: Yes, he said something like that.

TATSUNO: And they're lies?

IWAKAMI: That's putting it rather strongly . . . But I suppose so. He was an evacuee from Manchuria and lost his father over there.

(*Short pause.* SHIMA *slowly turns around and gazes at* TATSUNO *as*

she supports herself against the drainboard. Returning a stern look,
TATSUNO *speaks gravely.*)
TATSUNO: Shima, you knew this before, didn't you? Am I right?
(*Silent,* SHIMA *remains frozen.* TATSUNO *addresses* IWAKAMI, *who
appears dumbfounded over the current mood.*)
    I'm sorry, sir. Could you show us Mr. Murai's composition?
    Or, perhaps, if you don't mind, could you read it?
IWAKAMI: It's not as interesting as you think. Besides, it's half
    torn and rather short.
TATSUNO: Never mind that. Please let us hear it.
(SHIMA *covers her face with both hands.*)
IWAKAMI: Well, in that case . . . (*He takes out a stack of old com-
    position paper from the inside breast pocket and slowly turns the
    pages.*) The title . . . Oh, yes, it's called, "Trees." They're the
    kind growing in the mountains . . . Well, let me begin: "I was
    repatriated from Manchuria. There is no country of Manchuria
    anywhere. It never existed from the beginning. My father
    worked as an official of Manchuria. So if he died, it would not
    be in the line of duty. My friends say he met a useless, 'dog's
    death.' When I asked them if that made me a pup, they said,
    'That's right.' A pup does not have a home into which it is
    born and no primary school from which it graduates. These, of
    course, did not disappear. They never existed from the
    beginning. My friends ask me if I miss my home and school in
    Manchuria. This question does not mean much to me. While I
    was being raised in Manchuria, my parents told me I should
    never miss my home in Japan. And now my teachers say I
    must forget the past and live for the future. So, wherever I go
    from here on I will probably never long for the past or feel
    lonely. Maybe I will become the most cheerful and the liveliest
    person in Japan. Still, I sometimes wonder. Is someone like
    that really happy?" . . . Unfortunately, the rest is torn off. The
    title was "Trees," but there's no mention of it here. Since I did
    give him a grade of ninety, he must have written about it fur-
    ther on in an interesting way. Ha, ha, ha, ha. I still remember.
    He had been reading Sōseki's[7] *I Am a Cat*[8] at the time, outside
    of class. And there's a touch of that in his writing.

[7] Born 1867, died 1916. An important modern Japanese novelist.
[8] *Wagahai wa Neko de aru* (1905), one of Natsume Sōseki's earlier satirical novels
with a cat as a narrator.

(*Silently,* TATSUNO *gazes at* SHIMA.)

TAKAI (*excitedly*): Now, isn't that interesting! How about it? I think Mr. Murai is quite talented.

TATSUNO (*ignoring* TAKAI, *he blurts out*): You knew about this, Shima? And about everything else?

(SHIMA *twists herself around to face away from him.*)

IWAKAMI (*as if trying to determine* TATSUNO's *feelings*): Even so, I wonder what it's all about? If he was so well liked at work, why couldn't Murai settle down in one spot? He's sociable, and I think it's about time he found a suitable marriage partner.

TAKAI (*becoming enthusiastic*): I asked Mr. Murai about that. He said he has a strange habit. As soon as he gets good at anything, he wants to run away from it . . . When I asked around, everyone agreed he's a fantastic fellow. He took first place in a photography contest in senior high school and sold a number of pictures to magazines and advertising agencies. He could have become a professional if he had kept it up. But he didn't want his entire life decided so soon. He majored in law at college and quickly passed the bar examination. After that, he started painting, and his work impressed an American art critic. He was invited to New York and spent three years studying leisurely. Still, for some reason, a career as an artist didn't agree with him. According to Mr. Murai, he finally had to get away from himself. He's worked at several jobs since then, but as soon as everything began to go his way, he always wanted to run away. He's terribly afraid that he would be cast into a particular role. I just can't understand him. He's also a professional race car driver and has made very difficult climbs alone as a mountaineer.

TATSUNO (*listens nervously but finally unable to suppress his annoyance*): You're . . . You're so naive!

TAKAI: I beg your pardon?

TATSUNO: Of course, you are. Mr. Murai has a habit of lying. You were being teased.

TAKAI: That's not true. And I've checked on his mountaineering.

TATSUNO: But he seems to have displayed quite a different side of himself to Shima.

SHIMA: Murai wasn't lying! (*Finally, unable to contain herself,*

SHIMA *cries out in a gasping voice.*) He was exactly as Mr. Takai described him! I lied!

(*Sighing deeply,* TATSUNO *closes his eyes.* SHIMA *sits down limply in a nearby chair.*)

IWAKAMI: Ah, we must be getting along . . .

(*Sternly,* TATSUNO *restrains* IWAKAMI, *who is timidly beginning to rise from his chair, intimidated by the eerie atmosphere.*)

TATSUNO: Please wait! You must stay a little longer! (*With a trembling hand,* TATSUNO *reaches into his pocket and frantically searches for a pack of cigarettes. The first two he finds are empty, and finally from the third pack he pulls out a single, bent cigarette and holds it in his mouth. The packs, which had been roughly thrown on the table, are all of different brands.*)

TAKAI (*somewhat overwhelmed by all this development and now trying to restore the mood in this setting*): Oh, you mix your brands, too. Like Mr. Murai.

TATSUNO: What do you mean by that?

TAKAI: He was different, you know. He never settled on a single brand though even a student like me usually has his own favorite . . .

TATSUNO: Maybe he had an insensitive taste.

TAKAI: It wasn't that. He said he couldn't make up his mind because he was able to clearly distinguish the unique flavor of the various brands. When Mr. Murai was still young, different brands were introduced and taken off the market in rapid succession. He was laughing as he said his generation might be characterized by its absence of a favorite brand.

TATSUNO (*suddenly, crushing the cigarette he was smoking, he rises. He struggles to hold back his impulse to shout.*) Mr. Iwakami, what did you think of Mr. Murai as a student?

IWAKAMI: What do you mean?

TATSUNO: Did you like him? Or, dislike him?

IWAKAMI: Does that really matter?

TATSUNO: I absolutely despise kids like this Murai. There were plenty of them around. They'd transfer from other schools and frantically try to become part of the class. When we saw a kid like that, we'd all gang up on him. We'd hide his lunch, and—oh, yes—we'd tear up his composition—like *that*.

IWAKAMI: But why? That's so . . .

TATSUNO: No special reason. We just didn't like them. Kids who timidly but cleverly make their way in class. They're vile like fungi or parasites. A majestic tree growing in the forest dies gallantly once it's transplanted elsewhere. Even kids understand that much among themselves. Anyone would hate them. Let's be honest, Mr. Iwakami, didn't you really dispise kids like that? (*He is almost shouting as he ends his speech.*)

IWAKAMI (*even he grows angry and rises*): I'm sorry. What's wrong with all of you? What's this about? This is too much!

(*Firmly grasping the table with both hands,* TATSUNO *lays his face down. Pause.*)

SHIMA: I'll . . . I'll try to explain it to Mr. Iwakami. (*A single tear runs down her cheek.*) You see, Murai left me because he couldn't love me anymore. It was my fault. I pressed him for an answer . . . I didn't want to be simply treated gently or playfully . . . I said I wanted to be loved . . . He was honest. He just couldn't respond to my demands.

TATSUNO: Excuse me. I'm going out to cool off. (*Briskly crossing the room and going out into the hallway, he closes the door behind him.*)

SHIMA (*shutting her eyes and as if struggling to convince herself*): And I also realized that it was impossible for him to love anyone, including me. (*Slowly shaking her head.*) No one . . . Yes, like his cigarettes. (*Suddenly burying her face in her hands.*) I was afraid because Mr. Tatsuno resembled him. And I didn't want to repeat that same mistake. I was determined to make it work this time.

(*After a single cry escapes from* SHIMA's *throat, she trips along after* TATSUNO, *who has already left the room, and rushes out into the hallway. She brushes aside* TATSUNO, *who happens to be leaning on the door, and presses her forehead against the opposite wall. Inside,* TAKAI *half rises from the chair in surprise but appears helpless. Silently, he and* IWAKAMI *gaze at each other;* TAKAI *sits down again. Long pause.*)

TATSUNO (*finally, as though in a monologue, self-mockingly*): This farce was more complicated than I thought. And the plot was different from the one I had in mind. I don't mean just Murai . . . Shima, you turned out to be a very ordinary, gentle girl.

And you needed someone with whom you could share a mutual understanding like anyone else and a man who could express his love for you with conviction.

(*A faint sob escapes from* SHIMA's *throat.*)

Don't you agree? Then why didn't you tell me this honestly, from the beginning? I'm not Murai. If you had been honest with me, everything might have worked out fine.

(*Turning around completely,* SHIMA *silently gazes at* TATSUNO.)

Why did you think up that farce? Why didn't you try to speak for yourself rather than speak to me through words picked up from Murai?

SHIMA: Then let me ask you. Why did you go along with this farce? Why did you try to assume the role I assigned to you, which was the exact opposite of your real character? (*Her quiet voice is drained of all emotion as if she had become totally resigned.*) You assumed so happily and completely the role of Murai I created for you as though you had been spared the responsibility . . .

TATSUNO (*forcefully, as if brushing aside her remark*): I'm not Murai. I don't even look like him. You had no reason at all to fear me.

SHIMA: That's not true! You were actually afraid of yourself. I knew that from the instant I saw you. That's why it didn't matter whether it was a farce or not. I wanted somehow to keep myself from pestering you for an answer.

TATSUNO: That's ironic. And thanks to this farce, you've done exactly that by pressing me for an answer.

(*Long pause.*)

SHIMA (*whispering*): I guess we're through . . .

(*Without responding,* TATSUNO *turns his back on her. Again, pause.*)

SHIMA (*in a low, firm voice*): That's right. Now that you thoroughly despise yourself.

(*Deliberately,* TATSUNO *looks back, and the two gaze at each other, sadly. At that moment,* NISHIKI *suddenly emits a strange, low laugh from the bedroom.* IWAKAMI *and* TAKAI *stand up in surprise.*)

NISHIKI (*still on his back and without looking at them*): Ha, ha, ha, ha. Don't be fooled, everyone. That fellow may call himself Tatsuno, but he's lying through his teeth. He's actually Murai

Toyojirō, using an alias. Of course, Murai may be an alias, too. And beginning tomorrow, Tatsuno may use another name. Ha, ha, ha, ha.

(*That laughter resounds mysteriously; it suggests a clearly abnormal state of mind.*)

Listen, everybody, do you know why that guy uses a train of aliases? Ha, ha, ha, ha. It's because he's afraid of me. And he's afraid of my wrath and the wrath of my dead wartime comrades. Yes, it's no use trying to escape. You pandering coward!

(IWAKAMI *and* TAKAI *gaze breathless at* NISHIKI. *Outside the apartment, both* TATSUNO *and* SHIMA, *who faces him, slowly back away as if they are retreating from a frightening thing. As* NISHIKI'*s long, low weird laughter fills the entire stage, the curtain falls slowly.*)

Epilogue

Toward evening on a clear day, about two weeks after Act Three.

The setting is still TATSUNO'*s apartment, but all the household furniture has been piled up in one corner, and the footlocker and the bedding bag have been pulled out to the center of the large room, suggesting the preparation for moving has been completed. The suit is placed in such a manner so that the audience's attention is naturally drawn to it.*

(*Sitting on the footlocker,* SATOMI *begins to address* TATSUNO, *who stands by the window with the rays of the evening sun on his face.*)

SATOMI: How many months have you stayed in this apartment?

TATSUNO: Nearly six.

SATOMI: I never liked this apartment from the very beginning. Still, things have taken a surprising turn.

TATSUNO: That's right.

SATOMI: Don't worry. I'm finished talking. I've got nothing more to say.

TATSUNO: I'm sorry, Satomi.

SATOMI: Never mind. Once I've resigned myself to it, I feel this may be the best thing for you. It's just like you to go back to the country and start a business of your own. Maybe it's fate. Only, take care of yourself.

TATSUNO: Thanks.

SATOMI: And thanks to you, I can quit being a matchmaker. I'll miss that, but it's a relief, too.

TATSUNO: I'm sorry.

SATOMI: Don't be silly. You can't win against ghosts and evil spirits.

(*Short pause. As* TATSUNO *stares out of the window, he whistles "The Boat Is a Sailboat."* SATOMI *addresses him from the back, rather somberly.*)

What I say now may sound like crying over spilt milk, but wasn't that Sawada girl crazy about you? Frankly, I'm more worried about her. Haven't you made a mistake again?

(TATSUNO *stops whistling and slowly turns around but remains silent.*)

Listen, Tatsuno, everything else may be hopeless, but what about seeing her just once more? I think there's still a chance.

(*Silently,* TATSUNO *shakes his head.*)

Then it's all finished between you two? But this time weren't you more serious?

TATSUNO: Yes—at first. In any case, we were meeting in that rather bizarre fashion . . . Now, I think that girl still loved Murai.

SATOMI: But how about your own feelings?

(*Short pause.*)

TATSUNO (*sitting on the window ledge*): As a matter of fact, I met her twice after that.

SATOMI: And . . . How did it go?

TATSUNO: How can I put it? It's like suddenly coming across a lover in broad daylight after always meeting her in a pitch-black tunnel.

SATOMI: You were disillusioned?

TATSUNO: No. But I certainly became afraid of seeing her anymore.

SATOMI: Still, weren't you at least in love with her while the two of you were in that tunnel?

TATSUNO: That's what I'm not sure of. It might be several years before I can see that clearly.

SATOMI (*sighing and shaking his head*): And when you finally find out, it'll be too late. Isn't it always that way? (*Rising slowly.*)

TATSUNO:

> Did you come to me
> Or have I gone to you
> I do not remember![9]

. . . Do you know that poem?

SATOMI: What's that?

TATSUNO:

> Was it dream or reality?
> Was I sleeping or awake?[10]

. . . It's from the *Tales of Ise*. Long ago, a man spent the night with an altar virgin of the Great Shrine of Ise.[11] The woman casually steals into his bedroom as if she were possessed. And the two part company without saying much to each other. The next morning, the guy, saddened over this brief encounter, sends her the poem I just quoted.

SATOMI: Now that you mention it, it does sound familiar.

TATSUNO: The two definitely made love, but why did it happen? Which one was in love? Was it only a passing fancy? Though it's quite clear that it all happened, it's impossible to find out what it meant to the parties involved. It suddenly came to me. I feel kind of strange when I realize that lovers like Shima and me were living, even in those days.

(*At that moment,* THE MOVER *and* THE SECONDHAND DEALER *enter from the hallway into the apartment with their several assistants.* THE MOVER *takes out the footlocker and the bedding bag to the hallway.*)

THE MOVER: So, this is all the furniture you want shipped. And you're leaving the rest for the secondhand dealer?

TATSUNO (*cheerfully*): Not quite. Take along that old rocking chair, too. Mr. Secondhand Dealer can't seem to take this off my hands.

THE SECONDHAND DEALER (*scratching his head with an exaggerated*

[9] See Fritz Vos, trans., *A Study of Ise Monogatari: With the Text according to the Den-Teika-Hippon and an Annotated Translation* (The Hague: Mouton & Company, 1957), I, 227. This poem is found in section LXIX of *Ise Monogatari* (Tales of Ise), a collection of short prose tales cast around poems describing incidents in the life of a celebrated romantic hero. It is regarded as an early tenth century work.

[10] *Ibid.* The continuation of the above poem.

[11] See *ibid.*, II, 119–22, for a detailed analysis of the whole section and the present poem.

gesture): I'm sorry. It's not worth the trouble. Nowadays, this business is getting tough, too.

(*He orders his assistants to carry out the rest of the chairs and the table and leaves with* THE MOVER. *The room becomes bare, highlighting the solitary rocking chair.*)

TATSUNO (*glancing around the room once more*): Well, shall we go, Satomi?

YUMI (*enters hastily*): Ah, is there anything I can do to help? You haven't forgotten anything, have you?

TATSUNO: No, I don't think so. Thanks for everything.

YUMI: Not at all. It's too bad, though. I wanted to get to know you much better, Mr. Tatsuno. Father said you were a fine person and was delighted to have you stay here.

TATSUNO: Thank you. Give him my regards.

YUMI (*lowering her voice slightly*): That reminds me. Father said he spotted Mr. Murai yesterday. He's in Tokyo.

TATSUNO: Oh, really? Where did he see him?

YUMI: He's apparently a taxi driver. Father was waiting for the signal to change at an intersection. He was sure that the cab which stopped in front of him was being driven by Mr. Murai. It pulled away quickly, so he couldn't call out to him. But he says there's no mistake about it.

TATSUNO: I see. That may be true.

YUMI: Mr. Tatsuno, aren't you interested in Mr. Murai anymore?

TATSUNO: Of course I am. But I'm beginning to feel it's better to just wait until I happen to see him somewhere.

YUMI: You may be right. Besides, you're bound to meet him because he moves around so much. Well, I'll be waiting downstairs. And please don't forget to leave the apartment keys.

(YUMI *leaves in a flurry.* SATOMI *gently restrains* TATSUNO, *who is about to follow her.*)

SATOMI: Say, Tatsuno, I hadn't intended to tell you this. Nevertheless, you should at least know about it. I felt terrible doing this, but I asked a friend in the police department about Mr. Murai. Then the other day, the police came to question me. They wanted to know whether Mr. Murai looked like a certain suspected criminal. It sounds ridiculous but . . . (*Silently, he looks at* TATSUNO.) It seems that the outstanding features of this suspect has a marked resemblance to you. And the crime was committed in the same town where you were living at the time.

TATSUNO: And his name?

SATOMI: He apparently used many aliases. They don't really know his true identity.

(TATSUNO *smiles sadly*.)

Of course, I made no mention of you. Still, I think you should be careful.

TATSUNO: Thanks.

SATOMI: Well, I have my car parked away from here, so I'm going ahead to get it.

(SATOMI *makes a hasty exit. Alone,* TATSUNO *tries to whistle softly, but suddenly, as if he had remembered, approaches the phone and dials. Following the ringing, a mechanical voice of a woman is soon heard:* "This is the telephone office. The number you have called is no longer in use, so please check with the operator." TATSUNO *replaces the receiver and tries dialing again, more carefully. The familiar ringing is followed by the same feminine voice:* "This is the telephone office . . ." *Sighing, he replaces the receiver. As he is about to leave the room,* TATSUNO *bumps into* NISHIKI, *who is entering.* NISHIKI *looks silently at* TATSUNO.)

TATSUNO: I won't be staying here anymore, Mr. Nishiki. Please take a long rest and get well. Your museum director says he won't fire you.

NISHIKI (*half whispering*): It doesn't concern me. I don't know you at all. I'm here to see Mr. Murai. Come to think of it, he's still a fine person. He's bound to come back.

TATSUNO (*smiling gently, he firmly says*): Yes, he's a fine person. He'll certainly be back . . . Goodby.

(TATSUNO *bows lightly and goes down and out of the hallway.* NISHIKI *fails to see him off; instead, he goes into the apartment and sits in the rocking chair which has been left behind. After a while, the phone begins to ring. When he silently picks up the receiver,* THE WOMAN'S VOICE *in Act Two is heard on the other end.*)

THE WOMAN'S VOICE: Hello, hello!

(NISHIKI, *with a blank expression, remains silent.*)

Hello! Please get Kawahara. He's there, isn't he? Please, let me just talk to him.

(*When* NISHIKI *still refuses to respond, the caller draws a deep breath and changes her tone.*)

It's you . . . It's you, isn't it? Am I right? Say something! I can't stand it anymore. I've become terribly thin and might just die if I go on like this. Sometimes I go to the front of your apartment building and look up at your room. I don't have the courage to go in, but it does help me to calm down, a little. Besides, your building is made of concrete and built so solidly. And as long as that building stands there, we'll always be . . . Please, say something . . . Anything.

(NISHIKI *slowly replaces the receiver. As he mumbles to himself,* THE MAN *in Act Two enters the door.*)

THE MAN: Hello. Ah, I believe this apartment is vacant. Can I take a look?

NISHIKI (*glaring at him*): No, it's not for rent. Mr. Murai lives here.

THE MAN: That's strange. I was told it would be vacant this month.

NISHIKI: There's no mistake. Mr. Murai will always be living here. As long as this apartment is located on this spot.

THE MAN: I see. Then I'll ask downstairs again. I'm sorry to bother you.

(*As* THE MAN *exits,* THE SECONDHAND DEALER *returns with his assistants.*)

THE SECONDHAND DEALER: Come on, let's get it over with. They don't like it if the junkman hangs around too long. (*Noticing the rocking chair occupied by* NISHIKI.) Well, what do you know! The boss of the movers finally forgot the rocker. What can you do? I guess we'll have to take this over, too . . . Pardon me, can you get up for a second?

(NISHIKI *neither answers nor tries to stand up. The assistants move out all the rest of the household furniture and only* NISHIKI's *rocker remains.*)

Pardon me, sir. We've got to move this out. Can you get up?

(NISHIKI *pays no attention and fails to answer.*)

Can't you hear me! Please get up!

(*As* THE SECONDHAND DEALER *lays his hand on the rocking chair, without a word* NISHIKI *brushes him aside, briskly. Surprised,* THE

SECONDHAND DEALER *exchanges glances with his assistants, but after a few seconds, they signal with their eyes and nod meaningfully to one another. Then they scatter to the four corners of the stage; each, respectively, raises his hand and signals upstage left and upstage right. In the next instant, they all swiftly dismantle the stage setting and begin moving it backstage. The apartment, the kitchen area, and the scenery beyond the windows which appeared so realistic are quickly disassembled and disappear as ten or more panels.)*

(Later, a black curtain is introduced upstage center. In front of it: only NISHIKI *who sits in the rocker, the phone with the severed line, and Murai's suit, hanging on a post.* NISHIKI *wears a blank expression and appears oblivious to what has occurred around him. Finally, the phone begins to ring. Again,* NISHIKI *fails to respond.)*

(As the bell continues to ring, there rises "The Boat Is a Sailboat" sung by a chorus of primary school children:)

> The boat is a sailboat with three masts
> What is a mere thousand leagues of sea . . .

Curtain

The Move

A Play in Six Scenes with a Solemn Epilogue

MINORU BETSUYAKU

Originally published in Japanese as
Idō
(Tokyo: Shinchōsha)
Copyright © 1971 Minoru Betsuyaku
All rights reserved

This play was first performed at Kinokuniya Hall (Tokyo) on September 22, 1973. The performance was directed by Toshirō Hayano.

CHARACTERS
(in order of their appearance)
WOMAN, MAN'S wife
MAN
MAN'S FATHER
MAN'S MOTHER
YOUNG MAN
HUSBAND ⎫
⎬ BILLPOSTERS
HUSBAND'S WIFE ⎭
SECOND MAN
SECOND WOMAN

Scene One

A single telephone pole. Pasted around its base are various posters such as: "Cats To Give Away," "No Urinating," and "For Rent: A Cut-Rate, Six-Mat Room.[1] *Please Telephone." Farther up and girding the pole—a sign: "Yamagami People's Finance Company." Otherwise, the stage is bare. It is brightly lit.*

(Suddenly, a woman appears. She has on a nenneko[2] *and carries a sleeping child on her back. In one hand, she holds a shopping bag with a baby bottle and diapers; in the other, a parasol. She wears socks and a pair of wooden clogs.)*

WOMAN *(looking up at the sky and appearing dazzled by it)*: My, what a surprise! It's such fine weather! After all, yesterday it rained and for six whole days before that . . . Well, why worry about the weather. It only turns out the way it wants to. Mr. Yamada always said, "One thing you can't change is the weather." *(She tests the ground by kicking it.)* It's so hard! My clogs could break. Is it all rock? *(Glancing around.)* That's impossible! There can't be this much of it. "Japan doesn't have such rocky places." Who said that? Mr. Kobayashi. It's something he's likely to say. He wouldn't stop talking until he said something about rocks or mountains. Could be a desert? If that's the case, we've finally reached the desert. Yes, a desert . . . But how strange. There's a telephone pole here. *(Approaching it.)* Is it really a telephone pole? That's exactly what it is. It has wires, which proves electricity is flowing. Mr. Suzuki hanged himself from a pole. Poor fellow . . . *"Yamagami People's Finance Company"* . . . *"Cats To Give Away"* . . . *"No Urinating"* . . . That's terrible! I wonder why they're so concerned with household matters? Still . . . Why did he bother hanging himself from a pole? Even Mrs. Suzuki said, "What a strange way to die . . ." Mr. Yoshida took poison. That's far

[1] One mat is about three feet by six feet.
[2] *Nenneko[banten]*, a quilted, half-length coat used by a Japanese woman for carrying a child on her back during the cold weather. The garment is made to protect both of them comfortably. Along with the other traditional clothing the *nenneko* is fast disappearing from the modern scene.

more natural. I think so. Who committed suicide by gas? Mrs.
Tanaka . . . Yes, I'm sure that's who it was. They said she was
crazy. No wonder, with her husband a drunkard and her child
in *that* condition . . . *"For Rent: A Cut-Rate, Six-Mat Room.
Please Telephone."* Ridiculous! Who's going to read them? Oh,
I see footprints . . . (*Follows them toward stage right, turns
around and comes back.*) What was he doing? . . . Probably
thinking about something. That's why he was walking back
and forth. Mr. Yokota acted the same way. As long as you're
thinking, I think it's far more efficient to remain still . . .
(*Looking toward stage left.*) Oh, it's you, Husband. What happened? Please hurry. I've been waiting such a long time for
you.

(*A cart piled high with various household furnishings appears. The
man pulling it wears an old hat and a well-worn coat; his trouser legs
are rolled up to keep them from soiling.*)

Can't you walk a little faster, Husband? You're always so slow.
At this rate, we won't cover even twelve miles a day. I wonder
if you're overweight? Dr. Kawata said you were. He said you
should be more careful. Aren't you short of breath? That's
why.

(*The cart stops abruptly.*)

MAN: Damn it!

WOMAN: What happened?

MAN: Isn't something stuck in the wheel?

WOMAN: Oh, it's a stone. The cart ran into a stone. You must stay
clear of them. Wait a minute! Maybe I can remove it . . . No,
don't pull the cart! My fingers will get caught. (*Removing the
stone.*) All right, Please be careful. It would be awful if we
wreck this old cart. There's no one around to make repairs in a
place like this . . . Now, if Mr. Takada were here . . . He's so
good at fixing such things. Oh, dear! What happened to Father
and Mother?

MAN: Aren't they around?

WOMAN: Aren't they around, indeed! I told you to keep an eye on
them. After all, they're getting on in years. What if they get
lost? Oh, look! They're sitting over there—of all places! (*Calling
out to them.*) Father! You, too, Mother! You mustn't sit over
there. Husband, please go and fetch them.

MAN: So its *"Yamagami—People's—Finance—Company"* . . .

WOMAN: Husband!

MAN: All right. But get the prop for the cart, Wife. Or else I can't let my hands go!

WOMAN (*taking out the prop from the baggage*): Here you are. This cart has become quite rickety, hasn't it?

MAN: Don't worry. It won't break down so easily. (*Propping the cart, goes to stage left.*) I'm going.

WOMAN (*from behind* MAN): Please hurry! Tell them we should all take a break at the same time. They shouldn't do it on their own. (*After* MAN *is out of hearing range.*) This is impossible! They're old. Still, they travel lightly and . . . Oh, what happened to the tea kettle? Surely, we didn't leave it somewhere again. My husband's so careless. I'm quite sure . . . After we had lunch . . . It was . . . Here it is. It's hopeless. He'll never learn where the kettle belongs. I wonder why he's that way? Whenever we need anything, we have to turn everything upside down . . . It's his character. Maybe he's had poor childhood training. His father isn't that way, though . . . (*Suddenly the alarm clock in the baggage begins ringing.*) Oh! (*Taking the clock from the baggage and turning off the alarm.*) This is terrible. It's already three . . . Yes, actually three o'clock. Already time for tea. And I thought we just had lunch. It's hopeless. We seem to be drinking tea all the time. (*Shaking the child on her back.*) Are you sleeping? You're strangely quiet today. (*Begins taking off her* nenneko.)

(*Carrying* MOTHER *on his back,* MAN *returns leading* FATHER *by the hand.* FATHER *wears a shapeless, black formal suit and a hat. He has a canteen strapped slantwise down from one shoulder and uses an umbrella for a cane.* MOTHER *wears an old one-piece dress and a wide-brimmed hat.* MAN *holds her cane and one of her shoes.*)

My! My! My! What in the world happened?

FATHER: She has a corn. The shoe didn't bother her until now . . . Are you going to put down the baby, Daughter? (FATHER *helps her.*)

WOMAN: Thank you. Please be careful. Is it all right? (*Lets* FATHER *hold the child.*)

FATHER: Don't worry. There, there . . . Oh, is he sleeping?

WOMAN (*approaching* MOTHER): How's your corn? Oh, dear, it's raw. You'd better put on some medicine. It might get infected.

MAN: Wife! Make some room for me. I simply have to put Mother down. (*Setting her down.*)

MOTHER: Well, well! I thought the shoes were broken in. (*Examining the shoes.*)

WOMAN: The shoes have lost their shape. You've walked in them for quite a while. Did you buy them at Mr. Miki's? He's no good. It may be a little farther on, but you should have gone to the next store. You know . . .

MOTHER: You mean Tamura's?

MAN: Wife, where's the first aid kit?

WOMAN: I don't know. Must be somewhere. Didn't Father take some stomach powder last night? . . . Tamura's shoes last longer though their styles aren't as good.

FATHER: Yes. I'm sure it's somewhere below the refrigerator . . .

WOMAN: Never mind. Please get the chairs down, Husband. I'll find the first aid kit.

MAN: Get the chairs down?

MOTHER: I'm all right.

WOMAN: But it's already three. We can't help it. It's teatime.

MAN: Teatime? Well, well.

MOTHER: I thought it was getting to be that time. Have we any more cheese crackers?

WOMAN: I think so. (*Searching for the first aid kit.*) Where is it? I can't find it.

FATHER: Why bother? It's only a corn. Put some saliva on it.

MOTHER: Suppose it gets infected?

FATHER: It won't if you put saliva on it. Much better than some worthless medicine.

MOTHER: That's just superstition.

FATHER: How can you say that? Besides, you often did the same thing yourself . . .

WOMAN: It's here! We simply must decide on a definite place for the first aid kit. We're always in a flurry when there's an emergency.

FATHER: Was it next to the refrigerator?

WOMAN: No, on the other side of the dresser. By the way, could you take down the baby carriage first, Husband? It'll be hard on Father unless we do something about the child.

MAN: All right.

(MAN *had already started to take down the table and chairs to prepare for the three o'clock tea, but he interrupts this momentarily to attend to the baby carriage.* WOMAN *brings out the first aid kit and treats* MOTHER's *foot.*)

WOMAN: Please sit on this chair for a minute, Mother. That's fine. Where's the corn? Ah, right here. Let me see. Shall I put on some mercurochrome and cover it with an adhesive bandage?

MOTHER: Then I can't put on the shoes.

WOMAN: That can't be helped. Anyway, these shoes are worthless now. Next time, I'll find a pair for you somewhere.

MOTHER: What do I do until then? Go barefoot?

FATHER: That's a good one. Like some native. Or you might hop on one leg.

MAN: Father, please lay the baby down here. (*Pointing to the baby carriage.*)

WOMAN: Mother, you can wear slippers. They may be a bit hard to walk with, but it'll do. Mountaineers who get corns all do that.

MOTHER: Why should mountaineers carry pairs of slippers?

WOMAN: I don't know, but Mr. Kobayashi said so.

FATHER (*peeking into the carriage*): Daughter, isn't he ready for his milk?

WOMAN: He's still asleep, isn't he?

MOTHER (*to* FATHER): Leave him alone when he's sleeping. He'll wake up and start crying if he's hungry. Don't bother him.

FATHER: All right.

MAN: Raise that hood so the sun won't shine on his face. Father. (*To* WOMAN.) Which tablecloth do you want, Wife?

MOTHER (*to* WOMAN): How about the checkered one? I like that . . . It's English.

WOMAN (*to* MOTHER): Actually, that's more American. All American kitchens use them. (*To* MAN.) The red checkered one. (*To* MOTHER.) Mr. Okada said so.

MAN: That one needs washing. It's quite soiled.

WOMAN: It's good for one more meal. Then, I'll wash it. Besides, the weather's nice now and . . . (*To* MOTHER.) How's your foot?

MOTHER: Fine, thanks. Where were the slippers?

WOMAN: Bottom drawer of the dresser. Those red ones are good. They've got strong soles. (*Putting away the first aid kit.*)

FATHER: Get me the stomach powder.

WOMAN: Does your stomach still bother you?

MOTHER: You smoke too much.

MAN; Yes, Father. You smoke too much. Why don't you cut down a bit? You'll get lung cancer.

FATHER: Iwamoto smoked seventy a day. It didn't bother him. He lived to be ninety-two. Of course, I don't want to live that long.

WOMAN: I'll get the tableware. Husband, please heat the water.

MAN: Is there any more alcohol left? I'll have to buy some before we run out completely . . . Watch for a chance. It would be just too bad if we forgot.

(*Four chairs are placed around the small table, and the preparation for the three o'clock tea begins.* MAN *lights the alcohol lamp and heats up the water for the tea.* WOMAN *sets the table, and* MOTHER *attends to the crackers and the lemons.*)

MOTHER (*taking a bite of the cracker*): They're a bit soggy.

WOMAN: With that long spell of rain, it can't be helped. The can was tightly sealed, though. Father, do you want the newspaper?

FATHER: Which one?

WOMAN: Well, this one is rather recent. It was folded and placed in back of the kitchen cabinet. (*Offering it to* FATHER.) You may have already seen it.

MAN: The copy you want might be over there, Father. It's the latest issue and was used for wrapping the hard crackers in the food box.

FATHER: No, this is fine. I haven't seen it yet.

MOTHER: Shall I turn on the radio?

WOMAN: Isn't it about time we changed the batteries? It's been quite a while. The static is really bad now. The last time I turned on the radio, the noise was so bad that I couldn't understand a thing they were saying.

MAN: That's not the fault of the batteries. The radio's broken.

WOMAN: But the batteries are about gone, too. That's right— speaking of batteries . . . The ones in the flashlight are very weak, Husband. They're about to go out.

MOTHER: That's right, they must be replaced.

MAN: When they start to go, they seem to go all at once.

FATHER: Can't you keep them stocked?

MAN: No, you have to buy them along the way . . .

MOTHER: There must be quite a load of laundry. We haven't washed for a while.

WOMAN: Yes. Husband, let's stop for a day some place near the water.

MAN: All right. Do we still have detergent?

WOMAN: I think so . . . Mother?

MOTHER: Yes. After all, we've only used it two or three times since we bought it. (*Picking up a teacup.*) Daughter, isn't there a crack in it?

WOMAN: Oh, you're right. It's cracked. These delicate things just can't take it. After five, six hours of rough travel, it's bound to happen, I suppose. The road is bad, the cart is bad, and you pull so recklessly.

MAN: It can't be helped. Should we change entirely to plastic or aluminum?

FATHER: Don't be foolish. How can you drink tea from plastic or aluminum? We aren't horses, you know.

MAN: Well, the tea's about ready. (*Peeking into the baby carriage.*) He still seems to be sleeping. Shall we start?

MOTHER: Yes, let's start. How about you, Daughter?

WOMAN: Fine.

(*Everyone is seated.* FATHER *murmurs some words and crosses himself. Others follow.*)

MAN: Have you a cigarette, Father?

FATHER: Sure. (*Taking out a pack from his pocket.*) The sky is so clear.

MOTHER: Yes. For the first time, in quite a while. "*Yamagami People's Finance Company.*" What's that, I wonder?

WOMAN: It's a sign. Husband, if you climb on top of that sign, couldn't you see far away?

MAN: I suppose I could. Isn't this cigarette a bit soggy?

FATHER: Yes. And a little bitter, too.

MAN: Did you get them wet?

FATHER: Could have. We had so much rain.

MOTHER: Don't smoke wet cigarettes. They're poisonous.

WOMAN: That's right. Poisonous. They say nicotine gets stronger when it's wet. Better not smoke them. Fresh ones should be in that tea container. (*Starts to rise.*)

FATHER: Never mind. I'm not going to smoke now . . .

WOMAN: I see . . . (*Sits down again.*) Listen, Husband . . . (*Looks up at the telephone pole.*) You could climb up, couldn't you?

MAN: No, I couldn't. That's ridiculous. I'm not an electrician.

WOMAN: Husband, you were so good at climbing to high places.

MOTHER: And what's to be gained by climbing?

WOMAN: To look into the distance.

FATHER: I see. Shall I try climbing?

MAN: Don't do it, Father.

FATHER: Why not?

MOTHER: Suppose you fall and break a bone or something?

FATHER: Don't worry. I may look decrepit now, but I was always good at climbing.

WOMAN: No, you mustn't. It's too dangerous for you, Father. Husband, you should climb because you're stronger. But you're such a scaredy-cat!

MOTHER: What's to be gained by looking into the distance? You can't see anything.

WOMAN: I'm curious.

MAN: I'm not in the least! Isn't this marmalade a little stale?

MOTHER: It's certainly stale. When I took off the lid a while ago, it was slightly moldy near the top.

WOMAN: We'll have to throw it away, then. Let me see.

MAN (*giving the jar to* WOMAN): You can't tell by just looking. But it's a bit moldy when you taste it.

FATHER: Oh, that's nothing to worry about.

WOMAN (*tastes it*): You're right. We'd better get rid of it. It's poisonous.

FATHER: Molds are generally like medicine. Even rice cakes digest better when they're moldy.

MOTHER: Why are you so unscientific?

FATHER: I'm not unscientific. Don't you know that penicillin is a type of mold?

MOTHER: Of course. You must have asked Dr. Kawata.

FATHER: What difference does that make? I tell you, penicillin is a mold.

WOMAN: Anyway, I'm going to throw it away. It would be terrible if it was actually poisonous.

MOTHER: I agree. Nothing like being careful. We'd have a hard time looking for a doctor around here.

MAN (*peering into* FATHER's *newspaper*): Anything interesting?

FATHER: Yes. A fellow named Kodama won ten million yen in a lottery. He never missed buying a ticket from the age of twelve.

WOMAN: How old is he now?

FATHER: Forty-two.

MAN: For thirty years. That's quite a story.

WOMAN: Remember Mr. Aizawa who worked at the post office? He happened to buy a ticket which was worth . . . Was it three hundred thousand yen?

MOTHER: Five hundred thousand. Caused quite a stir. A lucky man can win on a single ticket.

WOMAN: I've never bought even one in any lottery.

MAN: We couldn't win even if we tried.

FATHER: I bought one once.

MOTHER: Really?

FATHER: I didn't win, though.

MAN: In other words, we're just average. Such people are born losers. They have neither fantastic good luck nor fantastic bad luck.

MOTHER: Is the baby all right?

WOMAN: He certainly sleeps well. Must be tired. (*Rising to take a look.*)

MAN: He's tired, all right. He's bound to be if you carry him on your back. You should let him ride in the baby carriage since the road isn't that bad.

FATHER: I'll do the pushing.

WOMAN: That would slow us down. Besides, I'm far more comfortable carrying him . . . Mother, he's fine when he's sleeping. We don't have to wake him up.

MOTHER: All right. For a while, anyway. He'll start crying if something's wrong.

MAN: Shall I fix the milk now?

WOMAN: No, after he wakes up . . . But, let me ask you, Husband, don't you really want to climb up that pole?

MAN: No, I don't. What's the use of climbing?

WOMAN: I can't understand it. If I were a man, I'd certainly climb it.

FATHER: Why can't a woman do it?

WOMAN: Because . . . After all . . . It's impossible for a woman. I think it's a man's job.

FATHER: Why?

WOMAN: Because . . .

MOTHER: Don't do it! A woman shouldn't do such things. That's obvious. It's immodest.

WOMAN: Don't worry. I won't climb. Still, I can't understand why you don't want to.

MAN: Don't be a pest. I don't want to, that's all. Father, you're not eating much, are you?

FATHER: No.

MAN: Why not?

FATHER: I've got heartburn.

MOTHER: You should eat. You get heartburn because you just smoke and skip your meals.

WOMAN (*sitting at the table*): Where's the stomach powder?

FATHER: That's a good idea. I'll have some.

MOTHER: In any case, simply eat as if you're taking medicine, even if you don't particularly care to eat. Otherwise, you'll get sick. We cover quite a distance every day, you know.

WOMAN: She's right. You didn't eat very much this afternoon, either.

FATHER: It's just age. I can go on without eating very much. Besides, I don't carry any baggage.

MAN: Still, you eat so little. Shall I bring out something? Please, tell me if you want anything.

FATHER: All right. If you insist. I'll try eating what's on the table.

WOMAN: Shall I slice some cheese?

FATHER: Yeah.

MOTHER: I want another cup of tea.

MAN: Certainly.

(A YOUNG MAN *dressed like a tramp and carrying a dirty bag saunters in from stage left. Everyone becomes somewhat tense.*)

YOUNG MAN: Hello.

MAN: Hello.

YOUNG MAN: Are you having tea?

FATHER: Yes; please join us if you like.

YOUNG MAN: No thank you. I don't take three o'clock tea. It's not my habit. It'll make me lose my appetite for supper. (*Pointing to the carriage.*) Is that your baby?

WOMAN: That's right. He's sleeping now.

YOUNG MAN: Then your group consists of: a baby, his father and mother, and also his grandfather and grandmother . . .

MOTHER: You're right. We're an entire family. Won't you have some tea with us, anyway?

YOUNG MAN: No, I think not. If I have tea, I'll want the other things on the table. Let me see: cheese crackers, butter, and jam. Yes, indeed, they're all here! Then I'll spoil my appetite for supper.

MAN: Are you alone?

YOUNG MAN: Yes. (*He goes around the cart, observing it carefully.*) It's a fine cart. Looks so sturdy. It should make traveling easy.

WOMAN: Even so, it's quite rickety now.

YOUNG MAN: Rickety? Not at all. It's solid. (*Standing beside the telephone pole.*) May I climb it?

FATHER: Climb? That pole?

YOUNG MAN: Yes. I just feel like climbing. Of course, if I'll be disturbing you during your tea . . .

WOMAN: No, that's all right. We don't mind. Please climb up. We were just thinking of doing the same thing.

YOUNG MAN: Well, in that case . . .

(YOUNG MAN *removes his shoes, spits on his hands, and climbs up the pole. Everyone looks up blankly. After reaching a certain height, he takes out an old telescope from a leather bag hanging from his shoulder and peers into the distance.*)

WOMAN: Can you see anything?

MOTHER: Don't bother him. Suppose you surprise him and he falls.

WOMAN: Don't worry.

MAN: He doesn't seem to see anything.

WOMAN: Why not?

MAN: Doesn't he seem that way to you?

FATHER: But he's looking at something. Yes, notice how still he is.

(*Returning the telescope to the leather bag,* YOUNG MAN *slides down. He begins to put on his shoes.*)

WOMAN: How was it?

YOUNG MAN: Well, there's nothing special to see.

FATHER: Did you see anything?

YOUNG MAN: No.

WOMAN: But you must have seen something.

YOUNG MAN: There's a line of telephone poles, that's all.

WOMAN: And beyond that? You see, we're going that way.

YOUNG MAN: And beyond that? A line of telephone poles extends far into the distance.

MOTHER: That's all?

YOUNG MAN: Yes, that's all.

MAN: And . . . Did you see any people?

YOUNG MAN: No one. Perhaps you should climb up yourself. They say, "One view is worth a hundred descriptions."

WOMAN: I've heard that one, too . . . "One view is worth a hundred descriptions." Remember? Mr. Kawano often said that.

YOUNG MAN: Who's Mr. Kawano?

MOTHER: He lived next door to us—before. We've bidden farewell to those people . . .

YOUNG MAN: I see. Well, I must go now. I'm sorry I disturbed you during tea.

(YOUNG MAN *leaves. The four sit in their respective chairs and silently drink tea for a while.*)

FATHER: Shouldn't we get started, too?

WOMAN: There's a little time yet.

MOTHER: How much more?

MAN: Let me see. (*Looking at his watch.*) About thirty minutes. In the meantime, we must feed the baby and change his diaper . . .

WOMAN: That's right. Then we can start out, too . . .

(*Motionless and silent, the four wait for time to pass.*)

The stage darkens.

Scene Two

The stage still has a single telephone pole. However, its position has shifted, indicating a different setting. The cart is at stage center, with *chairs and various household goods having been taken off. A string is drawn between one of the footholds on the telephone pole and the prop for the cart—now set up on the cart; several pieces of washing are being dried on it.*

(*It is daylight and very bright. The child, in the baby carriage, is crying fiercely. No one appears for a while. Finally, from stage left* YOUNG MAN, *still dressed like a tramp, wanders in, dangling a leather bag. He is about to pass by but becomes concerned over the child's crying and returns to peek into the carriage. He attempts to amuse the child by shaking the noisemaker that is in the carriage, but the crying persists. No one is around, and the baby bottle on the chair is empty. With no other recourse, he picks up the child rather clumsily. As he strolls around the area amusing the child, the cries finally subside.* WOMAN *appears from stage right, carrying a pail of laundry.*)

WOMAN: Oh!

YOUNG MAN: Hello. He was crying so hard.

WOMAN: My! And there was no one here?

YOUNG MAN: No. I happened to be passing by . . .

WOMAN: I wonder where they are? This is terrible. Thank you. I'll take the baby now. (*Taking the child.*) Do you mind putting this pail somewhere?

YOUNG MAN: I'd be glad to. (*Taking the pail.*)

WOMAN: There, there, you poor thing. Were you crying here all by yourself? Is that so? And there was no one here? Aren't they awful? (*Checking the diaper.*) Oh, just as I thought. It's wet. Do you mind? There's a bundle of diapers in the carriage.

YOUNG MAN: You mean in there?

WOMAN: Yes, it's wrapped in a vinyl bag. I'm sorry. It's the same old story. I have to do everything. Honestly, Mother could at least have minded the baby. Imagine, leaving him all alone . . .

YOUNG MAN: Is this it? (*Giving her the bundle.*)

WOMAN: Thank you. That's it. Please put the pail down— anywhere.

YOUNG MAN: Oh, this? How about here? (*Setting it on a chair.*)

WOMAN: No! The chair will get wet. Somewhere over there!

YOUNG MAN: Then, here? (*Setting it on the top of the cart.*)

WOMAN: I suppose . . . (*Somewhat annoyed.*) All right . . . There.

I'll tend to it later. (*Examining the soiled diaper.*) My goodness! It's soaked through. Poor thing. No wonder you're crying. I'm sorry, Young Man. Could you throw this in the pail on the other side of the cart?

YOUNG MAN: Glad to.

WOMAN: Be careful how you hold it. It's wet. Hold it *here*. Of course, it's not really dirty. After all, it's baby things. And . . . No, not in that pail. The other one—over there. This one has freshly laundered things in it. No, in the other one—the smaller one over there . . .

YOUNG MAN: This one?

WOMAN: Yes, that one. Throw it in there. Oh, hold on! Did you throw it in already?

YOUNG MAN: Yes, didn't you say . . .

WOMAN: Was there any trash in it?

YOUNG MAN: Why—yes.

WOMAN: How could you? That's stupid! You have to empty the trash first.

YOUNG MAN: I see. I'm sorry. Let me see. Where can I throw the trash?

WOMAN: Oh, anywhere. Just throw it out over there. (*To the child.*) It's hopeless. Why is everyone so useless? Now, don't you feel refreshed? This will take care of you.

YOUNG MAN: Madam.

WOMAN: What is it?

YOUNG MAN: I'd like to go now.

WOMAN: Oh, are you leaving?

YOUNG MAN: Yes.

WOMAN: I see. I wonder? Would you mind the baby while I fix the milk? It'll take only a minute. This child seems awfully hungry. I'm sure that's why he's crying.

YOUNG MAN: All right. I'll take care of him while you're fixing the milk.

WOMAN: You will? Thank you very much. Where has everyone gone? Then I'm counting on you. Just watch him. You don't have to pick him up. Let him alone. Look after him if he becomes restless because he might fall off . . .

YOUNG MAN: I understand. Don't worry. I've had some experience at this. (*Taking out the noisemaker from the carriage.*)

WOMAN: Don't do that! (*Grabbing it from* YOUNG MAN) Who brought that out? This noisemaker is bad for him. It shows poor taste in its use of colors. It might turn him into a nervous child. Anyone would get upset if this were rattled in front of him. Try something else. (*Puts away the toy.*)

YOUNG MAN: But there's nothing else around.

WOMAN: Never mind. Just leave him alone. He rarely cries. What can you do? They don't make good toys anymore. So children these days are all nervous. Mrs. Yoshimoto's child, for instance. Obviously, you wouldn't know about him . . . It's terrible. If my child became like that, I'd hardly be able to stand it . . . By the way, do you know where the canned milk is?

YOUNG MAN: I wouldn't know. (*Lighting a cigarette.*)

WOMAN: Please don't blow the smoke toward the baby. He might get asthma. (*Again, looking for the milk.*) It's a yellow can— about this size—with a picture of a cow on it. I'm sure I left it around here somewhere before I went to wash . . . You didn't see it?

YOUNG MAN: Of course not. I only got here. I haven't touched a thing.

WOMAN: I see. That's strange. It's always the same. Whenever we want anything, the whole place has to be turned topsy-turvy. If they'd only decide where everything should go. I've told them over and over again, but it's useless. They soon get everything mixed up again. Oh, be careful with the cigarette ashes. They fell near the baby's feet.

YOUNG MAN: Oh, I'm sorry. (*Dusts off the ashes.*)

WOMAN: Where's the milk, anyway? It's probably Mother's fault; she's always putting away everything. Excuse me, could you come here and help me lift this cart? The milk might have fallen on the other side.

YOUNG MAN: Why, certainly. Hold on a second. (*Snuffs out the cigarette; he approaches the cart.*)

WOMAN: Yes, it's heavy.

YOUNG MAN (*lifting it*): Any luck?

WOMAN: Oh!

YOUNG MAN: Did you find it?

WOMAN: I found a stocking. That's strange. It's mine. Why is it lying in a place like this? . . . (*Picking it up and staring at it.*)

YOUNG MAN: Did you find the can of milk?

WOMAN: Well . . . no.

YOUNG MAN: Then I'm going to put the cart down. (*Lowers it.*)

WOMAN: Thank you very much. It must have been heavy. It was worth it, though. I found this stocking. I was ready to discard its mate. (*Putting it in her pocket.*) I'm always losing a mate. That's the worst thing that can happen. You can't wear an odd pair. I know, Mrs. Mizuta always does it, but I wouldn't dare.

YOUNG MAN: How about the milk?

WOMAN: You're right. I must find the milk. Young man, please take care of the baby.

(MOTHER *rushes in from stage left, excitedly. Since she wears slippers, she has difficulty running.*)

MOTHER: Oh, there you are!

WOMAN: "There you are," indeed! How could you leave the baby by himself? He was crying so hard.

MOTHER: I know. But it's dreadful. Father has collapsed . . .

WOMAN: My! What happened!

MOTHER: I don't know. He suddenly collapsed.

WOMAN: Where?

MOTHER: Right over there. Your husband is taking care of him now. Do you have any stimulant?

WOMAN: Stimulant?

MOTHER: Yes, he wants me to get it.

WOMAN: What does he mean by stimulant?

YOUNG MAN: Don't you have any whiskey or brandy?

WOMAN: Yes.

YOUNG MAN: That should do.

WOMAN: But I wonder where it is? Don't you know, Mother?

MOTHER: Let me see. Isn't it on the shelf, along with the seasoning?

WOMAN: That's possible. (*Starts looking.*) Well, it's here . . . The milk, I mean.

MOTHER: Milk?

WOMAN: I'll find the stimulant and take it over. Could you go ahead with the water and the first aid kit, Mother?

MOTHER: Yes, I will. (*Goes stage left with the vacuum bottle and the first aid kit.*)

WOMAN: I wonder if he's anemic?

YOUNG MAN: Can I help?

WOMAN: Don't bother. Just mind the baby. Make sure he doesn't fall. He's always getting restless and falling. Luckily, he's never been hurt. But you can't tell. Let me see. There's nothing here.

YOUNG MAN: If you've found the milk, maybe I can fix it. I can, you know.

WOMAN: Never mind. Please stop chattering. You'll get me upset. You just mind the baby. And leave the rest to me.

YOUNG MAN: Is that bottle up there—whiskey?

WOMAN: Which one . . . where?

YOUNG MAN: That one, up there.

WOMAN: This one?

YOUNG MAN: Isn't that the soy sauce?

WOMAN: You're right, soy sauce.

YOUNG MAN: Above that . . . Yes, and to the right . . .

WOMAN: Oh, this one? You're right. (*Opening the bottle and sniffing.*) Yes, you have sharp eyes. It's whiskey. Mr. Umino's husband was just like you. When it came to liquor, he could find it, no matter where it was hidden. Well, I'm counting on you. I'll be back soon.

YOUNG MAN: How about a cup—a cup?

WOMAN: Oh, yes. I almost forgot the cup. (*Taking the cup.*) I'll be right back. Please be careful with the baby. (*Exits stage left.*)

YOUNG MAN (*talking to the child as he lights a cigarette*): What kind of a family do you have? Is it always this way? It's so unsettled. That reminds me, I may as well fix your milk. Don't you fall off now. Yes, it'll be ready soon. (*Starts preparing the milk.*) What's this? How did they manage to load up such an untidy assortment of things? I see, it's the entire family possessions. (*Walking around and examining the baggage on the cart as he prepares the milk.*) Refrigerator, dresser, quilt cover, kerosene stove, wall clock . . . sewing machine, phonograph, fan, camera, carpet, mirror stand . . . What's this, a back scratcher? . . . That's too much. Say, they're even taking a goldfish bowl. Lamp stand and a picture frame—a copy of the Mona Lisa. A scale, a potty, a bird cage . . . Are they serious? What for? All—right . . . The milk's ready. (*Approaching the child.*) Are you hungry? There, there! Don't choke on it. (*Allowing the child to drink.*) No wonder it's hard work. They plan to take along everything. What a big job!

(*Carrying* FATHER *in his arms,* MAN *stumbles in.*)

MAN: Hey, somebody! (*Looking back.*) Hey, make a place for me to set him down! Line up the chairs!

(MOTHER *and* WOMAN *appear. They had met* MAN *as he was already returning with* FATHER *and accompanied him back.*)

WOMAN: Please wait a minute! Why didn't you let us know beforehand if you were planning to bring him back? I'm sorry, Mother. Please hold on to these. (*Provides* MOTHER *with the whiskey and the cup.*) I'll line up the chairs.

MOTHER: All right. (*Receives them.*)

MAN: Get with it! My arms are ready to fall off! I kept waiting, but no one came. What else could I do? I couldn't let him lie in a place like that.

MOTHER (*speaking to* WOMAN, *who is lining up the chairs*): Shall I spread a blanket on top of these chairs?

WOMAN: Never mind. This is fine. It's so much trouble looking for one. Anyway, let's have him rest here. Husband, it's ready!

MAN: I'm putting you down, Father.

WOMAN (*noticing* YOUNG MAN): Oh, have you fixed the milk? Did you know the formula? Can't be too thick or too thin, you know. Or else, he'll get diarrhea. I would have fixed it myself if you had simply waited.

YOUNG MAN: Don't worry.

MAN: How are you feeling, Father?

FATHER: Umm . . .

MAN: Wife, I think he could use a cold towel. Where's the wash basin and the towel? And the whiskey. And a cup. And bring the first aid kit, too. Maybe there's a good medicine. You must lie still, Father.

WOMAN: I wonder if it was fatigue, after all.

MOTHER (*attending to the whiskey and the first aid kit*): Daughter, will you get the wash basin and the towel?

WOMAN: Yes, Mother. Where's the towel? (*To* YOUNG MAN.) Please be careful. If you don't, he'll choke on the milk.

YOUNG MAN: Don't worry.

MAN: The towel's over there. You know, in the top drawer of the dresser. They're the ones we bought the other day.

MOTHER: Don't use the new ones. We just want to soak it in cold water. You'll find a clean towel in the laundry basket.

WOMAN: I know. But where's the basket?

MOTHER: It's . . .

WOMAN: I've found it.

MAN: Well, I was shocked. You collapsed so suddenly . . . Drink this, Father. (*Offering him the whiskey.*)

YOUNG MAN: Is it sunstroke?

MAN: Sunstroke?

YOUNG MAN: I think so. He probably didn't wear a hat.

WOMAN: Yes, I'm sure of it. It's sunstroke. I once heard from Dr. Kawata . . . You'll get one if you go outside on a hot day without a hat. (*Approaching* FATHER *with the wash basin.*) Please move over. I'll take care of him.

MAN (*rising*): So, it's sunstroke . . . That reminds me. What happened to my hat?

MOTHER: It's here. Shall I get it out?

WOMAN: You'd better wear it. It would be terrible if you collapsed, too. How are you, Father? Feeling a little better?

FATHER: Yes, I'm fine now. I've recovered.

WOMAN: No, you must lie still for a while.

MOTHER: That's right. Here's your hat. (*Giving it to* MAN.)

MAN: Thank you. (*Approaching the baby.*) Well, we're really sorry about leaving you alone.

WOMAN: Oh, Husband! Please thank this person. He took care of the baby while we were gone. He fixed the milk and . . .

MAN: Thank you very much . . . We were in such a disorganized state . . .

YOUNG MAN: Don't mention it. I had nothing else to do, anyway. He's sleeping now. Cigarette?

MAN: Thank you.

WOMAN: Please be careful of the smoke. It's time we started again, Husband. What shall we do about Father? (*Looking at the child.*) Oh, is he sleeping?

YOUNG MAN: Yes, he's sleeping.

WOMAN: I was thinking, Husband. If Father doesn't mind, maybe we can have him ride in that baby carriage.

MAN: In the baby carriage?

WOMAN: That's right. It can't be helped, you know. He can't walk in that condition. He's got sunstroke. And I think he's also quite exhausted. Husband, I'll carry the baby.

MAN: And who pushes the baby carriage?

(MOTHER *takes care of* FATHER. YOUNG MAN *approaches, smoking a cigarette.*)

WOMAN: We can ask him to push . . . I know. Of course, it's an imposition. But it can't be helped, under the circumstances. There's no one else around. I'm sure he'll help us if we only ask.

MAN: But, Wife . . .

FATHER (*noticing* YOUNG MAN's *cigarette*): Could I have one, too?

YOUNG MAN: Of course. (*Offering him one.*)

MOTHER: Don't smoke now. Remember, you've got sunstroke.

FATHER: Don't worry about it.

(YOUNG MAN *offers him a light.*)

WOMAN: Listen, Young Man.

YOUNG MAN: What is it?

WOMAN: Which way are you going from here?

YOUNG MAN: Me? I wouldn't mind going along with you, for a while. I know—you're short of help, aren't you?

WOMAN: Really? I'm so glad. Please thank him, Husband. He'll be a great help. We didn't know what to do. But we'll make it worth your while. We'll provide all your meals.

MAN: I'm sorry. We're so demanding . . .

YOUNG MAN: That's all right. Then what must I do?

MAN: We'll put Father in the baby carriage. So, if you could push it . . .

MOTHER: You're putting him in the baby carriage?

FATHER: Who—me?

WOMAN (*To* MOTHER): But there's no other way. I know you won't like it, Father. But please give it a try. Are you sure you should be smoking? There's no hurry. Please stay as you are for a little bit longer. We'll take care of the baggage.

FATHER: Are we going already?

MAN: Fairly soon. Well, I'll take down the washing.

WOMAN: Please do.

YOUNG MAN: Shall I help you?

MAN: Thank you.

WOMAN: I'm going to carry the baby, Mother. Could you lend me a hand?

MOTHER: All right. (*To* FATHER.) Never mind, dear. Please lie still.

(*Everyone starts working except* FATHER, *who lies on a row of chairs and stares at the sky.*)

Have you changed his diaper, Daughter?

WOMAN: Yes, a while ago. He's had his milk, and he's fine now.

MOTHER: He's sleeping soundly. Wait a minute. His hat string is loose. What if he got a sunstroke!

WOMAN (*To* MAN): You don't have to fold the laundry. Throw it into the basket. I'll do it later. Roll up the clothes line. Put it in the dresser, third drawer from the top. I said, "the third drawer from the top." If you just put it anywhere, it'll disappear again. And we'll have a big hassle over it . . . Mother, where did you leave Father's hat? Do you remember?

MOTHER: Of course I do. Here it is.

WOMAN: Please leave it out. He should wear it when he's walking. And don't forget our parasols.

MOTHER: Good idea. I'll leave them out. You know, these slippers are hard to walk in.

WOMAN: If you'd prefer wooden clogs, you can have mine.

MOTHER: In that case, I'll borrow them. (*Heading toward the cart.*)

WOMAN (*clearing the table*): When you finish over there, Mother, please help me move this table. Unless we start with the larger things, we won't get everything on the cart. Oh, what's the matter, Father?

FATHER: Nothing . . .

WOMAN: All right, then. But you shouldn't be so sensitive. There's nothing to be ashamed of. You're sick. And it can't be helped. Besides, there's no one watching you. That reminds me. Is the baby carriage ready? (*Approaching the carriage.*)

YOUNG MAN: It's certainly a huge load.

MAN: Yes. Still, we've thrown away a lot. You see, there's no point if we can't move.

MOTHER: Can I borrow these clogs?

WOMAN: Of course. You might loosen the thongs a bit if they're too tight. Don't worry about the baby carriage. I've cleaned it up.

MOTHER (*trying on the clogs*): This is much better. We must buy some extra pairs. (*To* WOMAN.) I'll leave the parasols here.

WOMAN: Thank you, Mother. (*To the men.*) Please be careful with the pieces of furniture. Everytime we handle them they get full of scratches. Did you notice, Mother? The corner of this table is chipped. It must have been bumped against something.

MOTHER: I know. Well, it can't be helped, under the circumstances.

MAN: Hey, bring me the rope. And a towel, too. This hot weather makes me sweat. Don't you sweat, Young Man?

YOUNG MAN: No. I don't drink water. I'm trying to be careful. When you walk in regions like this, you can't last if you don't.

MAN: I see. But aren't you thirsty?

YOUNG MAN: No, I'm used to it.

FATHER: Hey! I'd rather walk!

MOTHER: No, you mustn't, my dear. How can you walk? You'll have to ride, at least for today.

WOMAN: Mother's right. He's been kind enough to help push you. When you're free, Husband, could you please help Father into the baby carriage?

MOTHER: Shouldn't you lay down a cushion first?

WOMAN: I guess so. Is there any?

MOTHER: Never mind. I'll find one.

FATHER: Then I'll walk by myself until I'm ready to ride.

WOMAN: No, Father.

MAN: We'll move you, Father. Don't get up. I'm sorry, Young Man, could you help me lift him?

YOUNG MAN: Yes, of course. (*Grabs* FATHER.) Please walk slowly.

MAN: Hey, someone hold the carriage!

WOMAN: Yes, it's safe now.

(*Having placed* FATHER *in the baby carriage,* MOTHER *provides him with a cushion for his back.*)

MOTHER: How does it feel?

FATHER: Umm . . . It's all right.

(*The men load the chairs on the cart and bind them simply with a rope. Taking the remaining small items,* WOMAN *stuffs them between the baggage.*)

MAN: You know, there was a Mr. Kinoshita in our town. You look like him.

YOUNG MAN: I do?

MAN: Yes. Wife, doesn't he look like Mr. Kinoshita when he was younger?

WOMAN: Why yes, now that you mention it. I knew he reminded me of someone when I first saw him. You're right! Mr. Kinoshita. When he was younger, Mr. Kinoshita looked exactly like him.

YOUNG MAN: What does he do?

MAN: Mr. Kinoshita? Let me see. What was he doing, Wife?

WOMAN: Wasn't he working in a business office? Right, Mother?

MOTHER: Yes. A small one . . . He was always complaining about the low salary.

MAN: He was a good man. Only, he was timid. He wasn't the adventurous type.

WOMAN: We asked him to join us—many times. Of course, there were others besides Mr. Kinoshita.

YOUNG MAN: They didn't come?

MAN: That's right. Wife, we're about ready! How is it over there?

WOMAN: Well . . . I guess we are, too.

MOTHER: Have we forgotten anything? It'd be such a bother to come back again.

WOMAN: Don't worry.

MAN (*looking at his watch*): Then shall we go?

YOUNG MAN: Are we leaving?

(*Everyone looks toward stage right, the direction toward which they are headed. The scene becomes rather solemn.* WOMAN *removes the prop holding the cart, and its weight suddenly falls heavily on* MAN's *hands. Both* MOTHER *and* WOMAN *open their parasols.* YOUNG MAN *grasps the baby carriage.*)

MAN: Here we go!

(*Everyone slowly disappears toward stage right.*)

The stage darkens.

Scene Three

A single telephone pole still stands on the stage. However, no posters cover its base. It is broad daylight.

(*Finally, from stage left a couple* (BILLPOSTERS) *appears.* HUSBAND *carries a bucket of paste and brushes;* WIFE *has a large bundle of posters. The two approach the base of the telephone pole and look up.*)

HUSBAND: Tell me, Wife. I've always felt that a concrete pole has no appeal whatsoever.

WIFE: You're right, no appeal. It's so smooth. A telephone pole must be made of wood.

HUSBAND: That's right. It must be wood. I tell everyone that. But, oddly enough, they don't seem to understand what I mean. They claim concrete poles are stronger. But what's strength, after all?

WIFE: You're absolutely right. Strength is a secondary matter. Individuality is what's important.

HUSBAND: Yes, individuality. A telephone pole must have individuality. And it's the wooden pole that has that, no matter how you look at it. That's what I tell them. I say, "Look at a wooden pole. Even the shape of its knots are uniquely different."

WIFE: And we can even become fond of wooden poles. Shall we start? (*Lays down her bundle.*)

HUSBAND: Yes. (*Also lays down his tools.*) You can become fond of them. That's very important. They're all unique. Take this pole and that pole, for example. How can I put it?

WIFE: They each give a different impression.

HUSBAND: That's right, a different impression. Each one does, you know. But take the concrete ones. How about them? They have no individuality or anything else.

WIFE: Remember, Husband? When you go up to a newly erected pole, you get that strong smell of creosote around its base.

HUSBAND: That's right. It's that smell. A telephone pole must have that.

WIFE: You can always tell whether it's new or not by that smell. Shall we start?

HUSBAND: Yes, you're right. You can tell the new ones that way. Next time I see them I'll tell them—about the smell, I mean. I'm sure they'll be surprised. They'll say, "How about that!" When you compare the two, a concrete pole has nothing to recommend it.

WIFE: That's right. Though people say it's easier to paste posters on them.

HUSBAND: Easier? For posters? That's absurd. What a . . .

WIFE: I agree. Perhaps it's easier to paste on, but they don't realize it's also easier to have them torn off.

HUSBAND: Right. It's easier to have them torn off. They tear off so easily.

WIFE: Right. You just slap them two or three times with a wet rag. They don't realize that.

WIFE: No, they don't. A wooden pole may be hard to paste, but the poster isn't torn off so easily.

HUSBAND: It certainly isn't. That's for sure.

WIFE: You use a slightly thick paste, spread it well into the grain of the wood, and apply the poster with plenty of pressure. The poster looks as though it's almost absorbed into the wood.

HUSBAND: You're right. Of course. As though it's absorbed into the wood. All of it, you know. Because it's a wooden pole. That's its good point, no matter how you look at it.

WIFE: That's right. Shall we get started?

HUSBAND: Yeah. But I guess I'll have a smoke first.

WIFE: Wouldn't it be better to smoke later, Husband? We'll be more relaxed.

HUSBAND: You're right. Then I'll have it later. I'll have a tiny bit of water, instead.

WIFE: Yes, don't drink too much of it. You had some only a while ago.

HUSBAND: All right. (*Drinking from the canteen.*)

WIFE: Isn't it warm already? It's so hot.

HUSBAND: You want some?

WIFE: No, I'm fine. (*Screws on the stopper.*)

HUSBAND: Why not?

WIFE: I don't want any.

HUSBAND: I see. That reminds me. Don't you have candy or something?

WIFE: Yes. Would you like some?

HUSBAND: No, I'm fine. I thought you'd like one because you're not smoking or drinking.

WIFE: No, I'm fine. I may have some when you're ready to smoke.

HUSBAND: I see. Then shall we get started?

WIFE: Yes, let's.

HUSBAND: It's such fine weather.

WIFE: Yes, it is. And we must make good progress on this work while this weather lasts . . .

HUSBAND: That's right. We must do it now. It's strange, though. Ever since the weather's improved, I keep thinking how I really hate it.

WIFE: Hate what?

HUSBAND: This job.

WIFE: It's so simple. All you have to do is hold the brush and apply the paste.

HUSBAND: You're right. I realize that. But, you know, that's exactly what I hate about it. How can I put it? It makes me irritable. That must be it. In other words, these poles are concrete . . .

WIFE: That's terrible. I thought that might have been the reason. I was right, after all. You hate concrete.

HUSBAND: That's right. I can't stand it. But it wasn't that way at first. Wasn't working fun when all the poles were made of wood?

WIFE: You seemed happy, all right. I could tell by just working beside you. Oh, you were so happy . . .

HUSBAND: I was. That's right. You could tell by just being close to me. I was really happy, you know. (*Kneeling and clutching his head.*)

WIFE: Husband, maybe we're not suited for this job.

HUSBAND: This job? Well, maybe . . .

WIFE: Shall we try something else?

HUSBAND: Something else? What, for instance?

WIFE: There must be some work which employs your talent more fully.

HUSBAND: I agree. But we've been at this for thirty years. (*Rising.*)

WIFE: But if you really hate it, I . . .

HUSBAND: Well, I hate it. Though I'm not saying it's all that bad. At any rate, let's get started. After another fifty-six poles we can start back, can't we?

WIFE: Fifty-five after this one.

HUSBAND: Yes. It'll be easy. If we paste twenty-five poles a day, it'll take just over two days.

WIFE: I've always thought we could easily do thirty, if we raise our efficiency a little. Everyone else is going at that rate.

HUSBAND: That's true. But they do such a sloppy job of pasting.

WIFE: You're right. They're all sloppy. Well? Shall we start?

HUSBAND: Yes. Let's get started. How shall we paste it?

WIFE: How? I think the usual way is fine . . . It's so efficient.

HUSBAND: Yes, it's efficient. That's true, but I can't help thinking there must be a more efficient way.

WIFE: I suppose. Still, doesn't it look all right the way it is? They draw immediate attention.

HUSBAND: I see. I guess that's true. Well, let's not change it, then . . .

(*He begins pasting the posters on the telephone pole.* YOUNG MAN *appears from stage left, pushing the baby carriage with* FATHER *in it.* YOUNG MAN *pauses at stage center and watches the couple at work.*)

HUSBAND (*applying the paste*): This one is about the cat. (*Backing up a little and looking at it.*)

WOMAN (*pasting the "Cats To Give Away" poster*): I think it looks splendid.

HUSBAND: Place it a bit lower. Better leave extra paste on the top rather than the bottom.

WOMAN: How's this?

HUSBAND: Yes, that's fine. (*Approaching the pole, he applies the paste for the next poster.*) Is this all right?

WOMAN: Yes.

YOUNG MAN: Hello.

(*The couple stop working, turn around, and are somewhat surprised.*)
I'm sorry to interrupt you in the middle of your work. I happened to be passing by . . . I was walking . . . From that direction. Isn't it hot? That heat was too much for me. (*Realizing they are looking at the baby carriage.*) He's sick. Sunstroke. It's terrible. But no wonder, in this heat. It must be difficult for you to work, too. Are you billposters?

HUSBAND: Why, yes. Well . . . (*To* WIFE.) Wife, the paste will dry up.

WIFE: That's right! (*Pasting the "For Rent: A Cut-rate, Six-Mat Room . . ." poster.*)

HUSBAND: A bit too thick?

WIFE: Yes, it seems to be. But it can't be helped. There's hardly any water left.

HUSBAND: I'll put it on sparingly. (*Approaching the pole to apply the paste.*)

YOUNG MAN: I didn't expect to meet you in a place like this.

(*The couple stop working and turn around.*)
I don't mean to imply we know each other. How can I put it? I mean, running into people who paste posters. Ah, this kind of work does require long experience . . .

HUSBAND: Well, not exactly . . .

YOUNG MAN: Well, to some degree. Are you going over there? (*Pointing toward stage right.*)

YOUNG MAN: Yes, over there. How long have you been working?

HUSBAND: Let me see . . . Nearly thirty years.

YOUNG MAN: Thirty years! That's a long time.

WIFE (*pointing to the carriage*): Is he sleeping?

YOUNG MAN: Yes. It's sunstroke. The most important thing is to have him sleep in the shade. I suppose any kind of work takes at least that much experience—I mean, thirty years. I could never do it.

HUSBAND (*pointing to the carriage*): A relative of yours?

YOUNG MAN: No, I'm just looking after him. He has a family who is following. They've brought along all their personal belongings. And they're apparently also on their way—over there. Are you heading that way, too?

HUSBAND: Yes. Of course, we'll be heading back after fifty-five more poles, posting the other side.

YOUNG MAN: I see, the other side. The return trip must be hard work, too. Pasting all the way, you mean?

HUSBAND: Yes, all the way . . .

YOUNG MAN: Is there someone in the family waiting for you?

HUSBAND: No, there's only the two of us.

WIFE: We have no children.

YOUNG MAN: Then why don't you keep going?

HUSBAND: But we have our job to do.

YOUNG MAN: I know, but after you've come all this way?

HUSBAND: Naturally.

YOUNG MAN: But isn't it a pity, not to go on?

HUSBAND: That's what we're not quite sure of. In other words, should we keep going or turn back?

WIFE: But, Husband . . .

HUSBAND: Yes, that's true. I want to go back, even a day early. I really do. It's strange, though. The closer we get to the point of turning back, the more I hate going on. If we hurry, we can get back that much sooner.

WIFE: We're tired, Husband. That's why. When we reach this point, we tire most easily. Once we start back, you'll feel better again.

HUSBAND: You may be right.

YOUNG MAN: I wouldn't turn back if I were you. I'd keep going. I'd keep going as far as I could. Yes, I'd certainly go on. I've made up my mind. I'll leave this fellow here and keep on going.

HUSBAND: Leave him here? Why?

WIFE: You're imposing on us! We have our work to do. Besides . . .

YOUNG MAN: I'm not leaving him in your care. I'm simply leaving him behind.

HUSBAND: Leaving him? You can't do that, Young Man.

YOUNG MAN: And why not?

HUSBAND: Why not? It's cruel. He's sick, you know . . .

YOUNG MAN: I realize it's cruel, but it can't be helped. I shouldn't have gotten involved with them in the first place. For some reason, I get soft-hearted when I travel alone and want to be helpful . . .

WIFE: No! You mustn't leave him. You're imposing on us!

YOUNG MAN: Don't worry. I won't cause you any trouble. You can put the blame on me. So, forget about him. Goodby.

WIFE: No, you mustn't go!

HUSBAND: Hey, you can't do this!

WIFE: No, take him with you. You're imposing on us!

YOUNG MAN: Goodby.

WIFE: Young Man! We won't take the responsibility!

(YOUNG MAN *leaves*.)

WIFE: What shall we do?

HUSBAND: What would you like me to do, Wife?

WIFE: We've got to go after him and bring him back.

HUSBAND: Bring him back? We can't do that.

WIFE: Then what shall we do?

HUSBAND: Well . . . I just don't know.

WIFE: He's sick, you know.

HUSBAND: I realize that.

WIFE: Suppose something happens to him?

HUSBAND: What can we do? He's gone. It's not our fault. Besides, he said his companions were coming later . . .

WIFE: You expect us to wait here for them?

HUSBAND: Yes . . .

WIFE: For his companions? You can't depend on them. And even if they come, we don't know when. Suppose something happens in the meantime? Don't go near him, Husband . . . I don't like this at all . . .

HUSBAND: All right, let's forget about him. It can't be helped. It's not our fault, anyway. Let's finish up our job and get out of here. Let's do that. That guy's to blame. (*Quickly applying the paste to the telephone pole.*) Hurry, Wife. Let's finish before anyone comes.

WIFE: Yes, there's no other way.

HUSBAND: You're right. If someone finds the carriage and asks us about it, we'll simply say that we didn't know.

WIFE: That's right. We really don't know, do we? Well, we knew that the Young Man left him. But we thought he'd come back right away. After all . . .

HUSBAND: Right! We thought he'd come back right away. That's exactly what he said: "I'll be right back."

WIFE: No, he didn't say that. Still, we thought he did. That's natural. Can you imagine anyone leaving a sick person among total strangers?

HUSBAND: That's right, we just thought so. It's only natural to think that way.

WIFE: Of course, it's natural. We'll tell it that way. (*Finishes pasting.*) How's that?

HUSBAND: Fine. Let's go. Don't forget anything. I'd hate to leave something behind and have to come back for it.

WIFE: I understand. We've got everything.

HUSBAND: Then let's go.

(*The couple start for stage right but stop, petrified, having looked into the baby carriage.*)

Wife, what'll happen to him if his companions fail to come?

WIFE: But the fellow said they were coming . . .

HUSBAND: I know, Wife, but you can't believe that guy.

WIFE: Still, they'll come. I think they will. What would he gain by telling such a lie?

HUSBAND: Yes. But suppose they don't come. That old man will die.

WIFE: That's absurd! He's just lying there with a sunstroke. That's not so serious.

HUSBAND: But suppose no one ever comes?

WIFE: How can you say that? He said they'd follow very soon. They'll come. And even if they don't . . . We can simply say we thought they would. Since we thought that the Young Man would come back immediately, we never dreamed the old man would die . . . That's true—no idea . . . Well, Husband . . . What else can we do? Take him with us?

HUSBAND: Of course not. We've got our job to do . . .

WIFE: Shall we at least give him a drink of water, Husband? Maybe he's thirsty . . .

HUSBAND: That's fine. But won't we get more involved if we do that?

WIFE: Don't worry. We'll give him a drink and find out how he is. And if he's well enough, let's ask him if he has companions.

HUSBAND: I see. Let's try.

(*The couple fearfully approach the baby carriage and peek in.* HUSBAND *looks at* WIFE. *Then extending his hand, he touches* FATHER's *face. He withdraws it quickly and holds his breath.*)

WIFE: What is it?

HUSBAND: He's dead!

WIFE: You can't mean it!

HUSBAND: It's true!

(*The couple stare at the corpse, petrified.*)

What shall we do?

WIFE: What do you mean?

HUSBAND: Shall we run away?

WIFE: Well . . .

HUSBAND: If we see anyone, we'll tell it this way. He was already dead before he was brought here. And his companion skipped out. We thought he'd be back, for sure . . . No good? Right, that won't work. Rather, we didn't know he was dead. We thought he was asleep. That's the truth. We aren't doctors, you know. Maybe he's not dead yet. That's possible. I'll say I just touched him, and he seemed to be sleeping soundly. Besides, that's true. We're completely innocent. You see, the culprit is *that* guy. He killed him. That's right, Wife. Of course, that's right. That guy killed him and ran away. And we chased after him. That's reasonable. He's the bad guy, you know. We ran after him to catch him and make him confess. That'll be our

story. Let's run away . . . Wife, haven't you anything to say?
Or . . . Do we wait?

WIFE: Yes, it can't be helped.

HUSBAND: Do you think they'll come?

WIFE: Let's wait and see. At least, today . . . They might come,
you know.

HUSBAND: What do we tell them when they come?

WIFE: Well . . . (*Approaching the carriage.*) Husband, look at him.
He's quite old. And seems exhausted. The rim of his eyes are
so dark.

HUSBAND: Don't look at a dead man's face.

WIFE (*taking a handkerchief from the fold of her dress, she covers his
face*): I wonder if the Young Man knew?

HUSBAND: Knew what?

WIFE: That he was dead.

HUSBAND: I wonder, too.

(*The two clasp their hands prayerfully, facing the baby carriage.*)

WIFE: Shall we sit down?

HUSBAND: All right.

(*The couple sit.*)

WIFE: Would you care for a cigarette?

HUSBAND: Well, I guess I'll have one. (*Takes out a cigarette and
starts smoking.*) Do you want something to eat?

WIFE: No.

HUSBAND: Then, how about some candy?

WIFE: Not now.

HUSBAND: How about some water, then? You haven't had any.

WIFE: You're right. I'll have some. (*Takes a drink from the canteen.*)

HUSBAND: He looks terribly exhausted.

WIFE: I've never seen a dead man before.

HUSBAND: I see. He lies there so quietly . . .

WIFE: Yes. I never thought they would look that way.

HUSBAND: Wife, do you think his companions will really come?

WIFE: Yes, I think so. I don't mean I trust the Young Man, but I
somehow feel that they will.

HUSBAND: Is there a little breeze now?

WIFE: Can you hear it?

HUSBAND: Yes, though it's blowing quite high up . . .

(*For a while, the two listen to the wind. Then, aroused by the sound from stage left, they rise in anticipation. Soon,* MAN *pulling a cart appears from stage left.*)

MAN: Oh, hello. Here you are, Father. We were so worried. Sorry to be late. At any rate, with all this baggage. (*Pointing toward stage right.*) Hey, he's here, he's here! It must be his youth, but that guy kept moving on. No, I didn't think anything would happen to Father. But, after all, he was sick. And I couldn't help worrying . . . It's sunstroke. And he's getting on in years.

(*Carrying a child on her back,* WOMAN *appears from stage left.*)

WOMAN: Well, well. Here you are, Father. How could you? If you had only waited for us. (*Shouting toward stage left.*) Please hurry, Mother! Here he is! Still, I wonder what happened to the Young Man. (*To* MAN.) Oh, can you wait a minute? You want the prop for the cart? I'll get it.

MAN: Hurry! You know, I'm really tired out today.

(MOTHER *appears.*)

WOMAN: We must all travel together, after all. That's right. That's the secret of traveling. If anyone goes ahead, the others are bound to worry . . . You must be tired, Mother. There was hardly any time for even a drink of water. (*To the couple.*) Hello. I'm so grateful. Were you looking after him?

HUSBAND: You see . . .

MAN: I've a feeling this cart has taken quite a beating, too. Wife, I was sure it was rattling—around here. Just look.

WOMAN: You're right. You'd better repair it as soon as possible. If you don't, it'll only get worse and worse. Don't sit there, Mother. Husband, please take down a chair for her. We must let her sit down immediately. And she needs water. Please wait a minute, Mother. We'll take the chair down right away.

MOTHER: I'm fine. How is he?

MAN: You mean Father? He's over there.

WOMAN: I'm sure he's sleeping. We must express our thanks, Mother . . . Those people were looking after him. We're so grateful to you. We'll attend to him now.

MOTHER (*to the couple*): I'm very grateful . . . (*Tries to approach the carriage.*)

WOMAN: No, Mother. We'll get the chair down now. I'll look after Father. Still, I wonder where the Young Man went?

HUSBAND: Listen, everyone . . .
(*Everyone looks at* HUSBAND. *Unable to speak further,* HUSBAND *simply points to the carriage.*)
    Your Father's dead!
(*For a while, everyone stands petrified.*)
    The stage darkens.

Scene Four

A single telephone pole as before. At upper stage center stands a crude cross, marking a grave. The cart is to the right of stage center. To left of stage center are the table, the chairs, and the baby carriage with the child. On the table is an old, hand-operated phonograph with a "morning-glory" horn.

(*It is dusk. The evening glow is about to disappear.* MOTHER, *with white lace on her head, kneels in front of the grave. Behind her,* WOMAN, *also in white lace, is standing. On the other side of the grave marker,* HUSBAND, *holding a shovel, and* WIFE *are standing.* MAN *stands alone near the table and turns the handle of the decrepit phonograph.*)

MAN (*addressing no one in particular*): It can't be helped. It really can't. These things happen. Moreover, we used to talk a lot about it—about what we'd do if anyone died along the way . . . That's why we decided at the beginning that we'd keep going. That's how it was. And we all agreed. That's right. We must go on. There's no other way . . .

WOMAN: Husband, please keep quiet for a while. Mother is praying.

MAN: It couldn't be helped. It's not our fault. We knew we should have taken better care of him. But actually what could we have done? That's obvious. No one could take the time. Everyone had his hands full. Maybe we shouldn't have trusted that guy. Maybe not . . . After all, he wasn't our kin. And he was so young . . . And he wasn't the type to devote himself completely to Father's care. But, mind you, the guy agreed to help us. And once he agreed, he should have taken the responsibility. Isn't that right? Since he did agree . . . Well, forget it. Well . . . forget it. Why go on this way? Maybe it would have turned out the same whether he agreed or not . . .

(*During* MAN's *speech,* HUSBAND *and* WIFE (BILLPOSTERS) *slowly retreat from the grave marker and approach the table. They stand directly in front of it.*)

MAN: Still, I wonder where that guy went? (*Raising his eyes and becoming aware of the couple.*) Oh, I'm sorry . . .

HUSBAND: We want to express our deep sympathy on this occasion.

MAN: Thank you for your kindness . . . We put you through so much trouble . . .

WIFE: Sorry we couldn't be of greater help . . .

MAN: Well, please sit down. You were so helpful. Anyway, it happened in such a desolate place, and so suddenly . . . Please give me the shovel . . . I'll stand it here. And . . . Oh, yes. There's water over there. Madam can at least wash her hands. Please help yourself . . . I'll leave the towel here. You've been such a help . . . We could hardly have managed by ourselves. That's right. Yes, use that towel. And, of course, a cigarette. Please sit here. It was hard work, I know. You must be tired. Will Madam also join us? Yes, the cigarettes are here. And the matches.

HUSBAND: Was it your Father?

MAN: Yes, it was the Old Man. It sounds disrespectful, but he was a good father. Still, we'll keep going. That's right, we have to. What for? Why, we'd already agreed. Are you surprised? But that's the truth. We're going on. Oh, Madam, please wait a minute. My wife will soon serve you something to drink . . .

WIFE: Please don't bother.

MAN: In other words, it's for *that* reason. Do you know what I mean: "To climb over the dead and advance forward . . ." You know, that spirit. Surely you understand. As you can see, we left as a family. We're all here. Before we left, we talked over many things together. That's to be expected. This sort of thing is quite an adventure, you know. Oh, Madam, here's something for you to eat. Will you try one?

WIFE: Thank you . . .

MAN: Well, we talked about the possibility of someone dying. That's only natural. Such things do happen, you know. We discussed many things. And we finally decided to go. It meant we'd go on, even if one of us happened to die along the way. You see, that's how it is. So we must go on. We simply must. Well, what do you think about that?

HUSBAND: I beg your pardon?

MAN: I mean, about our going on . . .

HUSBAND: Oh, about your going on? But haven't you already decided on that?

MAN: That's right. We've decided that we'd keep going. So we must . . . Still . . . We'd like to know your opinion. Well, look at it this way: what would you do in our case? Would you go on or not?

HUSBAND: Let me see. If I were you . . . I wonder what I'd do? (*To* WIFE.) Wife, what do you think?

WIFE: Me? You mean whether I'd go on or not? I see . . . What would I do? I'd have to give it careful thought . . .

MAN: Yes. You'd have to. This is something everyone often thinks about. And probably they tend to decide against it.

HUSBAND: Why should they? How can you possibly think that . . . Tell you not to go on? Of course not. Hasn't that been already settled? If I were you, I'd go on!

MAN: You would? But in your case it hasn't been decided. As you know, we've already committed ourselves. But you people still haven't. So, we want to ask the opinion of those who have yet to decide. Would you go on or not?

HUSBAND: Of course, I'd go on. That's obvious. The choice has been made already . . . Even if it weren't . . . If I felt that way . . . To go on, I mean . . . I would go on. That's the proper thing to do.

MAN: But, you can't really say that. Look here! My father's dead. He died, you know. You must consider that. He was a victim. Our decision has claimed a victim. What's more . . . (*Glancing at* WOMAN *and* MOTHER.) This may sound cold-blooded, but there may be other victims in the future. I want your opinion, taking this into account.

WIFE (*to* HUSBAND): That's right, Husband. You have to consider that, too. After all, that's the issue. That's right. I certainly wouldn't go on. No, indeed. (*Again, to* HUSBAND.) Of course not.

MAN: Don't you agree? When you take that into account, I believe that's a reasonable conclusion . . .

WIFE: That's right. You can't help feeling that way. I wouldn't go on.

HUSBAND: I see . . . Well, I suppose so. If you consider that factor.

MAN: Then, we shouldn't go on?

HUSBAND: Well, I suppose not.

WIFE: I certainly wouldn't.

(*Leaving* MOTHER *at the grave marker,* WOMAN *slowly approaches the table.*)

MAN: Of course, I thought so. If I followed my natural feelings . . . Oh, yes, we're going on. It's been settled. But, ordinarily, people won't go. In fact, if someone tried to go, they'd probably condemn him. Yes, absolutely! That's true. That's quite natural and proper. Still . . . We must go on.

WOMAN: I'm sorry. Everything is so disorganized. And we haven't even offered you tea . . . No, please, remain as you are. I'll prepare the tea immediately.

MAN: Yes, they're waiting. Wife, these people are opposed to our going on—after all.

HUSBAND: Opposed? We didn't mean to . . .

MAN: No, no . . . I understand. Don't worry. That's natural. And it won't affect us in the least. Yes . . . We were only asking for your opinion.

WOMAN: Husband, please lower your voice a little. We mustn't disturb Mother . . .

MAN: Oh, is she still praying?

WOMAN: If it's all right with everyone, shall I prepare coffee?

WIFE: Please don't bother. We must be going. Right, Husband?

HUSBAND: Yes, we must be getting along.

WOMAN: No, please, stay a while. It'll only take a minute. And please have supper with us if you can. Though, it's rather simple fare.

WIFE: Please, Madam. We've been of so little help . . .

MAN: No trouble at all. Please stay a while. Mother will join us as soon as she's finished praying . . .

HUSBAND (*to* WIFE): Well, why not, Wife? They're being so kind. Let's at least pay our respects to their Mother . . .

WIFE: Well, let's at least do that.

MAN: Then it's settled. Well, just as I suspected . . . In your case, you wouldn't go on . . . . I suppose so. That's how most people

would naturally feel. But, mind you, I'm going on. I'm absolutely committed to that. Remember? "To climb over the dead
and advance forward." That's the way I feel about it.

(MOTHER *finally rises and approaches the table.*)

WOMAN: Mother, are you all right?

MOTHER: Making coffee?

WOMAN: Never mind, I'll do it, Mother. Please sit down.

MOTHER: Make mine strong. Somehow, I feel very tired. (*To*
MAN.) What happened to the record?

MAN: Oh, that's right. The record. (*To the couple.*) I'm going to
put on a record. If you don't mind, please listen. Let me explain. Dad had a favorite one . . . This is it . . . (*Putting the
record on.*) It's old and quite worn, but . . .

(*Setting the needle on the record. The record sputters for while and finally, rather faintly, the worn sounds begin to be heard. Everyone
strains to listen. It is the old, popular tune beginning with: "The—
sun—sets—on—the—desert . . ."*)

. . . My Old Man loved it. Isn't it curious? A song about the
desert. He wanted so badly to go there.

(*Everyone moves closer to the phonograph, lest they miss any part of
the faint recording. Gradually, the stage darkens. When the stage
lights are again turned on dimly, it is already night. Everyone is sitting around the table, with supper apparently over. The record is still
playing. But no one is listening, except MOTHER.*)

MAN: How about turning it off, Mother? The record will wear
out. Besides, if you play it too much, it will annoy our guests.

MOTHER: I see. In that case . . . (*Stops the phonograph.*)

HUSBAND: No, we don't mind.

WIFE: It's such a lovely song.

WOMAN: Mother, aren't you cold?

MOTHER: I'm all right.

MAN: No, you'd better put something over your shoulders.
There's a little breeze.

WOMAN: I'll bring something to throw over her shoulders. (*Rising
and going toward the cart.*)

WIFE: How long has it been since we've eaten at a table—like
this?

HUSBAND: You're right. After all, a meal should be served at the
table.

WOMAN: Here, Mother. Please put this around your shoulders.

MOTHER: Oh, thank you.

WOMAN: We had many more things until rather recently. The tableware was complete, and we could prepare more elaborate meals. But the dishes were all either broken or thrown away because they were too heavy. How about another cup of tea?

HUSBAND: Thank you.

WOMAN: And you, Madam?

WIFE: Thank you.

MAN: Ah . . . There's something I want to discuss with all of you . . .

WOMAN: The household goods gradually get fewer, and our life is becoming simple. But that can't be helped. At least, under the circumstances. We'll eventually become just like you two. A single suitcase will serve all our needs. Shall I pour you a cup, Mother?

MOTHER: Yes. Did you see the sunset a while ago?

WOMAN: Yes, I did.

MOTHER: Wasn't it beautiful?

MAN (*to* WOMAN): Wife, sit down for a minute. There's something I want to talk over with everyone.

MOTHER: I just remembered. You could get a fine view of the sunset from the library roof, in back of the middle school. Do you remember? We used to go there all the time.

WOMAN (*sitting*): You mean with Father?

MOTHER: Yes . . . with Father . . .

MAN: Listen . . . There's something I'd like to discuss . . . (*To* HUSBAND *and* WIFE.) That's all right. Please stay. I'd like you both to listen, too. It's about our previous talk. . . . Wife, I was talking earlier with these people . . . Ah . . . About— whether we should go on or not. We're going, of course. That's been settled. So that's not the issue. And I intend to go on. Still . . . you know . . . Father's dead now. That won't stop us . . . So, I'm not bringing up a change in our original plans . . . Rather, whether there's a need for a discussion now . . . That's all. What do you think? Isn't this a good time to go over our plans again? I talked about this with our guests, but suppose—now just suppose—someone else in our group dies? Isn't that possible? You never can tell. What shall we do, then?

I think this is a very important issue . . . So, how about it?
(*Everyone remains silent.*)
   Wife, how about it?

WOMAN: What do you mean, exactly?

MAN: That's why I'm asking you. Should we go on or not?

WOMAN: You know the answer to that.

MAN: Of course, I know! But didn't I just finish telling you? We should take this opportunity to bring it up again . . . Oh, yes, before we get into that I should make it clear to you. I intend to go on.

WOMAN: But there's no need to bring it up again.

MAN: I know. I know, but still . . . Didn't I just tell you? I'm not raising this issue because I don't want to go on. I'm going! I want to go on! I'll keep going even if I have to do it alone. Still . . .

MOTHER (*to* WOMAN): Daughter, I don't want to go on any farther.

WOMAN: Why, Mother?

MAN: You see! I brought it up because I knew this could happen. It can, you know. That's natural.

WOMAN: Why, Mother?

MOTHER: I suddenly felt that way a while ago, in front of Father's grave. I just didn't want to go on.

WOMAN: Why?

MOTHER: I don't know. I didn't mean to talk this way. Please forgive me. You see, it can't be helped. You two go on.

WOMAN: But what will you do, Mother?

MOTHER: Go home.

MAN: Go home? By yourself?

MOTHER (*to the couple*): Say, aren't you going back now?

HUSBAND: Why, yes. Of course, we'll be pasting posters along the way.

MOTHER: I wonder? Can I go along with you? My luggage is only personal things. I can carry it myself . . .

WIFE: Please do. We're working as we go back, so it'll be slow. But that may suit you perfectly. You won't get tired that way. Naturally, it depends on whether it's agreeable with the rest of you . . .

WOMAN: No, Mother. There's no one back there.

MOTHER: I'll be fine. There's the Kimuras, the Yamadas, and the Kobayashis, and Dr. Kawata . . .

WOMAN: But they're outsiders, Mother. They aren't your kin. You see, that's the difference. You mustn't go. Please come with us. It's only proper. That's why we left together. You see, we're all related. We can't allow ourselves to become separated from each other.

MAN: Besides, you're imposing on those people.

HUSBAND: Not at all . . .

WOMAN: Come with us. That's best. If you sleep on it tonight, tomorrow you'll feel the same way.

MOTHER: But, you know, it's strange. As soon as I knew Father was dead, I suddenly lost my enthusiasm. Don't you see? Now that he's dead, I haven't any reason to go on from here.

MAN: Even if you went back, Father won't be there.

MOTHER: That's true. I know that. But if I go back, I'll still have various memories. That's right. I'm sure it's because of that. Frankly, I've had this terrible craving to go back, from a while ago. I want to see the Kimuras and the Yamadas and the Kobayashis. And Dr. Kawata, too. I've got to tell them. About Father, I mean. Then I'm sure they'll all mourn for him. I know he'd want it that way.

WOMAN: Don't get discouraged, Mother.

MOTHER: I'm not discouraged. Why should I be? Aren't you sorry for Father? We couldn't even give him a funeral . . . That's why I want to go back and give him a funeral—a real funeral . . . I'll have everyone come. And talk to them. I'll tell them what kind of a man he was. And how he behaved at certain times. And bring up other things in his life, too. That makes it a real funeral, doesn't it? What happens if we bury him in a place like this and go on? No one will know he's dead. And no one will ever think of him.

WOMAN: Now, Mother. We've already said goodby to everyone. And didn't they give us a grand farewell party? In other words, that was our funeral. When the townspeople talk of us now, I'm sure, they'd only speak as though they were recalling the dead. Isn't that right? When we left home, Father and Mother and the rest of us all cried, like at a funeral. You see, you're expecting too much if you want another funeral back there.

MAN: Wife, that's enough. Why not let her go? If she's so set on going, we should ask them, though it's an imposition . . .

HUSBAND: We wouldn't mind in the least . . .

WOMAN: No!

MAN: Why not? Let's you and I go on. I'm determined to go.

WOMAN: No, Mother. You just don't understand. Now listen to me. Suppose you go back. At first, everyone will treat you nicely. And they'll certainly listen to your stories. And about Father's death, too. But what happens after that? The funeral won't last forever. And even the Kimuras and the Yamadas can't stir up their emotions day after day. What happens then? Remember, we won't be there. And from then on your days will get long. Don't forget, Mother. We decided to leave in the first place because we couldn't stand those endless days.

MOTHER: I know you're right, but . . .

WOMAN: Of course I am. And that's how it was. You see, Mother, until now you never realized what leaving actually meant. So, whenever something happened before, you immediately began looking for a way to make a fresh start. But you know, Mother, that's impossible. For once we've started, there's no turning back. We've no other choice besides going as far as we can.

MAN: And after we get there, then what?

WOMAN: That's right. We might even die along the way . . . You see, Mother, that's how it is. Just as you suddenly wanted to go back home in front of Father's grave, I suddenly want to go on, running all the way. I want to run and run as far as we can go. And get there as soon as we can.

(*Long pause.*)

WIFE (*to* MOTHER): Please go with your family. I think that's best. It's just as she says. No matter how you look at it, there's nothing better than going with your own family.

MOTHER: I guess you're right. I suppose that's best, after all . . . (*Starts crying. It becomes increasingly louder.*)

MAN: What do you think, Wife? Maybe we could all have another cup of tea . . .

WOMAN: Yes, let's do that. We've taken so much of your time

. . . I'll make some hot tea right away. Husband, shall we have *that* . . . You know, there's some black tea, isn't there?

MAN: Ah, that's a good idea . . .

HUSBAND: The wind is getting quite strong . . .

MAN: Mother, please stop crying . . .

(*For a while,* MOTHER's *crying continues. Gradually the stage darkens. When the stage suddenly brightens, it is already morning, and the preparation for departure has been completed.* MOTHER *stands fixed in front of the grave, and* WOMAN *is behind her.* MAN *checks the baggage on the cart, and the couple are at left of stage center to see the family off.*)

WIFE: We're lucky to have such fine weather.

HUSBAND: Yes, That's most important.

MAN: Wife, we're ready. Shouldn't we get started?

WOMAN (*leaving the grave, speaks to the couple*): Thank you so much for everything. You've been a great help.

HUSBAND: No, don't mention it . . .

WIFE: Please be careful along the way . . .

WOMAN: Thank you. We're leaving, Mother.

MOTHER: Yes, I know. (*Leaving the grave, addresses the couple.*) You were so kind . . . I must say goodby now. I thought it over all night. And I think it's better to leave together . . .

WIFE: Of course, you're quite right.

MAN: Mother!

MOTHER: Thank you so much.

HUSBAND: Please take care of yourself . . .

MAN: Well, we're going. Goodby.

HUSBAND and WIFE: Goodby . . .

(MAN *pulls the cart,* WOMAN *pushes the baby carriage, and* MOTHER *follows, using a cane. For a while, the couple look on, waving occasionally.*)

HUSBAND: They're gone . . .

WIFE: Yes . . .

HUSBAND: Still, it was such a pity.

WIFE: Why?

HUSBAND: Of course it is. Their mother was quite feeble. She'll die. She's bound to collapse during the trip.

WIFE: I suppose so . . .

HUSBAND: Wife, why did you say those things before? Remember, you said it was better for her to go with them. I just don't understand why.

WIFE: You know, come to think of it, I don't either. But . . . at the time I felt that way. It was better for her to go with them. Wasn't that the proper thing? Of course, it is . . . After all, that was the thing to do . . .

HUSBAND (*approaching the grave and looking down*): What shall we do?

WIFE: About what?

HUSBAND: About us, of course . . .

WIFE: What do you mean? (*She also approaches the grave and looks down.*)

HUSBAND: Maybe it's strange talking this way, but I suddenly want to go back.

WIFE: I feel the same way. Suddenly, I want to go back, too.

HUSBAND: Then shall we do that?

WIFE: Yes. Wasn't that our original intention?

HUSBAND: What I mean is: Let's go now, without finishing the job.

WIFE: Without posting?

HUSBAND: Remember, Wife? Didn't you once say you wanted to change work? . . . Well, could we make a go of it if we start a small shop?

WIFE: How about money?

HUSBAND: We'll borrow somewhere.

WIFE: Yes, I suppose we could try . . . But, Husband, I still think we should go back putting up the posters.

HUSBAND: You mean these?

WIFE: Yes . . .

HUSBAND: I see . . .

(*The couple gaze up the telephone pole*)

The stage darkens.

Scene Five

A single telephone pole with no posters. The stage is brightly lit.
(*For a while it is empty. Finally,* MAN *appears pulling the cart. On top of the baggage,* MOTHER, *holding a parasol, sits alone. Arriving at stage center, the cart suddenly sways wildly and comes to a halt.*)

MAN: That's funny . . .

MOTHER: What happened, Son?

MAN: It stopped.

MOTHER: It stopped? Maybe a stone or something is stuck.

MAN: That's possible . . . (*He cannot let go of the cart.*) There's nothing I can do right now.

MOTHER: Can't you see what's wrong?

MAN: No, I can't. Besides, if I let my hands go, even for a moment, the cart will begin to rock . . . Well, haven't we walked quite enough?

MOTHER: Quite enough . . . We've covered a lot today. Tired?

MAN: Am I tired? That hardly describes my condition! I feel as if I'm in a daze. How's the scenery, Mother?

MOTHER: The scenery, Son? Why, it's all hazy . . .

MAN: Hazy? How are the telephone poles?

MOTHER: Just the same. I can't see too far, but they seem to be lined up, very persistently.

MAN: Disgusting! I wonder who put them up?

MOTHER: No doubt the electricians, Son. That's their job, you know. They go anywhere to put them up.

MAN: Aren't you hot?

MOTHER: Of course. But it can't be helped.

MAN: It can't? Well, that's true. It can't be helped. How about it, Mother? Can you get down from there?

MOTHER: Get down? From here?

MAN: That's right. I've thought it over carefully. And there's no other way to get around this desperate situation.

MOTHER: What happens after I get down?

MAN: After that, I want you to bring the prop for the cart that's over there—to here. Then, you see, I can get my hands free to check whether a stone is stuck in the wheel. And if it is, I can remove it. And maybe I can rest a bit and drink some water. What do you think of this scheme?

MOTHER: Not bad at all.

MAN: I thought so.

MOTHER: But I can't exactly jump down.

MAN: Of course not. You mustn't do a thing like that. If you break a leg, it would be terrible. It's a question of whether you can get down slowly by holding onto things.

MOTHER: Slowly, you mean . . . But tell me. What happens if I can't get down?

MAN: What happens then? Well, it can't be helped. We'll simply have to wait until my wife returns.

MOTHER: I have to stay up here?

MAN: Yes, up there. There's nothing else we can do, is there?

MOTHER: I suppose not. I wonder where she went?

MAN: Where did she go? Anyway, she's the type that likes to go on ahead. In other words, she's full of curiosity. She wants to see and probe everything. Just wait and see. She'll be back soon with something she picked up.

MOTHER: I don't mind that, but is it safe to let her wander off by herself?

MAN: If she's not safe, who is? Mother, let's get this straight. We're the ones who are in trouble.

MOTHER: Well, that's true.

MAN: Shall we wait, then?

MOTHER: No, I'll give it a try. I'll come down. I think I can make it.

MAN: Then please try.

MOTHER: Keep the cart steady!

MAN: Don't worry. I'll hold it down.

MOTHER: Anyway, the first step is to close this parasol, I suppose. (*Folds it.*)

MAN: That sounds reasonable. You know, Mother, an acrobat could walk on a tight-rope with a parasol in one hand. It's probably too hard for you.

MOTHER: And then . . . I guess I'll slip off my shoes. (*Begins taking off her shoes.*)

MAN: Please suit yourself. That way, you may avoid slipping. But do be careful. It'll be quite a sight if you slip and come crashing down.

MOTHER: Stop trying to scare me. (*Throwing off the shoes.*) I feel like a monkey.

MAN: You've just taken off your shoes, so far. Have some confidence in yourself. Please stop if you begin and find it dangerous. We only have to wait. Come to think of it, I'm surprised you managed to climb up in the first place. Besides, you were alone, weren't you?

MOTHER: Yes, all by myself.

MAN: Why did you climb up so high?

MOTHER: Well, I thought I'd feel better up here. But tell me, is it harder to get down?

MAN: We'll see.

MOTHER: I've a feeling it is.

MAN: Shall we start?

MOTHER: Shall we? Be sure you hold down the cart.

MAN: I told you not to worry.

MOTHER: Should I spit on my hands now?

MAN: Don't do that! It's bad manners.

MOTHER: But practically everyone does it when they're lifting something heavy.

MAN: Well, it's all up to you. But hurry. This is more frightening for the bystander.

MOTHER: Here I go . . . (*Slowly, she begins the awkward descent.*)

MAN: Some places may be hard to get a firm foothold, so you'd better test your footing. Press down with your feet, to be sure . . . That's right. You're doing fine. Yes, that's wonderful.

MOTHER: Son, it's rocking.

MAN: I'm sorry, Mother. You've just a little more to go. Keep calm. Try to get a foothold on something large. That's it . . .

(MOTHER *somehow manages to get down.*)

Congratulations. You've accomplished a difficult task. A most remarkable feat.

MOTHER: I shouldn't have climbed up there.

MAN: Oh, don't be so modest, Mother. Please get the prop for the cart.

(*When the cart is propped,* MAN *is finally free.*)

Now I'm free at last! Mother, will you have some water?

MOTHER: I'd love some. (*Examining the cart.*) I don't see any stone stuck here.

MAN: Maybe not a stone. But something must be stuck. It suddenly stopped with quite a jolt.

MOTHER: Nothing seems to be stuck.

MAN: Well, let me take a look . . .

(*Squatting, the two examine the cart.* WOMAN *with the child on her back appears from stage right, pulling an old, rusty bicycle.*)

WOMAN: Oh, what happened, Husband?

MAN: This cart suddenly stopped. (*Noticing the bicycle.*) What in the world is that?

WOMAN: A bicycle. Can't you tell? Isn't this the best thing I've picked up so far, Mother? Though it's rusty, it still runs. If we use a little lubricant, it'll run much better. When I first found the bicycle, I thought it wouldn't run. Well, it appears hopeless even now. But I took a chance and got a short ride on it— over there. I couldn't manage it too well with this child on my back, but it does run. So you see, it's still convenient. Might make a lot of difference. It's not too attractive, but who cares? After all, there's no one else around watching.

MOTHER: Was it lying somewhere?

WOMAN: Yes. Imagine finding something like this! I thought someone might be close by . . . But that's hardly possible. I'm sure it was thrown away because there was no more use for it. This wreck. Wouldn't you agree? Normally, it'd be thrown away. Husband, isn't this quite a find! You can use it, too. Why don't you take a ride?

MAN: Well . . . But why do it now? Haven't you already done it?

WOMAN: Yes. But why don't you try, too? You'll find out for yourself, it still runs. Scrapes a bit. The chain may be caught somewhere. See what I mean?

MOTHER: Son, why don't you ride it? After all, she did manage to pick up the bicycle. Looks a bit old but seems quite sturdy. Yes, it might be useful.

WOMAN: Yes, don't you agree? I thought so, too. Though it's rusty, it's quite substantial. Husband, once we take off the rust, it'll be in fairly decent shape. Why don't you ride it, Husband?

MOTHER: Son?

MAN: All right. I'll try. But this is not the time for it. The cart won't move.

WOMAN: I know. Something is stuck, for sure . . . I'll check. (*Offers* MAN *the bicycle.*) Isn't it sturdy? Not wobbly at all.

MAN: Well, I suppose so. Still, how could you do it? What made you pick up this thing?

WOMAN: I already told you it doesn't look too attractive. But the point is whether it runs or not. Shall I push you?

MAN: No! No!

(MAN *rides the bicycle. It slowly circles around the cart, making a scraping sound.*)

WOMAN: Well, how does it run?

MAN: Hmm.

MOTHER: I hear a noise.

WOMAN: I know. I'm sure the chain is rubbing against something. If that's all, it's easy to fix. Husband, isn't it easy to fix that?

MAN: Fix what?

WOMAN: That noise.

MAN: Fixing the noise won't solve anything.

WOMAN: Of course it will. Just simply tap the metal hood covering the chain.

(*The child begins to cry.*)

And, naturally, you need some oil. Lubrication will take care of the rest. (*Humoring the child.*) There, there. Oh, I forgot. I have to give him milk and change his diaper. Mother, I'm putting him down, so will you hold him?

MOTHER: All right.

MAN: You expect to take this along?

WOMAN: Of course. Don't worry. It's not that heavy. Besides, it's convenient. It's bound to be useful.

MAN: What possible use can this thing have?

WOMAN: Well . . . It'll be useful. Will you take down the table, Husband? I must put down the baby and fix his milk. There, there. Don't cry. I'm sorry, Mother. We'll take down the table, so please lay the baby on it.

MOTHER: Yes, all right.

MAN: How about using the baby carriage?

WOMAN: That'll do. Though it's a bit difficult to change the diaper . . . Well, why not? Husband, must I always remind you! The table should be stored where it's easy to get at. It's constantly used, though the carriage isn't. Mother, please lay him in the carriage when it comes down. Please don't hold him. I know you're tired. Husband, after you finish taking down the carriage, please get the diaper. I'm sure there's a clean one. I think it was in the bottom drawer of the dresser. And . . . Oh, yes, I'll fix the milk. Where's the water?

MOTHER (*laying the child in the carriage*): Shall I fix it?

WOMAN: Never mind. Instead, will you change the diaper when he finds it? I'm sure it's wet. No, don't bother, Mother. Husband, you take care of it. Mother's tired.

MOTHER: I'm all right.

WOMAN: Never mind, Mother. Husband, will you please take down a chair and let Mother sit down?

MAN: Yes, I'll do that. Don't worry, Mother. I'll change the diaper. Please sit here.

MOTHER: Are you sure? (*To the child.*) Stop crying, the milk will be ready soon. (*Sitting in the chair.*)

MAN: Well, I'm ready to change his diaper. But why does he cry so much?

WOMAN: He's healthy. That's proof that he is. Dr. Kawata said so, too. He said crying was a form of exercise. Exercise—that's right, Husband. That's good for exercising.

MAN: What is?

WOMAN: That bicycle. Won't you be exercising if you ride that around?

MAN: You know, I'm pulling this cart every day. That's enough.

WOMAN: But, Husband, exercise must train the whole body. You'll become a cripple if you just pull the cart. Oh, where's the parasol, Mother?

MOTHER: Oh, the parasol? I forgot it on top of the cart.

WOMAN: My, you're right. It's up there. It's bad for you if you go around bareheaded, Mother. Husband, can you find something that she can wear on her head? Or else she'll get a sunstroke. Here's the milk.

MOTHER: Maybe I should put on that towel over there.

MAN: Then please do that. I'll get *that* later . . . the parasol, I mean.

WOMAN: This child drinks like a starving puppy. Husband, Mother, aren't you hungry, too?

MOTHER: Now that you mention it.

WOMAN: Let's eat something. Is there anything, Husband?

MAN: Shall we prepare tea?

WOMAN: No tea. Right, Mother? We can't stay too long. A simple snack will do. Just look at him! That child must have been really hungry. He's not even stopping for a breath. Well, drink by yourself, then. Husband, aren't there some crackers wrapped in brown paper? (*Leaving the carriage and going to the cart.*)

MAN: That's what I'm looking for . . . Never mind. I'll find it.

WOMAN: I'm counting on you, then. It's a brown bag. But wait . . . Were they wrapped in newspaper, Mother? Remember? They were left over from some other teatime.

MOTHER: No, in a brown bag. I asked you if I should rewrap it in newspaper, and you said it was unsanitary . . .

WOMAN: Yes, that's right. Oh, did you find it?

MAN: I found it, but there's hardly any left.

WOMAN (*taking a cracker*): They were quite delicious. Oh, it's not soggy, yet. It must be the dry weather. Oh, please give one to Mother, Husband. It's delicious. I must have been hungry. Oh, that reminds me, Husband, where's the oil can?

MAN: The oil can? What for?

WOMAN: I just want to use it on that bicycle.

MAN: Why do you have to do it now? Can't you sit still for a while?

WOMAN: But why not? I want to. I think oil will make quite a difference.

MAN: Remember the tool box in the back of the cart? It's in there.

WOMAN: In the tool box?

(MAN *and* MOTHER *are eating crackers.* MAN *discovers something in the direction of stage right and tells* MOTHER. MOTHER *also notices.* MAN *approaches* WOMAN *at the cart.*)

MAN: Wife!

(*Pointing to stage right.* WOMAN *turns around and also gazes toward stage right. All three stare silently. After a long pause,* SECOND MAN *and* SECOND WOMAN *appear, looking very tired.* SECOND MAN *is pulling a push cart loaded with household goods.* SECOND WOMAN *has a baby on her back and is pushing the cart. It is a pitiful sight.*)

SECOND MAN (*noticing everyone*): Well . . . Hello . . .

MAN: Hello, it must be hard work . . .

SECOND MAN: Yes . . .

WOMAN: Won't you take a break? Husband, perhaps you can take down the chairs . . .

MOTHER: That's right. You should at least give the baby a chance to get off the mother's back for a while.

SECOND MAN: No, thank you. We're in a hurry . . .

WOMAN: I see. But the tea will be ready soon. Husband . . .
That's right . . . Maybe they could just have tea with us . . .

MAN: Yes. It'll be ready soon.

SECOND MAN: No, really, we're in a hurry. Well, goodby . . .

MAN: Are you going back?

SECOND MAN: Going back?

MAN: Ah . . . (*Pointing to stage left.*) Are you going in that direction?

SECOND MAN: That's right.

MAN: But why?

SECOND MAN (*pointing to stage right*): We started from over there.
Wife, I'm going . . .

MOTHER: Over there? From where—"over there"?

SECOND WOMAN: There's a town. We came from there . . .

(*A short pause.*)

SECOND MAN: Then I'll say goodby. Wife?

SECOND WOMAN: Yes, goodby.

MAN: Ah . . . Did you meet anyone along the way?

SECOND MAN: No, no one . . .

MOTHER: Is the baby all right? Doesn't he need rest?

SECOND WOMAN: Yes, he's all right. He's used to it.

WOMAN: Well . . . we have one, too . . . in that baby carriage.
Still, it must be difficult. Well . . . he does require attention
and . . .

SECOND WOMAN: It's difficult, but it can't be helped.

SECOND MAN: Wife, I'm going.

WOMAN (*pointing to stage right*): We're going over there. That's
what we decided to do and started out.

MAN: And how do you—ah—feel about it? That is . . . Why did
you start out—from over there?

SECOND MAN: We decided—to start out . . . That's all. I'm sorry.
We're in a hurry. Oh, yes, I forgot to tell you. Someone's dead
back there.

WOMAN: Dead? Who?

SECOND MAN: We don't know him. It's a young man.

MOTHER: Oh, dear!

SECOND MAN: Do you know him?

MAN: Maybe . . .

WOMAN: I wonder why he's dead?

SECOND MAN: I don't know.

SECOND WOMAN: Perhaps he died of hunger. He was terribly thin. And he only carried a single, tiny bag—like this . . . (*Gesturing.*)

SECOND MAN: Let's go!

SECOND WOMAN: Yes, goodby.

(SECOND MAN *and* SECOND WOMAN *slowly leave. The three look on, in a daze. For a while, the characters remain motionless. Then* MOTHER, *remembering, approaches the carriage and peeks in.*)

WOMAN: How is he?

MOTHER: Sleeping soundly. (*Sits in a nearby chair.*)

WOMAN (*approaches the bicycle and rather absentmindedly applies the oil*): What shall we do with this bicycle, Husband?

MAN: Hmm . . .

WOMAN: Shall we get rid of it, after all?

MAN: Hmm . . .

WOMAN: Of course, we should get rid of it. We need to travel as light as possible . . . Mother, shall we have tea? Perhaps we should take a little rest, have tea, and then start out again. Right, Husband?

MAN: Wife, why don't you forget it!

WOMAN: Forget what?

MAN: You're wasting the oil.

WOMAN: I suppose so. (*Rising.*) I'll get rid of it, after all. It's a shame, though. But we must be practical at a time like this. Did you see, Husband? Their baggage . . . it was so small! (*Gesturing.*)

MOTHER: I wonder why they're going over there?

WOMAN: Let's have tea. I'll pour you a tasty cup.

MAN: There's no time for that.

WOMAN: Oh, why not?

MAN (*pointing to the cart*): We have to do something about that.

WOMAN: That's right, I forgot. But isn't something stuck in the wheel? (*Examining the cart.*)

MOTHER: There's nothing stuck. I looked at it a while ago.

WOMAN: Then it needs oiling.

MAN: No, it doesn't! It suddenly stopped with a jolt. Isn't that so, Mother?

MOTHER: That's right—with a jolt. I was sure it struck a stone . . .

WOMAN (*rising*): I don't think there's anything stuck in the wheel.

MOTHER: I don't think so, either.

MAN: It was moving so smoothly until then. Not even rocking from side to side . . .

MOTHER: Ah—you don't suppose it broke down because I rode on it, do you?

WOMAN: That's impossible! It was much heavier before. And haven't we thrown away quite a lot? Husband, does it really not move?

MAN: No, it doesn't. But let's try just once more. Wife, try pushing from behind.

WOMAN: All right.

MAN: Good. Mother, please, will you hold on to this prop for the cart?

MOTHER: All right.

MAN: All—right! Do it slowly! The cart might break down if we pull too suddenly. Then we'll be in real trouble. Here I go! (*Pulls.*)

WOMAN: Wait! Wait, Husband! I know what's wrong! (*Going around to the other side of the cart.*) Look, Husband, this is terrible! Here's the problem!

MAN: Mother, the prop!

MOTHER: Right away!

WOMAN: You see, the pillow block is cracked. No wonder it won't move. If we don't take care of it, it'll split in two.

MAN: . . .

MOTHER: It happened because I was too heavy. That's why it broke . . .

WOMAN: Can you do anything, Husband?

MAN: Hmm . . . First, let's lighten the load. Let's throw away things. It can't be helped, can it? That'll keep the cart going until we have it repaired.

MOTHER: You know, I shouldn't have ridden on it . . .

WOMAN: Don't blame yourself. Anyway, Mother, let's throw *that* away—that dresser, I mean. Mother, do you mind? There's hardly anything in it now. And it's so heavy.

MOTHER: All right.

WOMAN: We'll take down the dresser and get rid of some old things. Won't that be enough, Husband?

MAN: Yeah. Let's try. Wife, lend me a hand for a minute.

WOMAN: All right.

(*The couple take down the dresser and a few small items.*)
Mother, will you check the drawers? If you want to keep anything, just put it in some cardboard box around here.

MOTHER: All right.

MAN: How about this phonograph and the records?

WOMAN: Let's throw them away. All right, Mother?

MOTHER: All right. Throw them away.

WOMAN: And what about the table and the chairs?

MAN: Let's keep them . . . By all means . . . And we don't want
to throw away things for our tea. The rest can go.

WOMAN: I suppose . . . Then I'll do that. I'll get rid of this tableware, instead. Don't you agree? We hardly use it . . .

MAN: Well, it can't be helped.

WOMAN: And that baby carriage.

MAN: Why?

WOMAN: We don't need it. Don't I usually carry him on my back?
Besides, those people didn't have one either.

MAN: I see . . . Then I guess it's fine . . .

WOMAN: Could you help me a minute, Mother? I'm going to carry
this child. And let's take out the blanket from the carriage and
load it on the cart.

MOTHER: Are you sure you'll be all right with him always on your
back?

WOMAN: Of course. I've done it so far. Isn't he sleeping soundly?
This child really likes to sleep. I wonder if he's sick?

(*Carrying the child,* WOMAN *cleans out the baby carriage and loads
everything on the cart. She assembles all the items to be discarded in
one spot.*)
Will this do?

MAN: Yes. I guess so.

WOMAN: In any case, let's try moving the cart. I wonder what
happened to *that* thing . . . I used it for pulling, when we
went up the hill before . . .

MAN: The rope's over there. Still tied to the cart.

WOMAN: Oh, here it is.

(WOMAN *places the rope tied to the cart on her shoulder.* MAN *grips
the handle of the cart.*)

MAN: Wife, here I go!

WOMAN: All right.

(*The couple apply all their strength and try pulling, but the cart fails to respond.* MOTHER *lays the prop she is holding on the back of the cart.*)

MOTHER: Shall I push?

WOMAN: No, Mother. Is it still too heavy?

MAN: Let's try once more. Are you ready?

WOMAN: All right.

(*They try again. The cart begins to move slightly.*)

MAN: A little more . . .

WOMAN: Yes . . .

(*Placing her hands on the back of the cart,* MOTHER *pushes. She applies her entire strength. The cart moves slowly.*)

MAN: It's moving!

WOMAN: Just a little more!

(*The cart begins to move, though swaying.* MOTHER *loses her strength and collapses. The cart disappears at stage right. For a while,* MOTHER *remains where she has fallen. Finally, she barely manages to raise herself.*)

MOTHER: Son . . .

(*Her arms relax, and she again falls on her face and lies still on the ground.*)

   The stage darkens.

Scene Six

   A telephone pole without any posters. It is nearly twilight.

(*For a while, the stage is empty. Finally,* WOMAN *enters, carrying the baby and gazing vacantly. She approaches the telephone pole and holds an ear to it. Soon* MAN *slowly appears, pulling the cart holding the household goods—now reduced to practically nothing. He stops.*)

MAN: What are you doing?

WOMAN: I hear a sound . . .

MAN: A sound?

WOMAN: I'm sure it's the sound of electricity flowing . . . Doesn't electricity also make a sound as it flows? Just like a river . . .

MAN: That's absurd . . . Isn't it the wind? The wind strikes the wires and that makes the sound . . .

WOMAN: The wind? (*Looking up at the sky.*) It doesn't seem to be blowing.

MAN: It's the wind . . . It doesn't seem to be blowing, but it actually is—higher up . . .

WOMAN: I'd have hardly suspected . . .

MAN: What?

WOMAN: That the wind is blowing . . .

MAN: The wind is always blowing. Up there, a wind is always blowing in the same direction. I mean, at this time of year . . .

WOMAN: The autumn wind?

MAN: No, this one is much higher . . .

WOMAN (*Again putting her ear against the pole*): Sounds like rushing water . . . Like a river flowing far away. I still think it's the sound of electricity. The wind should sound a little different. Remember? That one stormy day when the electric wires in back of our house were catching the wind and whistling loudly . . . That was the sound of the wind. The next day, the wires broke and someone got electrocuted.

MAN: This isn't a stormy day. It's such fine weather . . . In other words, I'm talking about a different kind of wind. It's blowing way up there and at a terrific speed. You can hardly hear it at all. It sounds as though something terrifically fast is flying over.

WOMAN: But . . . this is electricity. Why don't you try listening?

MAN: What? Well . . .

(*Releasing the cart,* MAN *approaches the telephone pole and places an ear to it.*)

WOMAN: Well?

MAN: Hmm . . . I can hear.

WOMAN: The wind?

MAN: Hmm . . . (*Removing his ear and looking up.*) I don't know.

WOMAN (*putting her ear to the pole*): I think it's electricity. I learned this once. You see, electricity travels seven and a half times around the world in one second. That's what is it, I'm sure . . . And it's that, flowing up there. Don't you think it's fantastic?

MAN (*placing the prop to the cart*): Why?

WOMAN: Seven and a half times around the world in just one second! It's fantastic!

MAN: I suppose so. (*Taking out a cigarette and smoking.*) Why don't you quit now?

WOMAN: Yes . . . (*Continues listening.*)

MAN: Why listen to the sound of electricity?

WOMAN: Why not?

MAN: I'm asking you.

WOMAN (*removing her ear*): Aren't you impressed?

MAN: Impressed? By what?

WOMAN: By electricity. A man invented it.

MAN: Of course he did. I know that. But is that any reason for being impressed now? Everyone was fully impressed when it was first invented.

WOMAN: I can't understand why you're not.

MAN (*taking down a chair*): Sit here.

WOMAN (*sitting*): I wonder how man ever thought up electricity?

MAN: I don't know. I'm sure that the guy who invented it didn't know either. He certainly didn't think that anyone would still be impressed years afterwards—listening to its sound from a telephone pole in the middle of a plain. That's right. Everyone is digging around in his own corner somewhere and finding all sorts of things. Later on, when he looks back, it seems awfully foolish. But no one ever thought so as he was busily working away at it. Isn't that right? Otherwise, why is a telephone pole standing in a place like this?

WOMAN: I suppose . . . I never imagined that telephone poles could be standing everywhere, in such a persistent fashion.

MAN: It's persistent, all right. They're all persistent. So is that chair.

(*Pointing to the chair in which* WOMAN *is sitting. She rises.*)

Take a look at it. Someone invented this. I don't know how he thought it up. I'm sure, at the time, he was terribly serious. How weird it looks! (*Kicking over the chair.*)

WOMAN: You'll break it! (*Picking it up.*)

MAN: So is this cart. Wife, take a look. Isn't it weird? It really is. If you ask me, this is weird no matter how you look at it. Why was it made in *this* shape? Why not differently? It's the fault of the guy who invented it. He could only come up with this shape. I'm sure everyone was surprised when it was first brought out in public. They must have gotten the creeps. It's so grotesque! Damn it! (*Kicking the prop for the cart. The cart tips and several items fall down.*)

WOMAN: Please stop, Husband! What are you doing? (*Picking up the fallen items and rearranging them.*)

MAN (*picking up the prop*): And this prop for the cart, too. Ha! Ha! Ha! Ha! . . . Take a look, Wife. We invented this! What an ugly, lousy invention! Ha! Ha! Ha! Wife, just take a look at it. If they found this lying on the roadside, no one would know what it was good for.

WOMAN (*arranging the baggage*): Haven't you done enough damage? Quite a few dishes must be broken by now.

MAN: They'll never know. They may realize it was made for some purpose, but they'd never know for exactly what. This—a prop for a cart? (*Grabbing the prop, he suddenly strikes the baggage on the cart.*) Damn it!

WOMAN: Husband . . . What's wrong with you, anyway?

MAN: Take a look at all those inventions and discoveries. A huge number of men worked a long time to invent and to discover them . . . They worked like hell. Damn it! Damn it! (*Striking the baggage.*)

WOMAN: Husband, please stop! They'll break! Husband! (*Trying to restrain him.*)

MAN: Leave me alone! I just can't stand this junk anymore. Junk! Junk!

(MAN *keeps pounding away. Bewildered,* WOMAN *looks on.*)

Every time this junk—all these small things—was invented, everybody must have gotten the creeps. That's right. You know, all of them are grotesque, each and every one of them. Damn it! (*He lifts one side of the cart and all the baggage falls down noisily to the ground.*)

(WOMAN *silently looks at the baggage.*)

Damn it! Damn it! Damn it!

(*While cursing,* MAN *continues to pound away at every piece of household goods on the ground with the prop.* WOMAN *stops restraining him. She goes to a fallen cardboard box, hastily examines the tableware, and sets it out on the ground.* MAN *gradually calms down and finally stands in a daze. Finding an umbrella among the baggage, he picks it up. Unfolding it:*)

MAN: Look, it's a "bat-umbrella."[3] I'll bet everyone calls it that because it looks like a bat. But why? Wife, have you ever thought about this? Why is it made in this shape rather than in another? That's a reasonable question. There must have been other ways to keep off the rain. Of course, it's well made. The handle's easy to grip and the mechanism of the metal clasp is quite good. And the ribs are sturdy and light. Besides, it folds up. It almost makes me want to weep when I think about the work going into making this umbrella before it finally turned out this way. Listen, I'm fed up. You know, I can't stand the fact that this is a "bat-umbrella." It should have turned out more differently. That's right! And I won't stand for it. Damn it!

(*Still holding the umbrella, he continues to strike the ground with it until he finally destroys it. Glancing at the tattered umbrella,* MAN *throws it away. Taking out the dishes one by one from their newspaper wrappings,* WOMAN *sets them out carefully on the ground.* MAN *finds the alarm clock, gazes at it for a while, and then jabs it with the tip of the broken umbrella. His action becomes gradually more violent. Finally, the clock is destroyed. He stops and gazes at the broken clock. Picking it up, he holds it up to his ear. It has stopped running. He is somewhat nonplussed and lays it down on the ground; then he rises. Finally, he becomes aware of the wretched spectacle around him.* WOMAN *continues lining up the dishes.*)

. . . Forgive me, Wife. Wife! . . . What are you doing?

WOMAN: It's missing . . . I just can't find the saucer for this teacup.

MAN: Isn't it broken?

WOMAN: That's impossible. Besides, there aren't any broken pieces. It was wrapped carefully to keep from breaking. I was so sure it was in this box.

MAN: It's over there . . . Probably in that other box. (*Starts searching in another cardboard box.*) See, in here . . .

WOMAN: I didn't put it there. I put the matched pieces in this one.

MAN: Of course, it's here. It's bound to be somewhere. (*Looking among the scattered, old things.*)

[3] The Japanese word *kōmorigasa* literally means "bat-umbrella," referring to its resemblance to a bat.

WOMAN (*standing and still searching among the old things*): It's wrapped in newspaper. Please don't step on it by mistake. It wouldn't be in there. That's the laundry.

MAN: Hey, look what I found. (*Dangling a wind-bell.*) Remember, it's the one you found once. (*As* MAN *blows on it, the wind-bell rings faintly.*)

WOMAN (*holding up a framed photograph*): See what you've done, Husband! The picture of Grandfather and Grandmother is completely smashed.

MAN (*again, blowing on the wind-bell*): Whoever invented this must have had plenty of time on his hands . . .

WOMAN (*after taking out the pictures, she discards the broken frame*): We don't need this anymore. (*Rolling up the photograph and, as if reminded, holds it up to her eye and peeks through.*) Turn this way, Husband.

MAN (*stops searching*): What is it?

WOMAN (*looking at him*): I used to play like this once. I can see you.

MAN: How do I look?

WOMAN: . . . You've lost weight . . . (*Removing the rolled photograph from her eye.*) Husband, I wonder if I have, too?

MAN: Yeah . . . (*Looking at her.*) You have, too.

WOMAN: Do I look terrible?

MAN: Well, it can't be helped.

WOMAN: I think I'll wear *that* dress. Remember? I wore it to Yoshida's wedding . . . I wonder where it is?

MAN: Isn't it in that wicker trunk?

WOMAN: You're right, I'm sure of it . . . I'm putting the baby down. Could you lend me a hand for a minute?

MAN: Wife, what should I wear? (*Taking the child and laying him down.*)

WOMAN: You should wear *that!* Remember, Father's tuxedo. That should be somewhere.

MAN: Will it fit me?

WOMAN: Don't worry. It's not in there. It's in that suitcase . . .

MAN: I see, in here . . .

(*The two bustle about in their respective places and begin changing into their costumes. The child is left alone on a stand.*)

WOMAN: Find it?

MAN: Yes, I found it . . . But the smell of mothballs is awful . . .

WOMAN: Can you wear it?

MAN: I guess I can manage . . .

WOMAN: You know, this is my favorite dress. I wore it just once. Everyone said it looked perfect on me. Mother said it might be a bit dressy, but I think it's just right. Nowadays everyone's dressy. Women much older than me are in much dressier clothes.

MAN: Wife, something's missing . . .

WOMAN: What?

MAN: Oh, here it is.

WOMAN: Everything should be in there. I packed it myself. Actually, I wanted to wear this, that other time, too . . . I mean, at the celebration at the Kimuras. Oh, dear, what happened? There's a stain. I must have spilt tea or something. Will it come off? Unlikely. It might have if I noticed it right away. Husband, your handkerchief.

MAN: Oh, thanks.

WOMAN: Husband, can you take a look at my back? I think there's a hook unfastened.

MAN: Oh? It's fine. They're all fastened.

WOMAN: This stain still bothers me. I could have taken care of it if I noticed it a little sooner . . . But it can't be helped. There's no time. Husband, please turn this way for a moment. (*Straightens his necktie, etc.*) Your necktie's always on crooked. Everyone says so. Honestly, I feel as though they're blaming me. Please be careful. Feel it occasionally—like this.

MAN: You can't tell by just feeling it.

WOMAN: You can, if you get used to it. (*Straightening the handkerchief.*) A sharp dresser does it, at least once every hour. How about Mr. Yamada? I've never once seen his necktie on crooked. Your handkerchief doesn't quite match, but I guess. it'll do. Let's go. We must hurry . . .

MAN: Go? Where to?

WOMAN: . . . (*Looks puzzled for a moment but becomes herself again.*)

(*The sound of something windlike blowing over. Looking dazed, the two stand among the old things.*)

I can hear it . . .

MAN: Hear what?

WOMAN: You know, the electricity. The electricity is flowing. Listen . . . It's humming.

MAN: You're right . . .

WOMAN (*glancing around*): It's all desert . . .

MAN (*placing a chair in front of the table*): Sit down.

WOMAN (*slowly sits. Whispering*): I like that tablecloth . . . That red-checkered one . . . (*Her eyes meet* MAN's, *and she remembers. Rising.*) I wonder what happened to it? (*Again, sitting.*) Perhaps we've come too far . . .

MAN (*bringing a chair and sitting opposite her*): Shall we take a rest?

WOMAN: Rest?

MAN: Like, say, about a week?

WOMAN: Here?

MAN: Right here.

WOMAN: In a place like this?

MAN: It can't be helped.

WOMAN: We can't. Not in a place like this. Let's go on a little farther. If we do that, there's bound to be a better place.

MAN: You say that every time, but there never is.

WOMAN: But it's true. This place is no good.

MAN (*sitting motionless for a while, then rises. Speaking to* WOMAN, *who looks up anxiously*): I'll make you some tea. Let's have tea. It's too early, but why not? Once in a while . . . (*Begins preparing tea.*) It's formal tea. And we'll spread out a tablecloth . . . That red-checkered one. And the teacups from the set with flower patterns . . .

WOMAN: That's right. There's a saucer missing from that one.

MAN: Forget it. Why worry about that now? We don't need a complete set of six, anymore. Just sit there. I'll fix it! We're finally having formal tea—after a long time. Let's slice some of that choice cheese.

WOMAN: Don't do that.

MAN: Why not? Why don't you leave it to me, for a change? You've got to relax sometime.

WOMAN: Do you know where the sugar is?

MAN: I know. In that round can?

WOMAN: That's right . . . There should be black tea in there, too. The red package has the better tea. After you take it out, be sure to put the lid back on tightly, or else it'll get soggy. Well, I'll fix it, anyway.

MAN: I told you not to. Today, I'll do it.

WOMAN: But, Husband, you don't know where everything is!

MAN: Of course, I do. Don't worry. That's right . . . You set the table, then.

WOMAN: All right. Then I'll do that. The tablecloth. Where was it?

MAN: Over there . . .

WOMAN: Oh, here. I know. (*Becoming somewhat lively.*) It's been quite a while since we spread this out for formal tea . . . What are you looking for?

MAN: What? Oh—for a match . . . Ah, here it is.

WOMAN: You never put back anything in its proper place. The tableware is lined up here, so please watch your step. It's been some time since I used this set of teacups. A saucer is missing, but the rest still managed to survive on top of that cart . . . Husband, do you know where the cheese is?

MAN: Of course.

WOMAN: Husband, we've got *that*, too.

MAN: What?

WOMAN: A small can of caviar . . .

MAN: Oh, really? Let's get that out, too.

WOMAN: It's near the bottom of the box and wrapped in newspaper along with the cheese . . .

MAN: Oh? (*Searching.*)

WOMAN: But, Husband . . .

MAN: What is it? (*Taking out the caviar.*) Is this it?

WOMAN: . . . Don't you feel a little decadent?

MAN: About what?

WOMAN: Having tea at this hour . . .

MAN: Why not? Okay! Let's be decadent. That's the way to be— once in a while.

WOMAN: I feel a little guilty.

MAN: Guilty? (*Laughs.*)

WOMAN: It's not an unpleasant feeling, though.

MAN: Why should it be unpleasant? It's always good to be decadent. Can you slice the cheese?

WOMAN: All right . . . I know I've asked you before, but do you want to slice this? There's one that's already opened. It may not taste as good, but shouldn't we finish it up first?

MAN: Now, now. Don't be so stingy. I'd rather have the one that tastes even a little better. We're decadent now . . .

WOMAN: We shouldn't have thrown away that phonograph. That would make a great difference at a time like this. Don't you remember, Husband? How many days after our departure was that? We put on records and danced, with the flags of all nations tied to the telephone poles? Did we throw away those flags?

MAN: Of course, we threw them away . . . that junk. Hey, is the table ready?

WOMAN: Yes, but please wait. The tablecloth is on crooked. (*Straightens it out.*) Lately, this sort of thing bothers me a lot. I wonder why? Oh, the saucers aren't out yet. Aren't they over there, Husband?

MAN: Where?

WOMAN: Where the tableware is lined up.

MAN: You mean the ones matching the teacups?

WOMAN: That's right.

MAN: They're not here.

WOMAN: You can't mean that!

MAN: But that's the truth.

WOMAN: Oh! (*Approaching* HUSBAND.) I remember now! They haven't been taken out of the box. The table looks fine. (*Bringing them out from the box.*)

MAN: Good.

WOMAN: Oh, I found the saucer.

MAN: Where?

WOMAN: In this box.

MAN: Wife, you said earlier it wasn't there.

WOMAN: It wasn't there before. I looked again and found it. Strange, isn't it?

MAN: Nothing strange about it. You didn't do a good job of looking before.

WOMAN: But it's still strange. I did look for it. I'm glad. This means we have at least a complete set of six . . . And we can serve up to four guests without being embarrassed. Do you remember, Husband? Once, on our way home, we all went to make a call on sick Mr. Kimura. Were there five of us? Yes, five—the Uedas, Dr. Kawata, and us. But the Kimuras didn't have enough teacups . . . It made me laugh. The Kimuras said they only had a set of four and were one short. Teacups usually come in sets of five or six. Strange, there were only four. Husband, do be careful. You're wearing a tuxedo. I wonder if there's an apron?

MAN: Don't worry. I'm fine. I'll be careful.

WOMAN: You should still wear one. It's nothing to be especially ashamed of. Even men wear aprons when they work in the kitchen. That's right, Dr. Kawata said so. All Western men do that. I'm sure it was around here . . . That's what they tell me. When the men come home from the office, they take off their suit jacket, wear an apron, and help out in the kitchen. I found it. Husband, please put it on.

MAN: Do I have to? We're almost ready . . .

WOMAN: Of course, you do. And you'd better wear it, even when you're eating. (*Putting it on for him.*) It's hard to get a tea stain out of this suit. Though a dark suit may seem to cover up the stain, it's still noticeable. Looks slightly soiled. But by then, it's too late to do anything. We must brush the suit a little. It's quite dusty.

MAN: Wife, shall we begin?

WOMAN: Yes, shall we? Where are your cigarettes, Husband?

MAN: That's right, I forgot.

WOMAN (*pouring the tea*): They're in the tea can. The recent good weather has dried them out, and they're no longer firm. The cigarettes aren't soggy, though. The bottom of the can has quite a bit of powdery tobacco. Isn't there any use for that? What a shame to throw it away . . . Well, the tea's ready. Mother! Mother! Mother!

(*Her eyes meet those of* MAN, *who has been slow in returning to the table. Becoming silent,* WOMAN *avoids his gaze.*)

I know. I know, but it still happens. Even as I call out her name, I've a feeling, I'm mistaken . . . That's why, I know Mother's gone.

MAN: You've got to rest. You're tired. You've been working too frantically. Wife, let's rest. Why, you'll be all right as soon as you get a little rest. You're mentally exhausted. So many things have happened. Too many things have happened. Well, the tea's ready, so let's have some.

(*The couple sit at the table and drink tea. For a while, they remain silent.*)

MAN: It's been quite a while . . .

WOMAN: Yes . . .

MAN: How about some cheese?

WOMAN (*standing up*): Husband, let's go!

MAN: Go?

WOMAN: Of course!

MAN: Go where?

WOMAN: We're leaving. We mustn't dally around in a place like this. We still have a long way to go. Please, we must go, Husband. We mustn't take time for tea. We mustn't get lazy. That's our problem. That's the cause of all our troubles. We'll be fine once we start.

MAN: But, Wife, you're tired! Let's do this. We'll just take off a day. Just one day! Then we'll go. So we'll start out day after tomorrow—in the morning.

WOMAN: No, Husband, let's go now. I mean it. We'll be finished if we stay here any longer. Does it matter if we're tired? We're always tired. Well, let's start packing.

MAN: You want to get started now? It's already dark.

WOMAN: What's the difference. Let's walk all night, then. And I want to keep going until I fall over. Husband, please help me carry the baby.

MAN: Wife, you mustn't. I'm not talking about starting out. That's fine with me. I'll go. But don't take the baby. We must bury him now. Do you understand? You must understand that!

WOMAN: No, I'm taking him along. We simply can't afford to lose any more members. Please, lend me a hand.

MAN: No, you mustn't. Do you know what I'm talking about?

WOMAN: Of course. Don't worry. I'm in my right mind now. Really. Please, lend me your hand.

(*With no other recourse,* MAN *helps* WOMAN *carry the child.*)

Let's start packing . . . Just what we really need. We don't need the table and chairs, the red-checkered tablecloth, or the set of teacups. We'll take along food, clothing, and other things—just a few of the barest essentials . . .

(*In semidarkness, the two busily begin to pack . . .*)

The stage darkens.

Epilogue

One telephone pole. The stage is brilliantly lit.

(*For a while, no one is on the stage. Finally, from stage left,* WOMAN *appears with a child on her back. She holds a parasol and carries a shopping bag with diapers and a baby bottle. At stage center, she stops, tips the parasol, and—looking up—is dazzled by the sky. Then she lowers her gaze and looks back.* MAN *enters pulling a cart containing their pitifully meager baggage. She waits until they have joined at stage center and both leave toward stage right.*)

The stage darkens.

SELECTED BIBLIOGRAPHY

General Works

Bowers, Faubian. *Japanese Theater*. New York: Hill and Wang, 1952.

Keene, Donald. *Japanese Literature: An Introduction for Western Readers*. New York: Grove Press, 1955.

Komiya Toyotaka, ed. *Japanese Music and Drama in the Meiji Era*, trans. and adapted by Donald Keene and Edwin G. Seidensticker. In *Japanese Culture in the Meiji Era*, vol. 3. Tokyo: Ōbunsha, 1956.

Michener, James A. *The Hokusai Sketch-Books: Selections from the Manga*. Rutland, Vt. and Tokyo: Charles E. Tuttle, 1958.

Pronko, Leonard C. *Guide to Japanese Drama*. Boston: G. K. Hall, 1973.

Sansom, George B. *The Western World and Japan*. New York: Knopf, 1958.

Modern Japanese Theater

Akiba Tarō, *Nihon Shingekishi*. 2 vols. Tokyo, 1956.

Clurman, Harold. "Notes from Afar (Part 1): Report on Traditional and Western Theater in Tokyo." In *Nation* (August 16, 1965), 4:84–86. A perceptive commentary on the general Japanese theatrical scene by a noted American stage director and drama critic.

Dōmoto Masaki. *Dentō Engeki to Gendai*. Tokyo, 1971.

Goodman, David. "New Japanese Theater." In *The Drama Review (Spring 1971)*, 15(3):154–168. A general discussion of the modern Japanese theater, which also includes its latest developments beginning in the sixties.

Kawashima Jumpei. *Nihon Engeki Hyakunen no Ayumi.* Tokyo, 1972.

Kawatake Shigetoshi, ed. *Engeki Hykka Daijiten.* 6 vols. Tokyo, 1960–62.

—— *Nihon Engekizenshi.* Tokyo, 1959.

Kurabayashi Seiichirō. *Shingeki Nendaiki (Sengohen).* Tokyo, 1966.

—— *Shingeki Nendaiki (Senchūhen).* Tokyo, 1969.

—— *Shingeki Nendaiki (Senzenhen).* Tokyo, 1972.

Kurahashi Takeshi. "Western Drama in Japan—the Japanese Shingeki Movement." *Japan Quarterly* (April–June 1958), 5(2):178–185. A brief survey of the modern Japanese theater by a drama specialist.

Japanese National Commission for UNESCO, ed. *Theater in Japan.* Tokyo: Japanese National Commission for UNESCO, 1963. See especially ch. 3, which covers the modern Japanese theater from the early 1900s to the present; offers information on the main theatrical troupes today.

Nagihira Kazuo. *Kindai Gikyoku no Sekai.* Tokyo, 1972.

Ochi Haruo. *Meiji-Taishō no Gekibungaku.* Tokyo, 1971.

Ortolani, Benito. "Fukuda Tsuneari: Modernization and Shingeki." In Donald H. Shively, ed., *Tradition and Modernization in Japanese Culture,* pp. 463–499. Princeton, N.J.: Princeton University Press, 1971. A detailed essay on Tsuneari Fukuda (1912–), a major Japanese theater director and playwright, setting forth his personal views on the history and significance of the modern theater movement.

Rimer, J. Thomas. *Toward a Modern Japanese Theater: Kishida Kunio.* Princeton, N.J.: Princeton University Press, 1974. A well-presented study of an important playwright in the modern theater movement whose career spanned over thirty years until his death in 1954.

San'ichi Shobō Henshūbu. *Gendai Nihon Engeki Taikei.* 8 vols. Tokyo, 1971–72.

Sugawara Takashi. "Prospects of Contemporary Theater in Japan." In Japanese National Commission for UNESCO, ed., *Proceedings of the International Symposium on the Theater East and West,* pp. 81–94. Tokyo: Japanese National Commission for UNESCO, 1965. The report discusses the traditional theater, the current state of affairs of the Japanese theater, and proposals for promoting the theater arts—both traditional and modern.

TEATRO Henshūbu, ed. *Shingeki Benran*. Tokyo, 1975.

Yamazaki Masakazu. *Gekiteki naru Nihonjin*. Tokyo, 1971.

Magazines on Modern Japanese Theater

Higeki-Kigeki
Shingeki
TEATRO

List of Plays in Print

Among the modern Japanese dramatists of the prewar period, many of their works translated into Western languages have long since gone out of print and are difficult to find except at larger libraries or at educational institutions, which may have collections specializing in Japanese literature and drama. The older plays listed here, however, are reprints and should be accessible to the general reader.

Abe Kōbō. *Friends* (Tomodachi). Donald Keene, trans. New York: Grove Press, 1969.

—— *The Man Who Turned into a Stick: Three Related Plays* (Bō ni natta Otoko). Donald Keene, trans. Tokyo: Tokyo University Press, 1975.

Endō Shūsaku. *The Golden Country* (Ōgon no Kuni). Francis Mathy, trans. Rutland, Vt. and Tokyo: Charles E. Tuttle, 1970.

Kikuchi Kan. *The Madman on the Roof* (Okujō no Kyōjin). Yōzan T. Iwasaki and Glenn Hughes, trans. In *Three Modern Japanese Plays*. New York: Steward-Kidd, 1923. Reprinted in Donald Keene, ed., *Modern Japanese Literature*, pp. 278–287. New York: Grove Press, 1956.

—— *The Saviour of the Moment* (Toki no Ujigami). Noboru Hidaka, trans. In *The Passion and Three Other Plays*. Westport, Conn.: Greenwood Press, 1971 (first published in 1933).

—— *Tōjūrō's Love and Four Other Plays*. Glenn W. Shaw, trans. Tokyo: Hokuseidō, 1925, 1956. Contains:

Better Than Revenge (Katakiuchi-ijō).

The Father Returns (Chichi kaeru).

The Housetop Madman (Okujō no Kyōjin).

The Miracle (Kiseki).

Tōjūrō's Love (Tōjūrō no Koi).

Kinoshita Junji. *Twight Crane* (Yūzuru), A. C. Scott, trans. In *Five Plays for a New Theater*, pp. 129–159. New York: New Directions, 1956.

Kishida Kunio. *The Roof Garden* (Okujō Teien). Noboru Hidaka, trans. In *The Passion and Three Other Plays*. Westport, Conn.: Greenwood Press, 1971 (first published in 1933).

Kitano Shigeo. *A Volcanic Island: The Sound of Night* (Kazantō). Andrew T. Tsubaki, trans. Tokyo: TEATRO, 1971.

Kurata Hyakuzō. *The Priest and His Disciples* (Shukke to Sono Deshi). Glenn W. Shaw, trans. Tokyo: Hokuseidō, 1922, 1969.

Mishima Yukio. *Dōjōji*. Donald Keene, trans. In *Death in Midsummer and Other Stories*. New York: New Directions, 1966, pp. 119–138. A modern Nō play.

—— *Five Modern Nō Plays* (from *Kindai Nōgakushū*). Donald Keene, trans. New York: Knopf, 1957. Contains:
  Sotoba Komachi
  The Damask Drum (Aya no Tsuzumi)
  Kantan
  The Lady Aoi (Aoi no Ue)
  Hanjo

—— *Madame de Sade* (Sado Kōshaku Fujin). Donald Keene, trans. New York: Grove Press, 1967.

—— *My Friend Hitler* (Waga Tomo Hittora). Hiroaki Satō, trans. In *St. Andrews Review* (Fall–Winter 1977; Spring–Summer 1978; Special Double Translation Issue), vol. IV, nos. 3–4.

—— *The Three Primary Còlors* (San Genshoku). Miles K. McElrath, trans. In *Occasional Papers No. 11, Japanese Culture II*, pp. 175–194. Ann Arbor: University of Michigan, 1969.

—— *Tropical Tree* (Nettaiju). Kenneth Strong, trans. In *Japan Quarterly* (April–June 1964), 11(2):174–210.

—— *Twilight Sunflower*. Shigeo Shinozaki and Virgil A. Warren, trans. Tokyo: Hokuseidō, 1958.

Mushanokōji Saneatsu. *The Passion* (Aiyoku). Noboru Hidaka, trans. In *The Passion and Three Other Plays*. Westport, Conn.: Greenwood Press, 1971 (first published in 1933).

Suzuki Sensaburō. *Living Koheiji* (Ikite iru Koheiji). Noboru Hidaka, trans. In *The Passion and Three Other Plays*. Westport, Conn.: Greenwood Press, 1971 (first published in 1933).

Yamamoto Yuzō. *Three Plays of Yamamoto Yūzō*. Glenn W. Shaw, trans. Tokyo: Hokuseidō, 1935, 1957. Contains:
Sakazaki, Lord Dewa (Sakazaki Dewa-no-Kami).
The Crown of Life (Inochi no Kammuri).

For the most recent and helpful list of modern Japanese plays, see *A Brief Bibliography of Modern Japanese Plays in English Translation* compiled by Japan Society, Inc. (1978). This booklet cites additional translated plays and offers information on unpublished playscripts, which are only available through agents. Other translated texts it mentions can be ordered from specific individuals: for example, an English version of Minoru Betsuyaku's *The Elephant* (Zō) that appeared in a theater magazine issued briefly in Tokyo, starting in late 1969.

To receive a complimentary copy of *A Brief Bibliography*, write to: The Japan Society, Inc., 333 East 47th Street, New York, N.Y. 10017.